Deleuze, Altered States and Film

Deleuze, Altered States and Film

Anna Powell

Edinburgh University Press

Edinburgh University Press Ltd
22 George Square, Edinburgh

Typeset in Monotype Ehrhardt by
Servis Filmsetting Ltd, Manchester, and
printed and bound in Great Britain by
Biddles Ltd, King's Lynn, Norfolk

A CIP record for this book is available from the British Library

ISBN 978 0 7486 3282 4 (hardback)

Contents

Acknowledgements

Many thanks are due to Berthold Schoene and the English Research Institute, and Sue Zlosnik and the English Department at Manchester Metropolitan University. They have encouraged my research, agreed to host the Deleuze Studies Website and provided me with a term's sabbatical. PhD and MA students past and present have offered further mental stimulus. I also acknowledge support from the UK Arts and Humanities Research Council for a further term's research leave to work on this project. David Curtis of the Arts Council kindly lent me Belson's cine films and the viewing tables at the ICA in London long ago. Lux Cinema, Hoxton was an excellent source of rare films. Sarah Edwards, James Dale and the team at Edinburgh University Press have again been helpful and efficient in bringing the book to completion.

Thanks to friends and fellow-travellers for their inspiration, support and love through this book and always. David Deamer, Alan Hook, Rachael McConkey, Venetta Uye and Ana Miller are the regular *A/V* team who input long hours of creative work filming, editing and helping to make our webjournal what it is today. Rob Lapsley takes the reading group to the outer circuits (and beyond). Fiona Price offered musical insights. Janet Schofield re-checked the proofs. And finally, special thanks to Ranald Warburton for companionship, patience, sound advice and mind-stretching debate at untimely hours.

Acknowledgements

Introduction: Altered States, Affect and Film

A man hangs suspended in the blue-lit water of a flotation tank. A fish-eye lens and pale, grainy images compress his naked body and enlarge his head, a human foetus close to birth in the womb of a machine. A slow tracking-shot glides the camera back from peering through the riveted metal port-hole of a flotation tank. The long shot reveals neurologist Edward Jessup (William Hurt) in deep trance. He is the subject of a laboratory experiment under observation by fellow scientists. The extensive paraphernalia of experiment: computers, monitors and alpha-rhythm flow charts, form a sharp visual contrast to Jessup's intensive visions, yet both are researching altered states of consciousness.

I want to take this pre-title sequence from the movie *Altered States* (Ken Russell, 1981) as a figure to launch my own exploration of cinematic altered states. My project sets out to accomplish a distinctive remapping of the film experience *as* altered state, using both the film-philosophical insights of Gilles Deleuze and his broader investigations with Félix Guattari as inspiration. So how might this image of Jessup in his tank work as an opener for the book's agenda? In order to clarify what my approach actually does, I will play devil's advocate with it first, to anticipate some possible objections.

Read as a metaphor, the sequence could be used to parody the film-theoretical project itself. The scientists in the lab do not share Jessup's intensive experiences directly, but merely watch body parts projected on a screen and log EEG rhythms. Thus, Jessup might be the film director in the ineffable throes of creation, running the film in his/her head. Developing this parody further, film theorists, as clinically detached intellectuals like Russell's stereotypical scientists, are not 'normal' viewers enjoying a movie. They interface the auditorium with theoretical abstraction, making it into their own kind of lab. Here, they tabulate data and mentally write a report with conclusions pre-formed by hypothesis. From this viewpoint, film theory appears as a mere jargon-ridden dilution of the cinematic experience.

If we shift from the limited focal length of such metaphors to open up the wide-angle possibilities of Deleuzian film-philosophy, the impact of

Russell's sequence looks very different. The work of Deleuze, solo and with Guattari, offers a set of tools to help us grasp our encounter with the art-work and consider the potential of its affective forces to alter us.

For Guattari, aesthetics are viral in nature, being known 'not through representation, but through *affective* contamination'.[1] In its broader, verbal usage, to affect is to 'lay hold of, impress, or act upon (in mind or feelings)' or to 'influence, move, touch'.[2] Affection as noun is 'a mental state brought about by any influence; an emotion or feeling'.[3] Although it retains connection to more general meanings, Guattari uses affect in a special sense here and in his work with Deleuze. Affect also permeates Deleuze's solo-authored cinema books, with both the movement-image and the time-image as distinct but congruent explorations of it.

Henri Bergson is the main philosophical precursor of Deleuze's temporally based cinematic affect. Bergson accused early cinema of representing the flux of matter in time as a series of static 'snapshots' that, strung together by mechanical movement, prevent awareness of duration.[4] Despite this explicit distrust of the 'cinematograph', Deleuze identifies a more fundamentally 'cinematic' philosophy in Bergson's implication of 'the universe as cinema in itself, a metacinema'.[5] Both regard the world as 'flowing-matter', a material flux of images and the human perceiver as a 'centre of indetermination' able to reflect intensively on affect.[6]

For Bergson, perception is extensive and actual but affection is unextended and virtual. Unlike perception, which seeks to identify and quantify external stimuli, affection is qualitative, acting by the intensive vibration of a 'motor tendency on a sensible nerve'.[7] Rather than being 'geographically' located, affect surges in the centre of indetermination. Its pre-subjective processes engage a kind of auto-contemplation that participates in the wider flux of forces moving in duration.

Deleuze likewise locates affection in the evolution from external action to internal contemplation. While 'delegating our activity to organs of reaction that we have consequently liberated' we have also 'specialised' specific facets as 'receptive organs at the price of condemning them to immobility'.[8] These immobile facets refract and absorb images, reflecting on them rather than reflecting them back. Deleuze echoes Bergson's definition of the affective process as a 'motor effort on an immobilised receptive plate'.[9] In his Bergsonian approach to the cinematic image, which I detail later, affection is not a failure of the perception-action system, but is its 'absolutely necessary' third element.[10]

Affect is produced by the formal grammar of film working through the medium of images moving in time. In *Cinema 1*, affection-images express 'the event in its eternal aspect' by foregrounding affects over representational content as 'pure singular qualities or potentialities-as it were, pure "possibles"'.[11] Particular affects (as 'qualisign') or power (as 'potisign') are 'dividual': they vary their quality according to the connections they enter into and the divisions they undergo. Emotions like terror and optical sensations like brightness manifest power-qualities, virtual possibilities waiting to be actualised in particular conditions.

So why is affect vital to Deleuzian film-philosophy? A specialised element in the continuum of flowing images, affects occur in the temporal gap between perception and action and occupy the interval without filling it up. Internal and self-reflexive in nature, affect operates by 'a co-incidence of subject and object, or the way in which the subject perceives itself, or rather experiences itself or feels itself "from the inside"'.[12] The processing of an image's affective quality occurs in the temporal pause between action and perception, an interval potent with possibilities for change.[13] As Claire Colebrook reminds us, cinematic affect 'short-circuits' our perceptual habit of selecting images that interest us only for potential action.[14] Colebrook asserts that 'freedom demands taking thinking, constantly, beyond itself' and the power of affect is crucial to such violent forcing of thought out of accustomed patterns by shifting them from spatial extension to intensive temporality.[15]

Deleuzian and DeleuzeGuattarian affect is pivotal to my own project in this book. I identify the affective properties of a special cluster of films that induce altered states by techniques to break up spatial conventions of linear time and sensory-motor movements linked by action. Affective techniques mobilise gaps and fissures in image content (such as the out-of-frame) and linear continuity (such as editing). Whenever I use the terms affect and affection, I intend to deploy them, like Deleuze and Bergson, to suggest a self-reflexive pause, a temporal hiatus catalytic for change.

Some intensive short films are, I assert, pure affective gaps per se. Rather than being a fixed 'altered states' canon, this fluid category of moving images is growing fast even as I write. Drawing on a uniquely enabling set of conceptual tools, I advance the argument that, in its radicalising 'special effects' that foreground the operations of time, altered states film is *the* primal cinema of affect.

Film theory thus starts to look less like a kind of perverse vivisection and more like a method of speculative thought with potent creative impetus. The qualitative power of cinematography far exceeds its narrative function (such as the thematic representation of Jessup's personal psychodrama here). Although film is the inspired product of a creative team and might well stimulate 'personal' fantasies, it is a medium that already undercuts both human subjectivity and matter through technologies that capture movement and techniques that fragment linear time. Film watching is, then, both a sensorial and a mental experience. In its dynamic combination of sensory impact and unique qualities of abstraction, film is a unique temporal stimulus for speculative thought.

So what do I mean by 'altered states'? The full term 'altered states of consciousness' became current in 1970s psychology-speak. Each component has a range of meanings relevant to my usage here. The verb 'to alter' is to 'make some change in character, shape, condition, position, quantity, value of [. . .] without changing the thing itself for another'.[16] The last clause about retaining some essential identity will prove contentious. To alter also means 'to affect mentally or disturb' (of pivotal significance to our argument) and 'to administer alterative medicines' (of special relevance in the chapter on drugs).[17] I use the noun 'alterity' to indicate 'a being otherwise. The state of being other or different, diversity, "otherness" '.[18]

Consciousness is basically definable as 'a condition and concomitant of all thought, feeling and volition'.[19] Although I sometimes use the word in default of a more fitting one for the job, I admit here that Deleuze, after Baruch Spinoza, problematises 'consciousness'. For both philosophers, conventional consciousness is the locus of a 'psychological illusion of freedom'.[20] Just as the body surpasses our knowledge of it, so the mind 'surpasses the consciousness we have of it'.[21] By registering effects rather than knowing causes, consciousness is inferior to thought and remains 'completely immersed in the unconscious'.[22] The limitations of consciousness lead to 'confused and mutilated' ideas that are 'effects separated from their real causes'.[23]

A state of consciousness, or 'mental or emotional condition', then, is for Deleuze inherently ripe for alteration.[24] State here means 'a physical condition as regards internal make of constitution, molecular form or structure'.[25] As we discover, Deleuze and Guattari's use of 'molecularity' explores the fluctuating properties of molecular structures in mental as well as physical conditions. I confess that I also want you to get into 'a state' in its colloquial use as 'an agitated or excited state of mind or feeling', as the most receptive approach to a cinematic encounter with alterity.[26]

Arguing that 'the brain is the screen' Deleuze (in his eponymous essay) presents cinema as both expressing and inducing thought.[27] Like film, the brain itself is a self-reflexive moving image of time, space and motion. Working with Deleuze's cinema books and his projects with Guattari, I expose cinematic 'altered states' as an under-researched area. I set out to offer new insights into the cinematic experience of a special body of films that trigger alterity in their own ways. Although some of my film choices grow from Deleuze's own, most of them have never been considered or linked together in this way. Asserting their distinctive qualities, I present them as significantly affective cultural experiences.

Mixed Planes and Singular Encounters: Methods

The use of a film 'clip' to open this section is typical of my methodology. My aim is to approach film in its specificity, as an experiential process as well as a stimulus to philosophical thought. I identify inductive film techniques and suggest their functions. As well as contributing to the hitherto under-researched aesthetics of special effects pivotal to altered states film, I want to convey a sense of each film as a singular encounter. To do this, I detail the impact of cinematic techniques and explore their affects and the mental shifts of gear they engineer by following Deleuzian methods of concept-formation via stylistic expression.

My project is, of course, practising productive 'interference' between disciplines in two of the ways identified by Deleuze and Guattari: 'extrinsic' and 'mixed plane', detailed in my conclusion to the book.[28] Rather than applying a unified methodological template, I remain responsive to the distinctive qualities of both films and concepts. Some sections separate out theoretical discussion and textual analysis (extrinsic), while others intermesh affects and concepts more closely (mixed plane). In my case, the 'interfering' discipline is Film Studies. By interfering with philosophy from a Film Studies background, I am reversing Deleuze's own process, but hopefully moving within the same mixed plane of film-philosophy.

Deleuze and Guattari's perspectives encourage innovative development rather than purely scholarly exegesis. Rather than wanting to produce a philosophical explication of Deleuze, and Deleuze and Guattari, my interest lies in mobilising their concepts by engaging them in critical and creative action. I use their suggestive force as a springboard to launch my own explorations of film and altered states. My concern here is to link aesthetic theory and practice in a mutually creative assemblage as part of my larger, non-written project to encourage Deleuzian-inflected arts.[29]

My eclectic approach also seeks to link traditionally separate areas of inquiry such as psychology, philosophy, aesthetics, film studies and cultural history to find ways they can cooperate as a viable assemblage. To this end, following Deleuze and Guattari, I draw on insights filched from physics and neurophysiology, but unlike them, I mesh this with debates about 'high' art and popular culture. I mix a selection of films chosen by Deleuze himself with little known experimental works and recent popular box-office successes.

I extend Deleuze's work in deploying art as a tool to investigate the nature of cinematic perception. In doing this, I mobilise a productive assemblage with the work of other practitioners from the fields of both art and philosophy. I want to flesh out some of Deleuze and Guattari's own more briefly acknowledged connections by a closer look at the metaphysics of counter-cultural writers like Carlos Castaneda. I consider Deleuze's networking with the theories of experimental filmmakers such as Stan Brakhage and Andrei Tarkovsky. The insights of artistic explorers of delirium, like Antonin Artaud, are linked with those of philosophers of space, time and perception. In particular, I engage the work of Henri Bergson, so crucial to Deleuze's own understanding of movement and time in cinema.

There is, of course, a plethora of material analysing the psychology of altered consciousness, ranging from depth psychology to neurology. Unlike the scientists of Russell's film, I am not a specialist in fields that collect the data and seek to chart the pathologies of altered states. I engage solely with ideas that offer insight into the cinematic encounter or throw light on Deleuze and Guattari's own philosophical project of alterity. Having identified the book's agenda and my methodology, I will outline the context and motivation of my intervention.

Critical Contexts

There is still an urgent need to introduce the film-philosophy of Deleuze to newcomers and to strengthen its force in contemporary Film Studies. This is particularly the case in the UK, which, till lately, lagged behind European, American and Antipodean work. There is also a body of substantial work in French and German which awaits translation for readers like myself with too basic a grasp of these languages. Recent headway has been made by Deleuzian theorists in the UK in the critique of specific art forms: literature, music and art.[30] Literary studies has offered a more fertile soil for Deleuzians, its ground already prepared by engagement with French theory via Kristeva, Irigaray, Foucault and Derrida for over twenty years. There is a small but now growing contingent of film applications in the UK, begun in the work of Barbara Kennedy, David Martin Jones and myself.[31]

So why has UK Film Studies been relatively slow in testing out Deleuzian methods? In some ways it is still governed by the violent reaction against 1970s and 1980s 'Screen theory', a French-theory-influenced critique led by the British film journal Screen from the 1970s on. The journal approached film via the substantial critical perspectives of Althusserian Marxism, structuralism, Freudian and Lacanian psychoanalysis and theories of the gendered gaze.[32] Screen theory provided valuable insights into ideological interpellation, the position of the viewer and fantasy formations of gender and ethnicity. It was reviled and rejected for its dense theoretical jargon, and its weighty theoretical approach was accused of being inappropriate to a popular medium by a particular school of thought.

Film Studies in the UK has been permeated at all levels from academic writing to classroom textbooks by a hegemonic culturalist presence too substantial not to be addressed in any preamble to a distinctive approach.[33] Culturalism, whose influence has spread, particularly to the USA (and now dominates *Screen* itself), draws on sociologists like Pierre Bourdieu and locates film as a popular cultural form.[34] I do not intend to negate or underestimate its valuable contributions to its film-historical and culturally based studies of cinematic representation, reception and production. Over my years of involvement with Film Studies, I have respected and learned from culturalist work. Yet, the sweeping rejection of *Screen* theory has, by 'throwing the baby out with the bathwater', led current UK film studies into a theoretical impasse.

I do not advocate a return to *Screen* theory, or its replacement by a new Deleuzian orthodoxy, but hope to invite productive dialogue and initiate mutual work across existing interstices. From a culturalist perspective, Deleuze's philosophy might be accused of obscurantism and of a relevance limited to the *cinéphile* canon. If Deleuzian theory is to be of substantial use-value to current Film Studies in the UK, we need to extend the Deleuzian canon to include more widely viewed films that use special effects that challenge and disorientate. By focusing, in clear, accessible terms, on altered states as a vital element in our viewing experience, and by celebrating the low-budget, the trashy and the mainstream as well as art-cinema and experimental work, I consider my own very different approach as complementary rather than oppositional to existing input in our lively and productive field.

The politics of film representation and the economics of the cinematic institution have generated a substantial body of research within culturalism. Deleuze and Guattari's work is always informed by an astutely radical political awareness. They worked to oppose both local and international abuses of power, including prison reform, gay rights and opposition to French imperialism in Algeria. Guattari's work with the anti-psychiatry movement and his eco-criticism is well-known.[35] Actively involved in the events of May 1968 and their aftermath, Deleuze and Guattari do not indulge in pure aestheticism. Rather than being for its own sake, art is always used as 'a tool for blazing life lines'.[36]

Deleuze and Guattari also offer a substantial remapping of the cinematic psyche, of vital interest to psychoanalytical film theorists even though they might reject it. Although they critique a paternalistic strand in Freudianism as an inadequate account of psychic dynamics, Deleuze and Guattari's challenge to dominant psychoanalytical approaches was the catalyst for a dynamic new psychic topography that yet retains roots in Freud and Lacan. Working at the micro level of the film experience on body and brain, my book complements both broader explorations of cinema history and more traditionally structuralist approaches to psychosexual fantasy. I set out to explore the percepts, affects and concepts of film *as* experience *as well as, not instead of*, political allegory or primal scene.

My work on cinematic perception differs from that of James Peterson and Noel Carroll on avant-garde spectatorship.[37] They build on the approach of hypothesis-testing and problem-solving pioneered by structuralist film theorist David Bordwell.[38] This uses schema from cognitive psychology as tool for interpretation. A schema is an orderly pattern imposed by perception on a mass of sensory information to make meaning more manageable. They argue that although experimental film makes more demands and offers spectators more complex stimuli, it is still limited to a finite range of interpretative patterns and styles partly fixed by critics. Rather than inviting such problem-solving interpretations, I assert that experimental films aim to derange the senses and the mind.

Although there is now a substantial body of sociologically inflected work on spectatorship, the impact of the film experience as encounter has so far been downplayed.[39] Theories of spectatorship could also learn from thoughts (literally) on our nerve endings, and from cinema's potential to alter consciousness. Like the human body, film techniques engage dynamic technological forces mobilised by projection and perception. The eyes are an extension of our brain. They are a working component of the imagination's operations; the camera's machinery and the social 'machinic assemblage' of cinema as cine-literacy becomes ever more culturally central as a mode of perception.

Two main strands have developed internationally in English-language Deleuzian Film Studies. The first locates Deleuze's work in critical theory and philosophy, as exemplified by David Rodowick's *Gilles Deleuze's Time Machine*, which also references C. S. Peirce's semiology.[40] Such work gives primacy to theory, using film as an illustrative example. The second strand evokes the 'aesthetics of sensation' in a lyrical prose style. Steven Shaviro's pioneering work draws on Deleuze in his reading of cinematic affect via body-horror and masochism.[41] Barbara Kennedy considers the corporeal and non-corporeal dynamics of 'becoming-woman'. I want to broaden the scope of Ronald Bogue – who keeps rigorously to those films referenced by Deleuze himself – and to engage with popular, if not necessarily blockbuster, cinema.[42] In this respect, my work extends that of Patricia Pisters, who reads canonical, popular and art cinema with equal interest.[43] My current project develops my last book *Deleuze and the Horror Film* in opening Deleuze's film-philosophy to the wider Film Studies community.

I want to increase Deleuze's accessibility by integrating his concepts with more mainstream films like *Donnie Darko* as well as art-house and experimental cinema. As well as considering 'classic' altered states movies such as *2001*, *Performance* and *Easy Rider* from an innovative perspective, I will be addressing a surprising absence in Deleuze's own 'canon' by giving lesser-known 'experimental' and 'underground' movies the attention they deserve. In its relevance to the wider context of the altered states practices of audiences (including sex, dreams, drugs and meditative trance) my book can contribute more broadly to debates about the significance of popular culture in the field of UK Film Studies.

Altered States: Menu

Justifying his own aesthetic 'canon', Deleuze says that 'if you don't love it, you have no reason to write a word about it'.[44] My selection of movies is inevitably shaped by the specificities of my personal and cultural history and that nebulous, synaesthetic and contentious element, 'taste'. I reveal, for example, a decided fondness for the psychedelic movies of my late teens and undergraduate years. Yet my interest here is not limited by nostalgia. I have watched them repeatedly, but repetition need not lead to entropy. Each time, these films open up a new encounter: as I change and become with my changing contexts, so do they. My case studies are both singular experiments and culturally shared examples of what might be done with Deleuzian alterity and film, but the DeleuzeGuattarian approach can be applied to whatever 'turns you on' (to use a decidedly machinic, albeit dated, catchphrase).

My examples range from early to recent material from Europe, Soviet Russia and the USA. Of course, cinematic altered states are internationally diverse, but the study of specific national identities in this context raises complex issues I do not have space to address here.[45] Detailed historical or production contexts are also outside the scope of this study. I am mainly working with film material currently available (as I write) for viewers at the cinema, on domestic-use videos and DVDs and by cine-hire.[46] I find that films by maverick directors such as Stanley Kubrick and David Lynch that straddle the art-house/mainstream divide are often most productive for Deleuzian applications.

I begin with dreams as the most familiar cinematic altered state, critiquing psychoanalytical dream-work through DeleuzeGuattarian 'schizoanalysis'. The second chapter analyses the popularisation of altered consciousness in drugs-oriented films. Having deployed a more familiar, theme-based approach, I move further into cinematic alterity. Chapter 3 explores the altered body maps of haptics and synaesthesia in short experimental films with spiritual and erotic material. Chapter 4 approaches cinematic distortions of space and time via Bergson and Deleuze. In my speculative conclusion, I open up new digital and fractal directions for film.

Each chapter works with films that simultaneously represent and induce altered consciousness in a way inspired by Deleuze. The chapters have a dual focus on mainstream narrative and the short, intensive bombardment of experimental work, often rapidly copied and toned down by the Hollywood mainstream. Particular chapters suggest specific benefits of using Deleuzian and DeleuzeGuattarian concepts to think film affects, percepts and concepts in order to mobilise further, more fundamental questionings.

In psychoanalytical film readings such as Michel Chion's on Lynch the cinematic encounter with dream sequences either remains opaque or is subsumed in the supposed universality of unconscious scenarios.[47] Instead of an 'archaeology' of dreams, Deleuze and Guattari offer the 'cartography' of schizoanalysis, which I use together with Deleuze's cinema books to indicate a distinctive approach to cinematic dreams. In Chapter 1, I explain why Deleuze and Guattari refute psychoanalytic dream-work as a critical technique and why Deleuze prefers a Bergsonian approach to film dreams. To extend this, I recap a debate instigated by the Surrealists on the power of art to radicalise consciousness and highlight Artaud's intervention.

I identify three types of film dreams, beginning with more recognisable forms. In classical Hollywood narration, dreams are bracketed off from the central plot, like the Salvador Dali sequence in Hitchcock's *Spellbound* (1945). Yet, even in this, the use of multiple images, displacements and temporal distortions undermine conventional punctuation. In Lynch's arguably surrealistic *Fire Walk with Me* (1992) and *Mulholland Drive* (2001), dreams intensify an already anomalous narrative. Set in the liminal state between dream and waking, these dream contents spill over into actuality by material manifestation. More experimental dream-films, like Maya Deren's *Meshes of the Afternoon* (1943), blend dreams and waking in a seamless continuum and the explicit dream becomes less central. I present Michael Powell and Emeric Pressburger's *The Tales of Hoffmann* (1951) as 'implied dream' to exemplify the optical and sound situation of the 'cinema of enchantment'.

I launch Chapter 2 with Deleuze and Guattari's consideration of intoxicants in art via 'pharmacoanalysis'.[48] The impact of hallucinogens on brain chemistry induces radical perceptual changes. In this, my most detailed chapter, I contend that cinema offers an aesthetic parallel in its capacity to expand mundane modes of perception and thought. I want to interrogate how far each film impacts on us as an affective agent of becoming and alters consciousness. To do this, I suggest how particular stylistic techniques, such as abstraction and anamorphosis, might induce virtual narcosis by cinematic hallucination.

This process is elucidated through Deleuze and Guattari's concept of molecularity, with its roots in biology, atomic physics and the shamanistic writings of Castaneda. My typography of drug-induced hallucination ranges from the multiple superimpositions of Kenneth Anger's botanical brew in *Inauguration of the Pleasure Dome* (1954) to the heroin and amphetamine 'hip-hop' style and the skewed space-time of Darren Aronofsky's *Requiem for a Dream* (2001). The LSD trips of Roger Corman's *The Trip* (1968) and Dennis Hopper's *Easy Rider* (1968) reflect the conventions and cultural mainstreaming of psychedelic consciousness.

Deleuze and Guattari's reconceptualisation of the body as 'anorganic' is both radical and contentious. My focus is on altered states of body in Chapter 3. Films stimulate virtual sensation and induce affect by haptics and synaesthesia. Sensations of sound and vision impact in the body-without-organs (BWO) of the film/viewer assemblage. Drawing on *Cinema I*, I trace the vibrant affective aesthetics of textures and rhythms, colours, flicker and strobe as well as sound effects. An experiential approach to these often abstract films replaces symbolic interpretation.

Here, I introduce an affective 'logic of sensation' and erotic multiplicity to think the sensory experience of Kenneth Anger's *Puce Moment*. The cinematic eye is remapped in Stan Brakhage's reflections on aesthetics as well as his film *Dog Star Man* (1961–1964). Tony Conrad's *The Flicker* (1965) uses stroboscopic editing to stimulate hallucinatory phenomena. I also suggest how James Whitney's *Lapis* (1966), with its concentric coloured dots, induces meditative trance through its expression of the molecular flux.

Erotic film is the chapter's second corporeally altered state. I suggest how sexual ecstasy breaks down individual identities in the sexual fusions of cinema. Deleuze and Guattari replace a genitally limited body by the infinite possibilities of 'a thousand tiny sexes'.[49] Among the films I approach from this angle are Kathryn Bigelow's virtual-sex-as-drug *Strange Days* (1995) and Donald Cammell and Nicolas Roeg's hallucinatory sex in *Performance* (1970). Carolee Schneemann's *Fuses* (1967) visualises explicitly sexual sensations in affective images of movement, colour and light. This chapter's cinematic examples work to unravel existing body maps in favour of a more processual and fluid BWO.

Chapter 4 focuses on time. Time is a central cog in movies. Reels of film take time to unwind through the projector (or DVD player for electronic versions) and we give up our time to watching them. If cinema, rather than normalising time in such techniques as linear editing, fragments and confuses it, the mind also experiences altered states of time that challenge familiar temporal perceptions. For Deleuze, the interval of the time-image is located in editing, framing, lighting and overlay. I draw on his cinematic insights to illumine philosophical debates on the nature of time and human consciousness. The insights of Bergson on duration are crucial here. Deleuze's adaptation of these produces a radical typology of the time-image.

Werner Herzog's *Heart of Glass* (1977) uses long-held shots of clouds and grainy superimpositions to suspend linear time (and uses literally hypnotised actors to disorientate further). In different genre, science fiction provides a language of 'cosmic' temporality far removed from the clock-time of Terra. My sci-fi examples include Kubrick's essay in Nietzschean cinema *2001: A Space Odyssey* (1968) which elides aeons and Jordan Belson's abstract animation *Re-Entry* (1964) which traverses space-time. I round off the chapter by considering how the apocalyptic visions of a popular movement-image film, *Donnie Darko* (2001) enable the protagonist to see time-lines and avert an already seen future. My application suggests that more mainstream forms of film are open to Deleuzian interpretation via gaps we can work to extend.

In conclusion, rather than repeating a detailed summary of findings, I suggest possible futures for cinematic affect, alterity and Deleuzian film studies. The implications of 'fractal logic' are located in Deleuze and Guattari's last joint work. New experiments in digital imaging and video raise new political issues via the changing landscape of electronic 'encephalisation'. In its concern to explode habitual ways of thinking and feeling, as well as in its own radical poetry, I also assert Deleuze and Guattari's affective theoretical writing as itself an altered state.

Altered states of awareness are not the preserve of a limited audience of cognoscenti. Mainstream popular cinema, aided by effects technology, has expanded its parameters to include lavish spectacles of alterity. Even in conventional narratives, ecstatic and visionary sequences engineer audience participation. It is an intriguing question how far and in what ways cinematic depictions of altered states shape our perceptions of actual experiences. It may be, for example, that some acid trips of the late 1960s and 1970s came to resemble those in *The Trip*, *Easy Rider* or *Apocalypse Now* (Francis Ford Coppola, 1979). Altered states are at once idiosyncratic and subject to changing fashions like the film technologies used to present them.

Working with cinematic altered states has made me more aware of the limitations of language to grasp the affective quality of the art encounter *as* an altered state. Critical writing on film can only ever produce an *approximation* to the cinematic experience as the viewer as writer replays them on a different plane. For me, the altered states of film demand a more creative style of interpretation than that of some 'transparent' scholarly ideal. As I engage with the film as experience, my written style shifts according to what I am working with, becoming more, or less, dense or structured as the materials change. Lesser-known films require more 'description'.

For Deleuze, art is 'always incomplete, always in the midst of being formed, and goes beyond the matter of any liveable or lived experience. It is a process'.[50] Analytical readings are far from exhausting the film's affective catalytic potential for becoming. So, our encounter with film and our theoretical exploration of it offer much more than a copy of a copy of a copy (of a copy). Read my speculative responses alongside your first viewing (or fresh re-viewing) of the films being explored. Use the sections in the order and the way that appeals. Jessup uses *himself* as his experimental subject. By connecting altered states film with Deleuzian concepts, this book invites you to do the same.

Notes

1. Guattari, *Chaosmosis*, p. 92.
2. *The Oxford English Dictionary*, Vol. I, p. 211.
3. Ibid., p. 213.
4. Bergson, *Creative Evolution*, trans. p. 306.
5. Deleuze, *Cinema 1*, p. 59.
6. Ibid.
7. Bergson, *Matter and Memory*, pp. 55–6.
8. Deleuze, *Cinema 1*, p. 65.
9. Ibid., p. 66.
10. Ibid., p. 65.
11. Ibid., p. 102.
12. Ibid., p. 65.
13. Deleuze, *Cinema 2*, p. 33.
14. Colebrook, *Gilles Deleuze*, p. 40.
15. Ibid., p. 38.
16. *The Oxford English Dictionary*, Vol. I, p. 365.

17. Ibid.
18. Ibid., p. 366.
19. *The Oxford English Dictionary*, Vol. III, p. 756.
20. Deleuze, Spinoza, p. 60.
21. Ibid., p. 18.
22. Ibid., p. 59.
23. Ibid., p. 19.
24. *The Oxford English Dictionary*, Vol. XVI, p. 551.
25. Ibid.
26. Ibid., p. 550.
27. Deleuze, 'The Brain Is the Screen', pp. 365–72.
28. Deleuze and Guattari, *What is Philosophy?*, p. 217.
29. For Deleuzian-inflected film, music and art, see http://www.eri.mmu.ac.uk/deleuze/.
30. See Colebrook, 'Inhuman Irony' and other essays in Buchanan and Marks, *Deleuze and Literature*, pp. 100–34; Buchanan and Swiboda, *Deleuze and Music*; O'Sullivan, *Art Encounters Deleuze and Guattari*.
31. Martin-Jones, *Deleuze, Cinema and National Identity*; Powell, *Deleuze and Horror Film*; Kennedy, *Deleuze and Cinema*.
32. Motivated by Laura Mulvey's seminal essay, 'Visual Pleasure and Narrative Cinema'.
33. Culturalist prime movers have been Mark Jancovich, Joanne Hollows and the e-journal *Scope*. See Jancovich, Faire and Stubbings, *The Place of the Audience*; Jancovich, Hollows and Hutchings, *The Film Studies Reader*.
34. Bourdieu, *Distinction*.
35. Guattari, *The Three Ecologies* and *Molecular Revolution*. Studies of Deleuze and politics include Buchanan, *Deleuzism*, and Thoburn, *Deleuze, Marx and Politics*.
36. Deleuze and Guattari, *A Thousand Plateaus*, p. 187.
37. Carroll, *The Philosophy of Horror*, *Interpreting the Moving Image* and *A Philosophy of Mass Art*; Peterson, *Dreams of Chaos, Visions of Order*.
38. Bordwell and Carroll, *Post-Theory*; Bordwell and Thompson, *Film Art*.
39. Following Stacey, *Stargazing*.
40. Rodowick, *Gilles Deleuze's Time Machine*.
41. Shaviro, *The Cinematic Body*.
42. Bogue, *Deleuze on Cinema*.
43. Pisters, *The Matrix of Visual Culture*.
44. Deleuze and Parnet, *Dialogues*, p. 144.
45. See Martin-Jones, *Deleuze, Cinema and National Identity*.
46. These films are available on DVD or video from sources like the ICA (http://www.ica.org.uk) and videos of broadcast TV series. Carolee Schneemann's *Fuses*, still limited because of its sexual explicitness, is available for hire (on cine) or personal viewing at the Lux cinema (http://www.lux.org.uk). Work with viewing tables gives a greater sense of each frame's

complexity. Region 1 DVDs from the USA can be played in the UK on multi-region machines.

47. Chion, *David Lynch*.
48. Deleuze and Guattari, *A Thousand Plateaus*, p. 283.
49. For more on Deleuze and Guattari's claim that there are '*n* sexes', see Grosz, 'A Thousand Tiny Sexes: Feminism and Rhizomatics', pp. 187–213.
50. Deleuze, 'Literature and Life', p. 1.

CHAPTER 1

The Dream Machine

The analyst seeks only to induce the patient to talk about his hidden problems, to open the locked doors of his mind. (*Spellbound* title sequence)

at the heart of dreams themselves – as with fantasy and delirium – machines function as indices of deterritorialisation.[1] (Deleuze and Guattari)

Spellbound

Good night and sweet dreams – which we'll analyse after breakfast. (Dr Brulov, *Spellbound*)

Alfred Hitchcock's *Spellbound* begins with an on-screen text identifying psychoanalysis as 'the method by which modern science treats the emotional problems of the sane'. Here, as befits a film about the 'talking cure', the opening prioritises words. The text is a curious mix of scientific certainty and gothic madness. It assures us that 'once the complexes that have been disturbing the patient are uncovered and interpreted, the illness and confusion disappear'. Yet, at the same time it pronounces that 'the devils of unreason' will be 'driven from the human soul' by analysis as exorcism. Such ambivalence recalls Freud's own suggestion that analysands who describe the return of the repressed, 'hint of possession by some daemoniac power'.[2]

From another perspective, though, the written text underlines the inadequacy of language to convey the special affective quality of the cinematic dream state. The film's highlights are not written or spoken text, but pure image and sound, opaque to Freudian word-association. They operate on a plane more amenable to a Deleuzian approach to films and dreams whether explicit (a character shown dreaming) or implicit (the broader film as dream world).

Yet psychoanalytical interpretations of film dreams have long been hegemonic and Hitchcock has attracted much cinepsychoanalytic interest.[3] One aim of this chapter's argument is to compare psychoanalytic and Deleuzian methods to underline their divergence. In some ways, this process reflects my own 'deconversion' from cinepsychoanalysis and this is why I have chosen *Spellbound* to launch this study.

So what kind of psychoanalysis informs *Spellbound*? On a thematic level, it makes an earnest attempt to validate the talking cure, but its Hollywood simplifications reflect the 'dollar book Freud' rapidly popularised after the analyst's death in 1939. For Dr Constance Petersen (Ingrid Bergman), John Ballantine (Gregory Peck) is in thrall to an Oedipal 'guilt complex over a sin that was only a child's bad dream'. Ballantine's repressed childhood traumas are transferred to a father-figure, the older analyst Dr Edwardes, who he kills by proxy and whose identity he steals. The parental function of transference is underlined by Dr Alex Brulov (Michael Chekhov)'s offer of himself as a surrogate father and reminder to Constance that she is not her lover Ballantine's 'mama'. The normalising function of analysis is seen not only in the 'cure' for paranoiac amnesia, but also in Constance's gradual exchange of professional for wifely role.

So what might a psychoanalytic approach unearth of symbolic significance in the explicit, recurring dream recalled by Ballantine? Its first shot sets up a theatre of the unconscious and the surveillance economy of the gaze via prominent eyes painted on curtains. One of these eyes, cut by scissors, replays a similar image in Luis Buñuel and Salvador Dali's *Un Chien andalou* (1928) to enact a symbolic castration both of Ballantine's vision and his ego-defences.[4]

The sound and vision experience of the dream in the card game's melting edits, is interrupted by the analysts' obsessive search for the word association as a magic key to unlock trauma. Constance and Brulov excitedly break into Ballantine's account, disrupting the dream's flow with attempted analysis, which of course increases suspense by delaying further revelation. As Ballantine sits in a trance, their aggressive questioning seeks to force word associations out of his memory. They hang over him, drawing the blinds on the external snow scene that offers a more effective trigger to recollection. Despite personal and professional therapeutic intentions their manner recalls interrogation. Hitchcock thus aligns psychoanalysis with the less significant and more off-track investigation by the police.

Hitchcock indicates further, by his play with eyes and spectacles, that they are looking in the wrong place. Myopic Brulov raises his glasses and attempts to scry Constance's handwritten notes. Shots of Constance deep in thought, highlight her eyes to suggest, along with her animated vocal tone and pace, an obsessive, manic quality to her epistemological drive to 'see' the truth of psychosexual secrets.

Analytical voices fade as the inner narrative unfolds a vast Dali dreamscape. Hitchcock, rejecting traditionally 'blurred and hazy' film dreams style chose Dali's artwork for its 'great visual sharpness and clarity – sharper than the film itself', but also to authenticate his own link with

Surrealism.[5] A large, distorted head hangs forward to overlook the murder witnessed by Ballantine. For psychoanalysis, this superhuman phallus marks the omniscience of a judgemental God/father. The villain (Dr Murchison) remains faceless and eyeless to enable Ballantine to project himself onto the blank space and kill Edwardes by proxy. As the camera moves into a close-up of a twisted wheel dropped by the murderer, the hole at the centre is both an ever-watching eye and the hole of castration. Winged shadows pursue Ballantine's flight, engulfing him in the darkness of displaced guilt and ego loss.

In the grounding model of cinepsychoanalysis the spectator distances the screen as an imaginary spectacle. Rather than engaging in the affective continuum, body is thus split from mind. The analysand's words in the 'talking cure' are displacements of preordained complexes. Here, there are significant theoretical fissures with Deleuze's attitude to cinematic dreams and his focus on affect rather than overt signification. A Deleuzian perspective might, for example, regard the play of lighting on Ballantine's forehead as intensive searching through layers of memory. Or we might consider the properties of a distinctively eerie sonsign: the high-pitched wail of the theramin in Miklos Rozsa's electronic scoring of psychic disturbance.

Deleuze's critique is not limited to actual dreams of characters, but dream-images can be 'scattered' through a film in ways that make it possible to 'reconstitute them in their totality'.[6] In classical Hollywood, dreams are bracketed off from the central plot. Yet the use of multiple images, displacements and temporal distortions undermine such conventional punctuation to mobilise potentially endless chains of interlinked images. In *Spellbound*, he writes, 'the real dream does not appear in the Daliesque paste and cardboard sequence' but is spread between widely separated elements, including

> the impressions of a fork on a sheet which will become stripes on pyjamas, to jump to the striations on a white cover, which will produce the widening-out space of a washbasin, itself taken up by an enlarged glass of milk, giving way in turn to a field of snow marked by parallel ski lines.[7]

In these series of images, a large circuit is mapped out in which 'each one is like the virtuality of the next that makes it actual'.[8] For Ballantine, confused by image overlay, the actual, hidden sensation is his accidental childhood agency in his brother's death.

Despite its uncanny impact, the recurrent dream is over-familiar to Ballantine through repetition and too far displaced to 'unlock' his secret. The dream is only part of a longer process of unravelling. Seeking the truth elsewhere than the analyst's couch, Constance and Ballantine visit Gabriel Valley, the scene of Edwardes's actual murder. In the train dining car, the flicker of passing lights induces a light trance and the gleam of a knife elicits a fixed stare from Ballantine, his growing hypersensitivity to environmental stimuli shared by the viewer. Constance misunderstands his response as murderous and shifts the knife.

Gabriel Valley's vast, impersonal snow scene recalls its displaced figuration in the dreamscape.[9] The film's movement climaxes in the exhilarating glide of the couple's skiing, out of synch with its static, back-projected ground. As they approach a precipice, Ballantine's sinister aspect is intensified by film-noir shadow. At the eleventh hour, he rescues Constance and himself from the fatal cycle of repetition and breaks the spell not by word association but through redemptive action.

Brulov and Constance have been looking for clues in a static space, abstracting movement from evidence, whereas enlightenment lies in the motion of the child's slide. Images of passing train tracks, the rubbing of a fork on the sheet and the slide of the camera-eye up the striped bedcover hold Ballantine's sliding secret. His brother's impalement on spiked railings has been expressed by the fork, the knife, sled blades and skis cutting into snow.

In seeking to unearth hidden structures of meaning, cinepsychoanalysis abstracts cinematic signs from their moving, changing medium. Clearly a new approach to cinematic dreams is timely, based on Deleuze's aesthetics. Rather than focusing on overt and covert symbolism with psychosexual significance, we can encounter images within the flux of dynamic forces and become aware of our own participation in their motion.

This means a shift away from symbolic meaning to the singularities of style and expression. Kinaesthetics replace language-like representation at the crux of the filmic event. Deleuze's approach offers a fresh encounter with even the most 'classical' film dreams. I am extending the debate between Freudian and Deleuzian oneirics from surrealist echoes, through hybrid forms to new cinematic grammars of dream. The next stage of my journey is driven by mixed fuel: Deleuze's time-image work on dreams and DeleuzeGuattarian schizoanalysis, which, I argue, remains a covert force permeating the cinema books.

Schizoanalysis, Becoming and Film

Deleuze and Guattari remap the unconscious to replace the unearthing of past trauma by psychoanalytic 'archaeology'. They neither centralise the ego nor pathologise mental anomalies. Developing Antonin Artaud's poetic images, they produce a new method of psychic cartography: schizo-analysis. Schizoanalytic maps do not depend on foundational relations but produce themselves. Rejecting traditional models of the body's organic layout, these 'intensive' maps chart a shifting 'constellation of affects'.[10] The schizophrenic experiences such pure intensities via the body-without-organs (BWO), a concept detailed in my Chapter 2.

Schizoanalysis foregrounds the intensive transitions of autoproductive desiring machines in states of immanence. Applied to film, it avoids trans-lating symbolic representation into a definite set of meanings, aiming instead to 'overturn the theatre of representation into the order of desir-ing-production'.[11] Melding style with form and theme, it maps assem-blages in process. It charts concepts generated in the dynamic perceptual encounter of film and viewer via the affective interval.

For schizoanalysis, the affective force of film exceeds the symbolic prop-erties of language and image. It works to release us from the schemata of representational equations and motivates us to think in new ways, freeing up desire to become. The Oedipal scenarios mapped onto film dreams by psychoanalysis are abstracted, deep structures rather than embodied acts. Sensory-motor responses to light, sound, colour and motion lead thought away from preconceptions into the realm of non-symbolic ideation, or 'intuition'. Schizoanalysis does not approach mental anomaly with the pathologising 'apparatus of capture', but instead explores an 'intense feeling of transition, states of pure, naked intensity stripped of all shape and form'.[12]

A psychoanalytical definition of schizophrenia identifies 'discordance, dissociation, disintegration', accompanied by detachment from reality in 'a turning in upon the self and the predominance of a delusional mental life given over to the production of phantasies (autism)'.[13] Guattari's experimental group work with schizophrenics at la Borde replaced Freud's hierarchical model of the unconscious with a dynamic, interactive mobili-sation of a 'desiring machine, independently of any interpretation'.[14] Rather than strengthening subjective ego defences, Guattari's technique favoured the creation of a dynamic group ego. As well as providing new methods of clinical practice the 'intensive voyage' of schizoanalysis opens up new modes of art and politics.[15]

Schizoanalysis refutes lack as primal condition and its consequent split-ting of subject from object. Deleuze and Guattari seek out 'regions of the orphan unconscious – indeed "beyond all law" – where the problem of Oedipus can no longer be raised'.[16] Oedipus colludes with the existing system, whereas schizoanalysis mobilises the micropolitics of desire in a 'neo-aesthetic/neo-sexuality outside psychoanalytic myths and theatres of the past'.[17] The schizo is anarchic, 'irresponsible, solitary, and joyous [. . .] a desire lacking nothing, a flux that overcomes barriers and codes, a name that no longer designates any ego whatever' (sic).[18] This model diverges sharply from the psychoanalytic use of fantasy to enable the return of the repressed, engineer sublimation and endorse social consensus.

Guattari and Deleuze distinguish clinical schizophrenia and schizo-analysis as critical method. Schizoanalysis operates as '*the outside of psycho-analysis itself*', discovered by 'internal reversal of its analytical categories'.[19] Their 'schizos' are experimental artists such as Artaud, Samuel Beckett and Franz Kafka, whose creative 'schizzes' both deploy and motivate becomings. So where do dream images fit in the schizoanalytic map in process?

Dreams in *Anti-Oedipus*

Deleuze and Guattari object to the centrality of dreams in analysis, arguing that the supposed 'royal road' of unconscious desire is actually a super-egoic domain ruled by an internalised repressor. In *Spellbound*'s dream sequence, for example, the gigantic head and ubiquitous eyes mark the territory of what they call a 'superpowerful and superarchaicised ego (the Urzene of the Urstaat)'.[20] At first glance, Deleuze and Guattari seem to reject the significance of dreams outright, along with Freudian strictures. Dreams have been read as Oedipal, they argue, because of their 'perverse reterritorialisation in relation to the deterritorialisation of sleep and nightmares'.[21] They identify the destabilising tendency of nightmares as potentially radical, but intriguingly leave this suggestion undeveloped.

Yet, despite the oppressive psychoanalytic colonisation of dreams, they still retain the possibility of redemption by machinic desire, asserting that 'at the heart of dreams themselves – as with fantasy and delirium – machines function as indices of deterritorialisation'.[22] Even in Freudian symbolisation, desiring machines circulate images in process of transformation, with potential for 'escaping and causing circulations, of carrying and being carried away' via

> the airplane of parental coitus, the little brother's bicycle, the father's car, the grand-mother's sewing machine, all objects of flight and theft, stealing and stealing away – the machine is always infernal in the family dream.[23]

A desiring machine uses guerrilla tactics to subvert symbolic interpretation by introducing 'breaks and flows that prevent the dream from being reconfined in its scene and systematised within its representation' via the empirical intervention of 'an irreducible factor of non-sense, which will develop elsewhere and from without, in the conjunctions of the real as such'.[24] The 'Oedipal stubbornness' of psychoanalysis cannot grasp the secret operations of desiring machines.

Deleuze and Guattari contrast the two analytical regimes through the concept of territory. While one 'reterritorialises' by fixing the significance of people and surroundings, the other 'deterritorialises on machines'.[25] Psychoanalysis 'settles on [. . .] imaginary and structural representations of reterritorialisation' whereas schizoanalysis 'follows the machinic indices of deterritorialisation'.[26] In the desiring machine, ideas are dynamic events, lines of flight leading off into a 'fibrous web of directions' like a tuber or map.[27]

Schizoanalytic approaches to art, then, replace representation by material capture. Denying psychic interiority, Deleuze and Guattari insist that art is an immanent 'being in sensation and nothing else: it exists in itself'.[28] Applied to film by Deleuze, it offers an experiential not a significatory approach to the moving image. The automatism of cinema deterritorialises perception. Anomalous states of consciousness can be celebrated rather than pathologised, both for their stylistic innovations and their impact on the audience who partakes of their affective contagion. Deleuze's reading of cinematic dreams shifts its overt focus from Freud to Bergson.

Deleuze, Bergson and Dreams

Bergson's dual model of the psyche has little in common with Freud's tripartite structure of ego, id and superego. The outer layer of Bergson's psychic topography is spatially and socially oriented. Interior affect vibrates intensively in temporal duration. In this schema, one 'self' is the external projection and social representation of the other. The fluctuating inner self is accessible by a process of introspection that enables us to 'grasp our inner states as living things, constantly *becoming*, as states not amenable to measure, which permeate one another'.[29]

Freud and Bergson each identify inner depth and complexity, yet their perspectives on time and the psyche are radically distinct. Freud's unconscious is a-temporal and its functions are '*timeless* i.e. they are not altered by the passage of time; they have no reference to time at all'.[30] Bergson's inner self is also formed of memory, but this is not limited by actual, familial experience: it belongs to the durational process of perpetual becoming and the continuum of memory and action. In my view, his fluid, multifaceted model of intensity is analogous to the affective multiplicity of schizoanalysis.

In Bergson's scheme, circuits of the past spread like ripples. The dream is the 'outermost envelope' of the circuits, furthest away from actuality.[31] The Bergsonian dreamer retains only tenuous connections with internal and external sensations via 'fluid, malleable sheets of past which are happy with a very broad or floating adjustment'.[32] The dream, then, lacks both the sensory-motor linkage of habitual recognition and the circuits of perception-recollection operant in attentive recognition. In Deleuze's Bergsonian time-image, the connections between 'an optical (or sound) sensation and a panoramic vision, between any sensation whatever and a total dream image' are 'weak and dislocatory'.[33]

Deleuze approaches film and dreams via commentary on Bergson's distinction between a dream-image and a recollection-image.[34] Bergson differentiates habitual and attentive recognition. Automatic recognition works by sensory-motor extension. Perception of an object's use-value is extended into movement. It operates on a horizontal plane via associated images. Automatic recognition superficially seems richer because of its extension into sensory-motor images.

Deleuze adapts Bergson's model to conceive a new approach to cinema as a philosophical as well as an aesthetic encounter. Attentive recognition mobilises intensive movements that focus on facets of the object as it passes vertically through different planes. We 'constitute a pure optical (and sound) image' in order to make a 'description' of the thing.[35] Rather than perceiving the concrete object per se, the pure optical image is more 'rarefied'.[36] Citing Robbe-Grillet, Deleuze asserts that such description actually 'erases' its original object.[37] It thus problematises the ontological status of the thing itself, enabling variant descriptions and rendering lines and features 'always provisional, always in question, displaced or replaced'.[38]

According to Deleuze's main types of descriptive cinema image, the movement-image is 'organic' (sensory-motor) and the time-image 'inorganic' (physical-geometrical).[39] A perception-image is actualised by recollection, whereas a 'pure' recollection remains virtual. A dream-image is distinct from either and can be identified by interlinked characteristics. Firstly, the sleeper's perceptions are reduced to the 'diffuse condition of a dust of actual sensations' that escape consciousness.[40] Secondly, the virtual image is not actualised directly, but appears in the form of another, different image, which 'plays the role of virtual image being actualised in a third, and so on to infinity'.[41] The dream, then, can be expressed in a range of distorted images, its non-metaphoric series sketching out a large circuit.

Deleuze traces the time-image's failures of recognition and recollection back to early European cinema's phenomena like amnesia, hypnosis, hallucination, madness, the vision of the dying and nightmare and dream in particular.[42] These altered states of consciousness are more prevalent in more philosophical and psychological types of cinema. Deleuze's examples are drawn from Russian Formalism, German Expressionism and French Surrealism. Here, I want to reprieve some basic premises of the historical Surrealists and view their most celebrated dream film, *Un Chien andalou* (1928) through a Deleuzian prism, drawing on both his remapping of cinematic dreams and his co-authored work.

Ultra-confusional Activity: Dreams and *Un Chien andalou*

As a starter, I will briefly recap what Freud's artist aficionados initially set out to do. Freud's psychosexual model centres on the fantasy displacements of desire in daydreams, night dreams and aesthetic expression. *The Interpretation of Dreams* (1900) offered the Surrealist movement a model of unconscious forces informed by secular humanism and scientific empiricism.[43] Yet, both Freud and the Surrealists were fascinated by extreme states of consciousness, particularly those labelled (often by Freud himself) as pathological. Rather than wishing to re-establish the ego's centrality, though, Surrealists sought to free the libidinal drives and challenge the reality principle. Their methods included dream-work, automatism (an inspirational technique of composition using trance) and *amour fou*.

Deleuze does not address Surrealism per se, possibly because of his repudiation of Freudianism and the politically problematic status of André Breton and other surrealists in postwar France. Deleuzian critique is not primarily focused on the evaluation of historical movements in art and cinema. Yet, it is possible to cross-reference Deleuze and Surrealist aesthetics both covertly (general tendencies) and overtly (specific references) via the crucial figure of Artaud whose concepts I address in a later chapter.

Buñuel's films are also a significant presence in Deleuze's work. Breton, after rejecting Germaine Dulac's 1928 film *Le coquille et le clergyman* (based on Artaud's scenario), gave his seal of approval to *Un Chien andalou* as the first 'true' Surrealist film. The film validated 'psychic automatism in its pure state' and expressed the 'actual functioning of thought. Dictated by thought, in the absence of any control exercised by reason, exempt from any aesthetic or moral concern'.[44] For Buñuel, it 'amalgamated the aesthetics of surrealism with Freudian discoveries'.[45] The scenario was conceived by the psychoanalytic practice of recounting dreams and selecting significant images for their sexual symbolism.

Unlike Dulac's film, *Un Chien andalou* does not feature a dreamer per se, but aims to be more 'realistic', which for Buñuel means 'animated by impulses, the primal sources [which] are those of poetry'.[46] Clearly intended to offend 'puritanical moral principles', it aimed not to please but to provoke radical awareness and 'a desperate appeal to murder'.[47]

According to Dali's 'paranoiac critical' method, the film subverts spectatorial control and pronounces 'the overwhelming importance of desire'.[48] Breton claimed that this intensive state of 'ultra-confusional activity' approaches insanity in its 'critical and systematic objectivisation of mad associations and interpretations'.[49]

Un Chien andalou's structural repetitions and retractions have a dreamlike interior cohesion. Its strongly affective images mobilise the haptic tactility of an eye slashed by a razor and a trapped hand crawling with ants. Skewed angles, varied focus, superimposition and spatio-temporal discontinuities disturb perceptual stability. Jump-cuts between long shots and close-ups, interiors and exteriors, fragment linear narrative.

For Breton, the film affirms the Freudian unconscious via dreams and presents it to the public with the didactic intent of a Surrealist manifesto. Deleuze's interest in early European avant-garde film is informed by his different philosophical and cultural agenda. For him, the value of such work as affective time-image is twofold. Via experimentation with 'visual and sound sensations (or tactile ones, cutaneous or coanesthetic) which have lost their motor extension', they are able to express philosophical concepts.[50] By creating a single 'automatic subjectivity' that unites 'image, thought and camera', they offer insight into 'the mystery of time'.[51]

Deleuze argues that perceptual disturbances are not dependent on extreme plot situations, but they can be produced by 'ordinary states' such as sleep, dream or disturbed attention.[52] They do not require motor extension or the memory-based recognition of specific recollections. In such receptive states duration is accessible via 'images of the past *in general*'.[53] These temporal images form an 'unstable set of floating memories', that move at 'dizzying speed as if time were achieving a profound freedom'.[54]

Motor powerlessness can trigger 'total and anarchic mobilising of the past'.[55] In dreams or other states of sensory-motor relaxation, images become those 'purely optical or sound perspectives of a divested present which no longer enjoys links with a disconnected past', such as childhood memories, fantasies or déjà vu.[56] A sleeper might experience the 'actual luminous sensation of a green surface broken with white patches', which evoke for 'the dreamer who lives in the sleeper' an interlinked chain of images in metamorphosis,

a meadow dotted with flowers, but this image is only actualised by already becoming the image of a billiard table furnished with balls, which in turn does not become actual without becoming something else.[57]

In cinematic terms, these transformations are conveyed by editing in the temporal ellipsis of superimpositions, or dissolves, which induce affective 'melting' states of consciousness.[58]

Un Chien andalou's events are linked by metamorphic associations: cloud bisecting moon/razored eyeball; underarm hair/sea-urchin/circular head of hair/circle of bystanders. Deleuze cites Buster Keaton's *Sherlock Junior* (1924) for its similarly constructed image string: unbalanced chair in garden/somersault into street/learning over precipice/jaws of lion/sits on desert cactus/little hill becomes island battered by waves/dives into snow/back in garden.[59] Such associated links set becomings in motion.

Deleuze notes that the production of dream-images in the 'metaphysics of the imagination' has polarised technical methods of linking images.[60] The first tends towards abstraction via 'rich and overloaded' techniques such as 'dissolves, superimpositions, deframings, complex camera movements, special effects' and laboratory manipulations.[61] The second, more restrained type uses non-continuity editing between concrete objects to effect 'perpetual unhinging which "looks like"' a dream.[62]

The relation of dreamlike states to the real is comparable to the anomalies of a language system in relation to current linguistic usage.[63] For the technically overloaded dream-image, the linguistic comparison includes 'addition, complication, over-saturation' as in the Dada film *Entr'acte* (René Clair, 1924) whereas the abstracted kind prefers 'elimination, ellipse, break, cut, unhinging' like *Un Chien andalou*. I will trace a shift from Freudian to Bergsonian affective dream-images via an experimental, surrealistic American dream film of Deleuze's first, 'complicated' type.

The Dreamer Entranced: *Meshes of the Afternoon*

> The mind begins with the matter at hand – the incidental curve of a road or the accidental movement of a passing figure. As it perceives these it possesses them as images, as the stuff of which it composes its day dreams and night dreams, in the forms of its desires and despairs.[64] (Maya Deren)

Although Oedipus is notably absent, Deren's work from the mid-1940s presents dreams as formations of desire. *Meshes of the Afternoon* (1945) and *At Land* (1945) are aligned to a Surrealism adapted to the cultural and artistic climate of the USA via her mentor, Chilean artist Encharito Matta, an ex-confederate and rival of Breton. Deren endorsed both Matta's rejection of Freud and his more conscious formalism via her own 'conscious control of form at variance with free association' and the 'Surrealist aesthetic of spontaneity'.[65]

Deren asserts that both films were misinterpreted by a critical ethos hungry for Surrealist work.[66] Although *Meshes of the Afternoon* might feasibly be read as psychotherapeutic in its enactment of tensions between Deren and her filmmaker husband Alexander Hammid, its intensive world of moving images expresses far more than psychosexual difficulties. Deren repudiates the Freudian curative attempt to subject the 'feminine' irrational to rational analysis.

Meshes of the Afternoon explores the mind's virtual imaging of actuality. For Deren, the film 'externalises an inner world to the point where it is confounded with the external one'.[67] This confusion of planes is assisted by fades, intercutting and repetitions. She foregrounds the continuum of virtual and actual and 'the imagined achieved [. . .] such force that it became reality'.[68] Rather than being driven by narrative action, her work is mobilised by shifts in perception and, according to P. Adams Sitney, a character's progress is 'marked by what he sees along his path rather than what he does' (*sic*).[69] For Sitney, Deren's 'trance film' offers a distinctive presentation of dreams as the visionary trances of

> somnambulists, priests, initiates of rituals, and the possessed, whose stylised movements the camera, with its slow and fast motions, can recreate so aptly. The protagonist wanders through a potent environment.[70]

So how distinct is the American dream/trance film from its European prototype and how might it look from a Deleuzian perspective? For Deleuze, *Un Chien andalou* concerns becomings rather than dreams. It presents the dream events of doubling, incongruity, violence and explicit sexuality, linking images in a potentially endless metamorphosis. Deren's piece unfolds a complex splitting of the self, dreams within dreams and defamiliarisation of the domestic space. Nevertheless, the two films share formal contiguity and oneiric inspiration.

Both Deren's and Buñuel's dream worlds elaborate an initial incident. Each splits the subject, but Deren's emanates five 'selves' (played by the filmmaker herself) and the schizophrenic figure is more central. Lacanian psychoanalysis might map the mirror phase onto the film's 'reflective experience' as well as its literal mirrors.[71] Both filmmakers render everyday objects uncanny and Deren uses cinematic technique to give 'malevolent reality to inanimate objects'.[72] The multiple sliding signifiers of *Un Chien andalou* are replaced by a more restrained set of symbolic objects, chiefly a knife, a key and a flower with context-dependent function.[73]

A further link of Deren's theory and practice with Deleuze's project is Eisenstein, whom she studied avidly in her period as a Marxist activist.[74]

In 1946, she published a substantial, Eisensteinian aesthetic statement.[75] Her typology of films as horizontal or vertical is clearly drawn from Eisenstein's elaborate theories. Vertical integration explores the complexities of consciousness within a moment rather than a linear temporal development.[76] She advocated the use of dynamic editing to transform content by sudden spatial and temporal shifts. Despite its oneiric immateriality, her film maintains the authority and potential of material objects as images.

Object-images appear in Deren's films for their own sakes as well as for their symbolic meaning because she believed that photography, as a reality equivalent, can work as 'a metaphor for ideas and abstractions'.[77] She emphasises the dynamics of memory activated by film-watching, when our 'continuous act of recognition' is like 'a strip of memory unrolling beneath the images of the film itself, to form the invisible underlayer of an implicit double exposure'.[78] Her suggestion that actualised images have a virtual dimension in connected acts of memory recalls the Bergsonian actual/virtual model I analyse later.

The 'sound situation' of *Meshes of the Afternoon* is Tijo Ito's abstract meshwork of plucked strings that varies the vibration of random notes with more structured passages. The music's reverberations entrance the auditory nerves. In this intensive, spatially static world, Ito's soundtrack operates a parallel process to the visuals with their subtly shifting replications. In its endless looping of intricate patterns, the music evokes a Bergsonian sense of duration via sounds congenial to the dream/trance state.

So how else can Deren's film offer a productive nexus for a Deleuzian approach? Rather than establishing locale, the opening shot refuses spatial orientation by focusing on the slight motion of swaying trees. Such intensive movements turn in on themselves to suggest a mysterious and diffused world of non-human energy. In counterpoint to these, the central character struggles to move swiftly and extensively via a more focused glide as though swimming against a current.

More extensive motion intrudes as an arm drops into frame, to disappear with equal suddenness after laying a flower on the pathway. By labelling such part-objects as uncanny schizoid formations, cinepsychoanalysis ignores the film's style, the very area where Deleuze chooses to work. He uses framing to think the presence of a durational elsewhere not subject to the limits of the spatial dimension. For Deleuze, the frame's inherent 'deterritorialisation of the image' depends on the determination of an out-of-field.[79]

The out-of-field opens up the frame to 'a more disturbing presence, one which cannot even be said to exist, but rather to "insist" or "subsist", a more radical Elsewhere, outside homogenous space and time'.[80] Deren's film insists on the presence of the out-of-field by her use of sudden intrusions or of fragments that fill the frame, such as feet and lower legs clearly cut off from a larger body by the limits of the frame. The film's subjectivity is fundamentally fragmented. When the woman (Deren's) face is eventually revealed, it is abstracted and diffused by the soft focus and averted gaze of a sleepwalker.

Unfolding the film's tapestry of moving shadows, a shadow hand lifts a shadow flower. The woman is preceded by her own elongated shadow, rendered sinister by its entrance into a domestic space. She leaves behind a triangular patch of darkness slashed with beams of light. Representation melts into an abstraction that underpins the autonomous force of light. When she sleeps in a chair bleached out by sunlight, her consciousness is similarly blurred and hazed over by afternoon sunlight.

For Deleuze, shadow has 'anticipatory function' in German Expressionist films such as F. W. Murnau's *Nosferatu* (1922) where it acts autonomously and forms disorienting 'virtual conjunctions' independent of character or object position.[81] Expressionism counterpoints light and shade to 'express an alternative between the state of things itself and the possibility, the virtuality, which goes beyond it'.[82] This 'beyond' is the Bergsonian virtual, spiritual dimension. Expressionism belongs to Deleuze's cinema of lyrical abstraction. Its Hollywood adaptation was the film noir contemporaneous with Deren's film.

Knocking unheeded at the front door, the woman takes a key out of her purse. Along with the Georgia O'Keefe style flower that she later lays between her thighs, these objects can be read as overt psychoanalytic symbols of a narcissistic yet active female sexuality that seeks to usurp phallic agency. Denied access, she drops the key, which slips down the steps autonomously to elude her slow-motion grasp, captured only by the temporal elision of editing. On entering, the camera obsessively pans the room then glides into close-up as the woman focuses on a cup and saucer and, for a Freudian, the further genital symbols of a knife in a loaf and a dangling telephone receiver, isolating the dreamer from the external world of linguistic communication.

The impact of these objects as antipathetic environmental forces is expressed by aggressive and 'overloaded' camerawork and special editing. A dizzying spiral undermines optical control as the woman climbs the stairs. In her later climb, the camera aggressively turns and tilts, shakes, swirls in a 360 degree turn, reduces her stature by high canting and suspends her from the ceiling, as gravitational laws are reversed in a possible nod to Jean Cocteau's *Le sang d'un poète* (1929).

The film's temporal dimension is insistent. In the empty bedroom, a still spinning record turntable suggests a recent departure. Stuck in the same groove, the record freezes progress. In an attempt to move the stasis, the woman takes the needle off. Time speeds up by fast motion and shadows stroke her closed eyes after the more jagged stabs of over-bright light and staccato editing of the stairs. The terrace outside darkens rapidly with her closed eyes, suggesting the onset of sleep. Shadows sweep across her twice with melting temporal fades that intensify the ominous atmosphere.

The film's dream worlds are multiple with overlapping edges. As the woman moves into closed-eye vision, the terrace enters an autonomous time zone and its own objective dream in the late afternoon sunlight. The insertion of one dream world into another is signalled by an irised-in terrace. This conveys the camera's own machinic point of view from within the lens and recalls the static record. The terrace replays the endless circuitry of the woman's pursuit of a mysterious, mirror-faced 'nun'. This gothic figure moves in fast motion while the pursuer is stymied by slowness, unable to narrow the gap between them. They remain in deadlock, temporally as well as spatially out of synch. Although the pursuer runs as fast she can, the nun's pace remains steady. Like the record, they are stuck in a frozen trajectory.

The film's interlinked dream worlds are not entirely repetitious cycles. Despite their deferrals, they lead to action and change. As well as multiple worlds, the woman is split into several personas of a schizoid trajectory. Multiple imagos appear in the same frame, interact and watch 'themselves'. Their identical appearance is distinguished by the cross-cutting of out-of-synch planes or dreams of sleeper, pursuer, lover and killer.

On one temporal plane, the knife lies on the stairs, while on another it is uncovered in the bed. The gleam of its blade distorts the woman's face in its polished surface. Deleuze uses a knife's gleam, intensified by close-up, to exemplify the limits of cinematic representation. Such affective qualities – brightness, terror and compassion in the case of his own citation from *Pandora's Box* (Georg Wilhelm Pabst, 1929) – are 'pure singular qualities or potentialities-as it were, pure "possibles"' that constitute eternal aspect of the event.[83]

The woman's fourth imago increases agency, transforming the key into a knife which she brandishes purposefully before it turns back into a key. In a complex play of multiple identities, the morphing key/knife is lifted twice. The second time, her palm is darkened as though with blood. The more passive imagos recoil and cover their mouths, turning their own clean palms outwards in horror while the sleeper stirs restlessly as though in the grip of nightmare.

The would-be killer wears a pair of goggles with lenses like silver balls. Together with the glinting knife, which she brandishes diagonally, this might (for cinepsychoanalysis) symbolise castratory re-appropriation of phallic power. The highly charged potential of this moment is emphasised by an insert of a foot stepping into four separate spaces: sand, soil grass, pavement, then back to carpet, edited smoothly as though one continuous location joined by the same movement. Deren herself described the metaphysical impact of this sequence as 'a crack letting the light of another world gleam through' in its glimpses of multiple, intersecting worlds.[84]

Continuing possible genital symbolism, the aggressor considers slipping the knife into the dreamer's mouth. Such 'matricide' would remove the central, controlling ego as the schizoid personae gain autonomy. The self-destructive threat wakens the terrified sleeper, yet the dream continues. A man in low-angle, traditional villain's shot leads her like a sleepwalker up the now steady stairs.

The knife, though still on the table, is no longer in the loaf, so dream events have impacted on several planes. With a territorialising gesture of control, the man replaces the phone before laying the flower on the pillow in a gesture identical to the nun's. The woman's face is bleached out by light and threatening musical notes accompany the man's reflection 'normalised' into a round shaving mirror. As he turns this face-down, she responds as though entranced, lying passively by the flower. His hand caresses her prone body and her close-up mouth is slick with saliva.

Yet her passivity is only apparent. Objects resume autonomous motion as flower becomes knife, radiating light before she throws it at his face with a rapid dart. The blow smashes the mirror and the shards of glass fall into the sea, suddenly visible through the hole left by his face as though no longer blocking it out. A complex pattern of waves wash over them as in *Un Chien andalou* and the camera tilts up to the vastness of the horizon.

As the film's structure comes full circle, the man locks into the same limiting trajectory as the woman. Lifting the flower and entering the house, his body is fragmented to feet and legs. He casts a dark shadow inside the room circled by his gaze. His eyes follow a trail of broken glass and fix on the woman, her throat cut by the shattered mirror. In unnerving close-up, the film closes on her dead face and staring eyes.

Through its densely layered, melting images, then, *Meshes* is more Bergsonian than Freudian. Time is reversed, accelerated or slowed as actions are frozen, condensed, repeated or expanded. Past and present, actual and virtual, are fused in an intensive oneiric continuum. There is little depth, and spatial orientation is tenuously held via continuous motion within a frame and across shots. Cutting on movements and elision maintains virtual continuity of action and the camera retains a central point of view. This smoothness is further augmented by slow motion. David E. James offers a provocative and stimulating study of American experimental film as structuralist 'meta-text' that I sometimes challenge.[85] Although accusing Deren's film of a historical essentialism, he identifies the 'density and intensity' of its 'lyric expressivity'.[86]

Made in 1945 just after *Meshes of the Afternoon*, *At Land* is likewise marked by European Surrealism, but Deren's subsequent work shifted even further from Surrealism to produce a more Bergsonian layering of temporality through the fluidity of dance. *Ritual in Transfigured Time* (1945–6) is a film ritual with intensive qualities achieved 'not in spatial terms alone, but in terms of Time created by the camera'.[87] Showcasing ritual and dance, it moves more in the direction of Deleuze's 'implied dream' in which the protagonist undergoes dreamlike encounters and moves between worlds without being depicted as asleep.

I have indicated the liminal status of *Meshes of the Afternoon* between psychosexual dream symbolism and a more fluid and multi-layered plane meshing consciousness and time. Its device of a dreamer makes a superficial fit into the first type of dream film, but its schizoid multiplicity is located in the spatio-temporal dynamic of the implied dream, which I consider later. Another liminal text located between dream and schizoid temporal layering, as well as between popular genres and art-film, is David Lynch's *Fire Walk with Me* (1992). I explore it via Deleuze's category of the waking dream.

Waking Dreams: *Fire Walk with Me*

the mind kicks in. And a lot of things that are going on in there become manifest.
(David Lynch)[88]

going back and forth in time.[89]

Like Deren, Lynch's dream-laden work consistently disavows Surrealist links. Valorising inspiration above historical imitation, he asserts that a 'forced, affected Surrealism would be horrible'.[90] He contrasts his own use of narrative and genre with the Surrealist preference for the film's medium and texture,[91] yet contrarily asserts his own work as 'primarily a sensory experience'.[92] For Chris Rodley, Lynch's surrealistic elements consist of defamiliarisation and the 'sensations and emotional traces of dreams'.[93]

Lynch's account of creative trance induction recalls Surrealist automatism or psychoanalytic free association. He focuses on certain words and phrases and 'pictures form' as though by unconscious linkage.[94] Yet Lynch dislikes psychoanalytical methods of unearthing buried material and prefers the machinic image of becoming a 'radio' tuning in to ideas and images and 'plugging in' to emotional states and qualities.[95]

Lynch also meditates on pure light or black, which has 'endless' depth, so 'you can go into it [and] it keeps continuing'.[96] Having induced a receptive trance state, he encounters images that act 'like magnets and they pull other ideas to them'.[97] This process recalls Bergson's description of recollecting powerful sense impressions that endure in memory and can be recalled as 'coloured and living' images.[98] If actualised, these virtual focal points reproduce corresponding sensations. Between actual and virtual, such images are the ideal raw matter for creative inspiration.

Yet Lynch seeks to control the random flux of images accessed. He prefers 'waking dreams' to the uncontrolled ones of sleep because their worlds are self-generated and chosen.[99] Among them is the town of Twin Peaks, the nodal point of interlocking worlds. Despite his controlling role, Lynch's techniques engage the psychic receptivity of waking dream via formal incompleteness, narrative complication and spatio-temporal elision. For him, 'fragments of things are pretty interesting. You can dream the rest. Then you're a participant'.[100]

Michel Chion's symbolically oriented critique of Lynch's aesthetics is of particular value for its insights into sound effects. I want to extend his substantial reading of *Fire Walk with Me* via Deleuzian perspectives. Lynch's potent blend of gripping storytelling and stylistic innovation validates my assertion that some of the richest Deleuzian encounters straddle the divide of high/popular art, to make experimental work more widely accessible.

Fire Walk with Me

the strangest dreams, in which two images overlie one another and show us at the same time two different persons, who yet make only one.[101] (Bergson)

Working in mainstream strictures with a degree of creative leeway, Lynch wanted *Fire Walk with Me* to be 'as free and experimental as it could be within the dictates it had to follow'.[102] Building on 'given' plot, characters and settings from his earlier TV Series *Twin Peaks*, he developed further dislocation of representational norms to induce profound unease. The exploding TV set of the titles sequence signals a shift of medium. More relevant to my agenda here, the hypnotic extended close-up of the screen's abstract flicker also suspends time and keys in the intensive states of perception the film demands.

There are many ways in which *Fire Walk with Me* could be considered Freudian. But their inadequacy as accounts of the film's events is overtly underlined by Lynch's use of interlocking worlds. In several scenes, the device of the sleeping dreamer is removed as the other world manifests itself independently. In the prologue, for example, when FBI agent Dale Cooper (Kyle MacLachlan) recounts his ominous dream to Inspector Gordon Cole (David Lynch), it recalls an analytical session. Yet, as a mysterious voice interrupts to insist that 'we are living inside a dream', another autonomous world swallows up the office in its own on-screen geography, characters and motivation.

In terms of symbolism and thematic content, the film is overtly psychosexual and familial. The Oedipal displacements of the family romance are stripped of the sublimation of Freud's Seduction Fantasy.[103] Freud's acceptance of clients' recollections of actual parental seductions was abandoned after 1897 in a gradual revaluation of infantile sexuality in which some accounts were reinterpreted as phantasmagoric reconstructions. This foregrounding of phantasy validated psychic activity and led towards the theory of the unconscious and the Oedipus Complex. Freud did, however, accept the pathogenic factor of actual incestuous seductions.

By positing spontaneous infantile sexuality and autoeroticism as well as actual erotic stimuli by others, Freud came to reject the notion that the child 'inhabits a private autonomous world until such time as a violation or perversion of this kind occurs'.[104] His controversial theory stresses the erotogenous nature of the infant/parent dyad, which, although not necessarily genital, may cause genital excitation. He argues that overly attentive parents are likely to dispose the child to neuroses by 'too much petting'.[105] The premature awakening of the sexual instinct before 'the somatic conditions of puberty are present' may later form the basis of nocturnal phantasies and dreams.[106]

Freud was aware of his theory's 'sacrilegious' import. *Fire Walk with Me* might almost be critiquing Jeffrey Masson's attack on the whole Freudian project based on this shift.[107] Laura's home, with its respectable neoclassical facade, is overdetermined as a site of Oedipal enactment. Her mother is severely disempowered and the household is run by Leland, the Freudian primal father of *Totem and Taboo* who takes all the women to himself.[108] Laura performs a range of essentialist feminine stereotypes, virgin, whore and her father's (other) wife. Her realisation of incest is the enforced surfacing of the already known.

Leland Palmer's transformation into the demonic 'Bob' is deeply uncanny in the Freudian sense. In back to the womb scenarios, the uncanny can produce the disturbing unfamiliarity of the doppelgänger. For Freud, doubling and repetition indicate unusually strong ego defences 'like the child, or of primitive man'.[109] In an attempt to ward off the death drive, self-repetition is 'an insurance against the destruction of the ego, as energetic denial of the power of death'.[110] Freud claims that such 'unbounded self-love' is driven by the retention of primary narcissism.[111] Leland's uncanny double could be read as the product of ego-inflation.

In response to ongoing trauma, Laura herself produces a less fantastical range of multiple personalities, from preppy high school queen to promiscuous coke addict. In order to suggest how Lynch's dreams move beyond Freudian themes to operate in more Deleuzian ways, I will consider Laura's explicit dream. I have chosen this sequence for its disturbing amalgam of waking dream in a complex torsion of planes.

Worlds Out of Frame

Deleuze compared the relation of dreamlike states to the real with the 'anomalous states' of a language system in their relation to current linguistic usage.[112] Technically overloaded dream images deploy 'addition, complication, over-saturation' as in *Entr'acte* whereas the more abstracted type uses 'elimination, ellipse, break, cut, unhinging' like those in *Un Chien andalou*. Both poles of the dream-image trace a large circuit via a chain of image actualisations but return to the situation that stimulated it initially. This return to a fixed point ultimately splits the 'indiscernibility of the real and the imaginary', as does the device of the dreamer and the viewer's supposed awareness of distinction between dream and reality.[113]

Like Dale Cooper's earlier, Laura's dream refers on one level to an actual dream overtly triggered by her father Leland's ambivalence. Yet, oneiric alterity is extended beyond the dream itself by unnerving ellipses, camera movements and lighting. Laura's eyes fix on a childhood picture of an angel feeding young girls. Rather than this being the Deleuzian image of a girl as inspirational model for all becomings, the girls are fixed in sentimental representation.[114] This image is intercut with its sinister counterpart: a framed photograph from grandmother Tremond. She is one of Lynch's 'abstractions', liminal entities that undermine divisions between worlds of sleeping and waking. Despite their apparently autonomous reality, their parasitic and demonic activities demand human hosts.

Tremond's picture shows the open door to another world. For Chion, these parallel worlds interact by 'oscillating dangerously from one to the other, each preying parasitically on the other'.[115] The waking world is always already mixed with its nightmare other. Despite identifiable singularities, they overlap and fuse in objects or places that act as two-way receivers. Lynch maximises contrast between worlds by insistent geographical location shots that encompass the totality of a place, enclosing characters in a static tableau.[116]

When propitious events align, parallel worlds conjoin and intercutting underlines continuity between dream and waking. Sudden dissolves between day and night mean than each is 'already present in the other'.[117] Although these phenomena could be used as evidence of a Freudian unconscious emerging from repression, the affective force of Lynch's cinematography exceeds symbolic labels.

The Tremond photograph is a dream gateway to the Black Lodge and its forces that engineer Laura's death. As Laura prepares for bed, a blue-lit medium-long shot keys in an atmosphere of expectancy. A close-up of the photograph through a brown filter throws the brightness behind the door into sharper relief before a closer shot takes us into the frame. As Chion indicates, the fluid camera leads Laura in, walking with her at her own pace.[118]

The camera's glide into darkness is accompanied by low-level machine-like humming and fluid horn notes. Chion notes how the film's 'uncontrollable forces' of constant, often sourceless sound make the screen into 'a fragile membrane with a multitude of currents pressing on it from behind'.[119] The most pervasive sound is the rhythmical drone of the ceiling fan linked to Leland's abuse of Laura. The wind it raises is a invisible current linking the worlds.[120] Despite its rich detail, Chion's musicology remains bounded by symbolic usage. As I discuss later, Deleuze's work on 'pure' sonsigns focuses instead on their affective immediacy to challenge consciousness.

Grandmother Tremond as malign doorkeeper beckons Laura into darkness as the panning camera teases us with the deferred revelation of her grandson. A perverse *puer eternis*, he wields incongruous authority in his adult suit and lights up the room's overblown roses wallpaper in a nauseous amber and blue light. The optical assault of flickering strobe jars our perception of the Red Room's velvet drapes and jags their lush tactility.

The disorienting camera skates low across the zigzag floor as the music climaxes on an electronic bass note. It pauses at a large gold shell and a green talisman ring on a polished table. Psychoanalytically of course, parted velvet curtains, blown roses, rings and shells symbolise the sexual preparedness of Laura as sacrificial bride. The black, white and red colour vibrations increase as the monochrome, funereal Dale Cooper emerges from behind the curtains as Laura's disempowered protector.

The liminal 'man from another world' specialises in the cryptic distortion of mundane language. Here, he announces 'I am the Arm and I sound like this' ululating a Native American war cry. Subtitled, his speech recalls the free association of automatic writing, irrational prose-poetry meant to articulate the surfacing unconscious, or else cut-ups in the Surrealist paper-folding game 'Exquisite Corpse'.[121] Such anomalies mark the coalescence of dream and actuality.

The failure of Dale's warning to wake Laura is signalled both by the sound overlap with the Red Room and the high-key blue lighting of her bedroom. Laura responds with dream detachment to her further warning by a young, dead woman who appears next to her in bed.[122] Though this apparition vanishes with a crash, Laura still clasps the fatal ring that marks this as a dream within a dream or a waking dream with frighteningly material components.

An objective jump-cut disrupts Laura's subjective point of view. The photograph on the wall reveals her still trapped inside the frame. A shot of her asleep in bed increases confusion when cut with a further image of her stuck inside the picture world. Like Deren's emanations in *Meshes of the Afternoon*, she watches herself coming though the door, each 'Laura' moving slightly out of synch in distinct temporal layers. The camera fully enters the frameless picture with Laura's point-of-view shot of herself asleep.

Gears shift between virtual and actual worlds, collapsing their multiplicity to a single layer. Light changes from shadowy blue to pink that lends a warm glow to the skin of Laura's hand. As the camera pulls back, she sits up in the morning light, convinced of the dream's malign continuity. She turns the picture face-down in an attempt to break its vampiric power over her and block egress between worlds.

So what might the Red Room, this anomalous locale accessed in extreme states, be? Unsurprisingly, Lynch refuses to fix its meaning. For him, it's 'a free zone, completely unpredictable' and ambivalently exciting and 'scary'.[123] Chion argues that its cellular rooms might be ventricles of the brain. As well as engineering Oedipal trauma, its inexplicable entities are also angels and demons.

According to Lynch, the Red Room has 'no problem with time'.[124] For Deleuze, the failure of attentive recognition produces a sense of being lost in time. Memory failure suspends sensory-motor extension so that the perceived image fails to re-establish contact by linking up with either motor- or recollection-images. At this stage, the actual image hooks up 'genuinely virtual elements', such as feelings of déjà vu, dream-images and fantasies.[125] They manifest what Deleuze calls states 'of reverie, of waking dream, of strangeness or enchantment'.[126]

Lynch's spatio-temporal 'abstractions' do indeed possess genuinely virtual elements. Their affective impact on the cinematic sensorium exceeds any symbolic significance. They could be durational composites from those distorted outer reaches of memory furthest away from the actual.[127] The Red Room scenes might thus be waking dreams of peculiar potency. Yet the Oedipal configurations that run through *Fire Walk with Me*, its geographical location, cultural extension and the foregrounding of overt dreams still gravitate against the cinema of pure optical and sound situations.

So how may anomalous modes of consciousness exceed the limits of the split in the large circuit caused by the retention of explicit dreams? Deleuze adopts the notion of 'implied dream' from Michel Devillers to describe states in which the optical and sound image is severed from its motor extension, but 'no longer compensates for this loss by entering into relation with explicit recollection-images or dream-images'.[128] It thus retains some of the qualities of the explicit dream-image of the sleeper but without its limitations.

As an example of Deleuze's second type of dream film, *Fire Walk with Me* moves over the borders into his third type, the implied dream, which dispenses with a sleeper altogether. In the more overtly Bergsonian *Mulholland Drive*, as I argue elsewhere, Lynch had developed a more seamless continuum between dreaming, sleep and waking in which the significance of the explicit dream within a dream is dwarfed by a smoother blend of actual and virtual.[129] To explore this further, I want to flesh out Deleuze's Bergsonian approach to recollection in cinematic dreams.

Beyond the Flashback: Recollections, Dreams and Thoughts

Deleuze draws extensively on Bergson's model of memory circuitry to analyse the cinema of the time-image. Moving vertically rather than horizontally, this model passes the image of the object itself through 'an infinite number of planes or circuits which correspond to its own "layers" or aspects', each mental image with its own descriptions.[130] During its passage, it encounters zones of 'recollections, dreams or thoughts' corresponding to specific elements.

Each of the circuits traversed by the image both 'obliterates and creates an object', presenting it to us afresh each time.[131] Yet, despite its vicissitudes, the object retains qualitative singularity. In this 'double movement of creation and erasure', these 'successive planes and independent circuits' by cancelling, contradicting, joining each other or forking 'simultaneously constitute the layers of one and the same physical reality, memory or spirit'.[132]

In the more philosophically dense and duration-centred cinema of the time-image, the planes coexist.[133] Sensory-motor links are replaced by more complex connections that circulate between pure optical and sound images and those from time and thought. Engaged in attentive recognition, the purely optical and sound description is an actual image on a circuit of interchange with a virtual one. In the gap between sensory-motor stimulation and response, the virtual image produces a new kind of auto-contemplation that fills it more completely. Like Bergson's recollection-image, this is neither motor nor material, but 'temporal and spiritual: that which is "added to" matter'.[134]

On one level, the cinematic flashback, as a closed circuit between past and present, illustrates the relation of actual and recollection images. Yet most flashbacks are clearly signalled as a 'conventional, extrinsic device' by the use of dissolve links and superimpositions.[135] However psychological or 'justified from elsewhere' their motivation might be, though, most flashbacks remain 'analogous to a sensory-motor determinism' and confirm the narrative's linear progression.[136]

Located at the other pole of the recollection-image, the flashbacks of Joseph Mankiewitz films such as *All About Eve* (1950) suggest 'an inexplicable secret, a fragmentation of all linearity, perpetual forks like so many breaks in causality' that recall Borges's convoluted short tale 'The Garden of Forking Paths'.[137] Mankiewitz's more 'theatrical' characters do not develop by 'linear evolution' but by sudden, inexplicable temporal forks that authenticate a more 'novelistic' method of unfolding the layers of the past through memory.[138]

Yet, such conditional and relative uses of flashback have not yet reached that pure, virtual recollection 'contained in the hidden zones of the past as in oneself'.[139] However convincingly the flashback might signal memory, if it is clearly bracketed off from the main body of the film, it remains part of the movement-image like clearly signalled dream sequences and other techniques representing distortion, discontinuity or extreme states of subjectivity.

These anomalous techniques may well weaken the sensory-motor scheme or widen its scope. Yet, as long as they are clearly signalled as dreams or memories in a temporary deviation from narrative norms, Deleuze asserts that they do not move freely in duration proper. Although the flashback's conventions might indicate psychological causality, it remains 'analogous to a sensory-motor determinism' and despite its circuits, still endorses linear narrative progress.[140] Thus the flashback, unable to form a virtual 'circuit of indiscernibility' with the actual, present image, gives us only an actualised recollection-image.[141]

Deeper time-images occur elsewhere. Moving closer to Bergson, 'abstract' cinema 'informs us' more fully when attentive recognition fails.[142] Here, remembering suspends sensory-motor extension and links the actual image to virtual affective elements that include déjà vu, dream-images, fantasies, theatre scenes or the 'past in general'.[143] The 'proper equivalent of the optical-sound image', then, is found in 'the disturbances of memory and the failures of recognition' as we travel further into altered consciousness through the realm of the actual or implied dream.[144]

From Dream-Image to Implied Dream: The Cinema of Enchantment and *The Tales of Hoffmann*

colour is dream, not because the dream is in colour, but because colours [. . .] are given a highly absorbent, almost devouring value. (Deleuze)[145]

To recap for a moment Deleuze's identification of the explicit dream-image's two poles cited earlier. One type leans towards abstraction via rich, overloaded techniques including complex camera movements, dissolves, superimpositions and special effects as well as post-production work.[146] The second kind prefers non-continuity editing between objects to produce 'a perpetual unhinging which "looks like" dream'.[147]

These poles trace out a large circuit via a chain of actualised images, returning to the situation that initially stimulated them. Along with such 'bracketing', both the device of the dreamer and the viewer's own distinction between dream and reality splits the 'indiscernibility of the real and the imaginary' in the large circuit.[148]

Yet Deleuze suggests a way to move beyond this split that keeps some qualities of the explicit dream-image while removing its limitations. The 'implied dream' dispenses with explicit dream images to express reverie and states of enchantment.[149] Although its return to the movement-image marks some degree of limitation, this new kind of image possesses special qualities of its own closer to virtuality.

The cinematic implied dream is characterised by '*movement of world*'.[150] Instead of depicting the character's response to an optical-sound situation, this kind of motion 'supplements the faltering movements of the character'.[151] Such ' "worldising" or "societising" ' results in a 'depersonalising, a pronominalising of the lost or blocked movement'.[152] Rather than recording characters moving through locales, the camera causes their world itself to move, shifting motion and agency from subject to environment.

For Deleuze, this type of film has a special relation to Bergson's circuitry of actual and virtual. Its virtual movement is actualised at the cost of spatial and temporal extension, thus it operates at the limit of the largest circuit.[153] Despite certain explicit dream-images themselves deploying techniques of world-movement, their momentum is limited by containment or retention. The implied dream, further away from actuality, 'liberates' them to a greater degree by engaging more closely with virtuality. It is, however, its extension into movement, however desubjectified, that prevents a fuller expression of the time-image here.

Among Deleuze's implied dream films are the 'infinitely stretched gestures which depersonalise movement' in the surrealistic distortions of *The Fall of the House of Usher* (Jean Epstein, 1928) and the anomalous motion of Charles Laughton's *Night of the Hunter* (1955).[154] Deleuze also cites the films of Louis Malle such as *Black Moon* (1975) for their desubjectified 'movement of world', via fantastic inversions and situations where 'each dream is a world'.[155] To move beyond these limitations, I want to introduce a new term from Deleuze's discussion of the implied dream and explore its dynamics of world movement.

At the far pole of the implied dream lies the 'cinema of enchantment'.[156] This is defined primarily by its 'universalised, depersonalised and pronominalised' movement.[157] Such movements, whether slow, fast or reverse motion, pass equally through nature as through 'artifice and the manufactured object'.[158] Deleuze's examples of this broad category are generically disparate, ranging from neo-realism to comedies of Jerry Lewis and Jacques Tati, in which the body's dance-like movements motivate the world-movement's 'sucking up and carrying away the living'.[159] This 'low-frequency wave-action' constitutes a 'kind of modern ballet'.[160]

Deleuze's main generic focus is the musical comedy, in which dance motion 'outlines a dreamlike world as it goes'.[161] He cites the song and dance numbers of Busby Berkeley with their 'great transformational machine' of enchantment.[162] Dreamlike dance is showcased by both the cerebrally controlled routines of Fred Astaire whose walk 'imperceptibly becomes dance' and the more organic acrobatic improvisations of Gene Kelly, who in *Singing in the Rain* (Stanley Donen, 1952) performs an improvised dance that originates in 'the unevenness of the pavement'.[163] Despite the convention that song and dance numbers are led by romantic lovers, motion exceeds subjective limits to open up to the 'supra-personal element, to a movement of world' outlined by the dance.[164]

Deleuze aligns the movements of dancing and dreaming. Astaire and Kelly 'get us into the dance' or 'make us dream', which 'amounts to the same thing' as, via oneiric cinematography, 'the dancer himself begins dancing as one starts to dream'.[165] Musicals explicitly feature certain scenes that function like 'dreams or pseudo-dreams with metamorphoses'.[166] But, beyond this, Deleuze claims, entire films can be 'a gigantic dream, but an implied dream, which in turn implies the passage of a presumed reality', however ambiguous the status of such a real might be.[167]

These musical implied dreams offer much more than the sensory–motor spectacle of a dream into which we are admitted. The world–movement that corresponds directly to opsigns and sonsigns also cancels customary sensory–motor links.[168] By operating pure optical and sound situations without motor extension, they make 'a pure description which had already replaced its object, a film set pure and simple'.[169] In this way, the implied dream's more 'comprehensive' focus functions on a deeper level than performance in 'the whole of an implied dream which even envelops walking': the spectacular rather than the spectacle.[170]

In the films of Stanley Donen, blatant artifice appears as 'flat' views in 'postcards or snapshots of landscapes, towns and silhouettes'.[171] These give colour its fundamental value, while 'the action, itself flattened, is no longer distinguishable from a moving element of the coloured film set'.[172] It is the 'dreamlike power' of dance to animate these flat views, opening up a space within and beyond the film set that 'gives a world to the image, surrounds it with an atmosphere of world'.[173] Thus world–movement corresponds to the optical and sound images of dream.

Minnelli has 'discovered' a multiplicity of worlds through dance. His fluid diegesis of music, song and dance creates 'as many worlds as image'.[174] Dance extends world movement to encompass 'passage from one world to another, entry into another world, breaking in and exploring' as in *Brigadoon* (1954).[175] In his films, 'every world and every dream is shut in on itself, closed up around everything it contains, including the dreamer'.[176] So the dreamer is being *dreamed by* the world instead of *dreaming it* and the object–world 'englobes' the character.

In this way, the set's centrality functions as 'pure description of world which replaces the situation'.[177] Colour is a pivotal expressive tool here. Deleuze explains that 'colour is dream, not because the dream is in colour, but because colours in Minnelli are given a highly absorbent, almost devouring value' with which we can 'become absorbed, without at the same time losing ourselves and being snatched away'.[178]

In Minnelli's musicals, dance acquires depth and agency to become 'the sole means of entering into another world, that is, into another's world, into another's dream or past'.[179] They develop the relations of sets as 'absorbent' worlds and dance as 'the passage between worlds'.[180] In their 'mystery of memory, of dream and of time, as a point of indiscernibility of the real and the imaginary', the musicals are the most Bergsonian examples of the genre.[181] The director's conception of implied dreams is 'strange and fascinating' because it always refers to another's dream or becomes 'a devouring, merciless power' for its subject.[182]

Non-Hollywood implied dreams include 'a new op'art, a new son'art' in the popular opera of Jacques Demy.[183] By using 'pure set valid for itself' and the artificial moves of chases and games, Demy's optical and sound situations are expressed in 'coloured set-descriptions' that give primacy to songs in a 'discrepancy' that unhooks the action.[184] Demy combines the sensory-motor city of social classes and passions with pure optical and sound situations, as it 'merges with what provides the set in it'.[185] Sound and vision thus surrounds the real with an implied dream to produce enchantment.[186]

The Tales of Hoffmann by Michael Powell and Emeric Pressburger (1951) offers such a state of enchantment. By layering and combining a multiplicity of art-forms – literature, film, set design, music, dance and opera – it unfolds interlocking planes of artifice. As well as capturing certain qualities of Hoffman's literary originals in their ballet and opera adaptations, it is a richly affective cinematic experience in itself. Sets, costumes and makeup insist on their own validity in this deviant diegesis of art for its own sake. In Plato's terms, the film's version of the world is at several removes both from reality and from the norms of postwar British cinema.

Each cinematic tale in Hoffman's collection unfolds a dreamlike *mise-en-scène* and a series of fantasy women. They are cued in by an image of overt artifice, a theatre programme's pages turned by hand. This both plunges us deeper into the enchanted world via the device of a magic book that comes to life, and contradictorily, retains an anchorage in the real that confirms and self-reflexively problematises the status of artifice. A taster of the forthcoming tale, the programme booklet features photographs of the cast in character, captioned by their real names with sketches of the set's motifs in the margin. Rather than the live performers and theatre stage replacing the printed page, here the film takes opera and ballet a step further into the virtual realm.

I will focus on 'The Tale of Giulietta' the Venetian courtesan (Ludmilla Tcherina). In the programme-prologue, sketches of bridges and gondolas key in a fantasy Venice. As the last page turns, the world of Giulietta fades in over a shot of Hoffmann's previous *inamorata*, Olympia, exposed as an automaton and dismembered. The dull gold ripples of a Venetian canal are superimposed over a close-up of broken springs protruding from Olympia's severed head as living doll makes way for enchantress in Hoffmann's series of elusive objects of desire. In the slowly melting fade, the pages are overlaid by flickering ripples on water as the gondolas and bridges of a flat plane studio set materialise. Hoffmann's Venice is an unreal world of light and colour that dominates performers, stymies their linear progress to trap them in a world of dreams.

Powell and Pressburger's cinematic devices include over-saturated, hot-house colours, distorted sounds and hallucinatory images. Their affective force mobilises mechanisms of perception that precede later cognitive processing. These mechanisms include kinaesthesia (the sense of movement and bodily orientation in space), synaesthesia (the mixing of different sense modalities) and hapticity (interaction between vision and sensory feeling or tactility).

Giulietta's tale enchants despite its two-dimensional stage scenery, stylised movements, sung dialogue and magic tricks. Its world moves by sonsigns: the refrain and dubbed voices, and by opsigns: shifting light, colour vibrations and dance that turns in on itself. I will consider some of these devices more closely to ascertain how they operate as a Deleuzian implied dream.

The blend of opera and ballet often unites singers and dancers on stage together. In Powell and Pressburger's film, the slow movements and static postures of singers constrain dancers from extensive leaps to the limits of a more intensive motion. Despite the magician Dapertutto (Robert Helpmann)'s transmutations of matter, the Venetian world appears curiously frozen. I want to discover, then, what *is* actually in motion in the world of these staged set-pieces shot by a static or conventionally tracking camera.

The very constraint serves to increase the dancers' affective potency. Dapertutto's pirouettes increase his magical force as he spins in the narrow bounds between candelabra to dance the intensive in-turning of narcissism. As well as casting a glamour on Hoffmann (Robert Rounceville) by their gorgeous appearance, Dapertutto the Satanic stealer of souls and Giulietta trap him by their encircling motion, spinning an invisible web of force around their prey.

The sequence is intensively laden with vibrations on the spot in counterpoint to more fluid movements. Prior to any characters, ripples or waves set the key rhythm of maritime Venice. They link up into visual rhymes by their parallel motion, seen in the floating gauzy backcloth of Giulietta's gondola, or the rippling veil masking a bas-relief of the sun in her palace, its power eclipsed by lunar forces. These gentle, continuous ripples have a soporific affect as part of the film's movement-assemblage of enchantment. They intensify the spectator's own sense of movement as part of the processual assemblage. We move within the film and it moves within us as the same affective event of images in motion.

Facial close-ups are sparse in the film, so impact on us more when used. Close-ups of Giulietta and Dapertutto suggest deceptive enchantment in the performative quality of their fantastical makeup with its unnatural colours, exaggerated shapes and glitter. The cold, statuesque property of Giulietta's pale, angular face is offset by the crimson lips and darkly outlined eyes of the femme fatale.

For Deleuze, the cinematic face in close-up has a special ability to epitomise the intensive vibration of the affection-image discussed in the next chapter.[187] What Deleuze calls the reflective face, such as Giulietta's here, expresses 'pure Quality' via something 'common to several objects of different natures' and is of a more contemplative nature.[188] Giulietta's face has commonality with carnival masks, Hoffmann's stolen reflection and more generally to Dapertutto's mirror-world of lost souls. But in its intensive motion it is far from being a static mask.

Hoffmann himself is a stolid physical presence, more often standing still to deliver a song than walking. Yet, even in one spot, he moves dynamically by the sonsign vibrations and modulations of his singing voice. For Deleuze and Guattari, music has a special status in relation to becoming. In *A Thousand Plateaus*, plane ten is 'becoming-music'. Patricia Pisters usefully contrasts psychoanalytic perspectives on sound with those of Deleuze and Guattari. For them, Pisters suggests, 'sound has nothing to do with castration-anxiety, jouissance, or an encounter with the Real', but is a potent catalyst for molecular becomings.[189] For Deleuze, sound is a more potent force of deterritorialisation than sight, because, as sound becomes more refined 'it tends to dissolve and connects with other elements easily in a machinic way'.[190] The sound quality of a song exceeds the signification of its lyrics.

Giulietta's advent in her gondola is heralded by an alluring song reprieved at the end as she fades back into the mist. This renowned *barcarolle* (named after the gondoliers or *barcaruoli*) was originally composed for Offenbach's *opéra-ballet Die Rheinnixen* (1864). The compound 6/8 time signature and relentless crotchet/quaver rhythm evokes the strokes of oars/pole or lapping waves.[191] A long tremolo leads into the swaying melody. The lyrics of 'Beautiful Night of Love' align Giulietta with the moon as queen of nocturnal love.

The device of dubbing means that the ballerina lip-synchs lyrics supposed to come from her heart, rendering their sincerity doubtful. Pisters reminds us that in psychoanalytic film theory,[192] the female singing voice is seen in 'a negative (lethal) although fascinating way'[193] and, specifically, the opera diva's voice functions as 'a classic *objet petit a*'.[194] Deleuze and Guattari's interest lies elsewhere, in the 'machining' function of voice in the assemblage.

Although Deleuze does not work extensively with music, he uses the ritornello or refrain, frequent in opera, to figure the operations of memory.

He applies the concept more broadly than its operatic use. For him, at moments of intensity, 'the image, whether sound or visual, is 'a little ritornello'.[195] He also uses it to describe the cyclical process of composition and decomposition that motivates extensive motor movements, so that space is 'a motor ritornello – postures, positions and gaits – to the one who travels through it'.[196]

Above all, the ritornello marks a stable territorial centre. What Pisters calls the 'lulling' lover's refrain acts to territorialise the loved one's sexuality as in Giulietta's ploy to enslave Hoffmann.[197] Nevertheless, as the ritornello invites improvisation, it also incorporates a deterritorialising function and opens itself to forces of chaos. Indeed, Deleuze gives the ritornello a metaphysical quality. He connects this sound, made 'at the limits of language' with the singularity retained by a soul 'when it takes to the open road' at the limits of the body that produces the sound.[198] Here, the occasional dissonances of the barcarolle only intensify romantic yearning.[199]

As well as powerful operatic sonsigns, Giulietta's tale, with its vibrant, clashing colours, induces what Deleuze calls the affective 'colouring sensation' modulated by the dynamics of tone and intensity.[200] His study of Francis Bacon analyses the painter's 'colour-force'.[201] Colours on canvas create virtual movement and release energy within the framed space of the painting.[202] Deleuze describes the dynamic interchanges of colour regimes and tonal harmonies as 'shores of vivid colours' and 'flows of broken colours'.[203] We can apply these insights to the colours of cinema's broader palette of affects and percepts.

For Bergson, each sense vibrates with intensive 'real action' in response to colour shade, light intensity and tone timbre. Cinematic affects interact at a micro level between themselves and at a macro level with other qualities. Deleuze writes that 'a colour like red, a value like brightness, a power like decisiveness, a quality like hardness or tenderness, are primarily positive possibilities' which, by referring 'only to themselves', exceed any narrative function.[204] This removes them from sensory-motor extension and shifts from linear time into duration.

For *The Tales of Hoffmann's* creative team, colour is a potent affective tool. The colour-image is expressed via intensive motion and extensive juxtaposition. Colours bleach out or intensify under different lighting. In decadent Venice, green and magenta, opposed in the spectrum, work in unnatural conjunction, their tension heightens affective discord. Yet their tones are not pure, but faded or highlighted by variations in shade. Performers wear modulations of the main colours to express dominant character traits.

Rather than the erotic couplings of flesh, the tale's orgy is a riot of light and colour demanding attention for its own sake. The masquers are barely differentiated as the camera focuses on the coloured detail of their writhing costumes, producing sensory overload as the predominant shades multiply and extend. The chaotic effect is enhanced by the reflective surfaces of green/mauve marble floor, its sheen increased by bright overhead lighting.

Strong contrast of black and white is overt in rejected lover Peter Schlemil's military uniform. The narrative justification for the loss of shading is his stolen shadow. Without this, he has lost all subtlety of colour tone, so replicates the affects of high contrast lighting in himself, condemned to obsessive extremes of desire, gratification and renewed need. His plaster-white face marks him prematurely with the pallor of death. Black and white feature in Giulietta's own colour scheme (as moon and night) and he belongs to her utterly.

The affect of colour is light-dependent. The tale displays the hypnotic affects of shifting light. It gleams, shimmers, shines and glitters with its own energy, providing movement even in the most static shots. The close-up reflection of Giulietta's face is seen through ripples, in a parallel mirror-world under water into which she sings with narcissistic delight. The water has a veiling effect. Like her, it shifts and changes, yet the glinting ripples insist on their own quality distinct from the human actants they enhance. Light is one element of cinematic perception that directly stimulates the nerve cells of the eye and can bypass cognitive processing for intensified affect. In tandem with Bergson, Deleuze refuses the Cartesian hierarchy of mind over matter to assert that rather than consciousness being light, it is 'the set of images, or the light, which is consciousness, immanent to matter'.[205]

The film's techniques of enchantment include actual magic acts by which matter is transformed. Yet the impact of these tricks entirely depends on their cinematographic expression. Glittering light, saturated colours and dancing that turns in on itself are showcased when Dapertutto appears from the depths of the mirror, like the devil of tradition. Skilful use of fades and soft focus extends the mirror's properties when he appears as a faint reflection without material body then steps out into an illusory reality of flattened perspective. As he crosses the threshold between virtual and actual, the magic act of materialisation is expressed in an inserted, abstract close-up of dazzling lights.

Dapertutto is a pragmatic magician who improvises workings with material immediately at hand, here colour and light. The glint of his gem-stone rings inspires the transformation of coloured candles into jewels. As the candle flames produce wax, he crystallises it in the palm of his hand to make coloured stones out of light. Both dripping and solid wax are formed into cut and uncut gems with a rough texture recalling their waxy origins. Dapertutto is master of appearances, becoming other for his own purposes. He transforms into a mooring post to eavesdrop on Hoffmann, his scaly tailcoat spins and parts like an insect's wings as he pirouettes between candles.

Distinction between living and inanimate matter is further blurred as the candles extend the colours of the revellers' costumes. Giulietta descends the steps dripping rose petals that extend the sensory range by evoking heady erotic scent. Like Dapertutto, she also becomes-insect in the scaly gleam of her tight black body and her wing-like, gauzy train. Despite the intensive motion of her wavy black hair, her dance steps are constrained by the magician's potent postures of command as he ensnares her.

Dapertutto sparks off a firework-like explosion and a necklace materialises amid the smoke. Its over-elaborate design and clashing colours are gaudy, with uneven, mismatched stones. Giulietta is allured by the glitter of the light itself, regardless of the simulated and transitory nature of the jewels revealed when Dapertutto turns them back to wax as a threatened punishment. Her spectacular seduction of Hoffmann will itself be fuelled by the magic of cinematic artifice.

In place of allegorical readings of psychoanalytic dream theory, I have approached *Tales of Hoffmann* as a Deleuzian implied dream. The sensory overload of dance, song, music and magic carry us far on the virtual plane. In the cinema of enchantment, set replaces situation and the 'to and fro' replaces action.[206] In tandem with the multiplicity of art forms, they produce the affective potency and durational implications of the implied dream. In my next chapter focusing on drugs in film, style also works intensively on the spectator's embodied consciousness.

Notes

1. Deleuze and Guattari, *Anti-Oedipus*, p. 316.
2. Freud, 'Beyond the Pleasure Principle' p. 308.
3. Among valuable examples, see Modleski, *The Women Who Knew Too Much*; Žižek, *Everything You Always Wanted to Know About Lacan*.
4. Psychoanalytic word-association might discover castratory significance in Ballantine's name: balls as testicles and tine as the prong of a pitchfork.
5. The director's disappointment led to his dismissal of the film as 'just another man-hunt story wrapped in pseudo-psychoanalysis'. Truffaut, *Hitchcock by Truffaut*, p. 234.
6. Deleuze, *Cinema 2*, p. 57.
7. Ibid.

8. Ibid.
9. For contemporary viewers, the blatant artifice of back-projections and corn-flake-snow has an additional alienation effect.
10. Deleuze, 'Real and Imaginary', p. 64.
11. Deleuze and Guattari, *Anti-Oedipus*, p. 271.
12. Ibid., p. 18.
13. Laplanche and Pontalis, *The Language of Psychoanalysis*, p. 408.
14. Deleuze and Guattari, *Anti-Oedipus*, p. 322.
15. Ibid., p. 319.
16. Ibid., pp. 81–2.
17. Kennedy, *Deleuze and Cinema*, p. 50.
18. Deleuze and Guattari, *Anti-Oedipus*, p. 131.
19. Ibid., p. 139.
20. Ibid.
21. Ibid.
22. Ibid.
23. Ibid.
24. Ibid.
25. Ibid.
26. Ibid.
27. Kennedy, *Deleuze and Cinema*, p. 69.
28. Deleuze and Guattari, *What Is Philosophy?*, p. 164.
29. Bergson, *Time and Free Will*, p. 231.
30. Freud, 'The Special Characteristics of the System *Ucs*', p. 191.
31. Deleuze, *Cinema 2*, p. 56.
32. Ibid.
33. Ibid.
34. Ibid., pp. 44–67.
35. Ibid., p. 44.
36. Ibid.
37. Ibid.
38. Ibid., p. 45.
39. Ibid.
40. Ibid., p. 56.
41. Ibid.
42. Ibid., p. 55.
43. Freud, *The Interpretation of Dreams*.
44. Breton, 'Manifesto of Surrealism', p. 26.
45. Luis Buñuel, quoted in Aranda, *Luis Buñuel*, 1976, p. 56.
46. Ibid., p. 58.
47. Ibid., p. 63.
48. Salvador Dali, in Aranda, *Luis Buñuel*, p. 64.
49. Breton, 'Manifesto of Surrealism', p. 20.
50. Deleuze, *Cinema 2*, p. 55.

51. Ibid.
52. Ibid.
53. Ibid.
54. Ibid.
55. Ibid.
56. Ibid., p. 56.
57. Ibid.
58. Ibid.
59. Ibid., p. 57.
60. Ibid., p. 58.
61. Ibid.
62. Ibid.
63. Ibid.
64. Maya Deren, on the sleeve of *Maya Deren: Collected Experimental Films: 1943–1959* (Amsterdam: Mystic Fire Video, 1986).
65. Deren, in Rabinowitz, *Women, Power, Politics*, p. 68.
66. Ibid.
67. Deren, in Sitney, *Visionary Film*, p. 31.
68. Deren, 'Notes, Essays and Letters', p. 1 (hereafter referred to as 'Notes').
69. Sitney, *Visionary Film*, p. 21.
70. Ibid.
71. Ibid., p. 11.
72. Deren, 'Notes', p. 30.
73. Ibid.
74. Deren was an initiated Voudun priestess. She filmed Haitian rituals and describes her ecstatic possession in Deren, *Divine Horsemen*, p. 260.
75. Deren, *An Anagram of Ideas on Art Form and Film*.
76. Deren, 'Notes', p. 1.
77. Deren, 'Cinema as an Art Form', p. 258.
78. Deren, 'Cinematography', pp. 154–5.
79. Deleuze, *Cinema 1*, p. 15.
80. Ibid., p. 17.
81. Ibid., p. 112.
82. Ibid.
83. Ibid., p. 102.
84. Deren, 'Notes', p. 30.
85. James, *Allegories of Cinema*.
86. Ibid., p. 30.
87. Deren video sleeve notes.
88. David Lynch, in Rodley, *Lynch on Lynch* (revised edn), p. 20.
89. Ibid., p. 187.
90. Lynch, in Chion, *David Lynch*, p. 25.
91. Kaleta, *David Lynch*, p. ix.
92. Lynch, in Chion, *David Lynch*, p. 25.

93. Rodley, in Rodley, *Lynch on Lynch* (revised edn), p. ix.
94. Lynch, in ibid., p. 270.
95. Rodley, in ibid., p. xi.
96. Lynch, in ibid., p. 20.
97. Ibid., p. 270.
98. Bergson, *Matter and Memory*, p. 133.
99. Lynch, in Rodley *Lynch on Lynch* (revised edn), p. 15.
100. Rodley, *Lynch on Lynch*, p. x.
101. Bergson, *Time and Free Will*, p. 136.
102. Lynch in Chion, *David Lynch*, p. 190.
103. Freud, 'Three Essays in the Theory of Sexuality', pp. 33–169.
104. Laplanche and Pontalis, *The Language of Psychoanalysis*, p. 407.
105. Freud, 'Three Essays in the Theory of Sexuality', p. 147.
106. Ibid., p. 148.
107. Masson, *The Assault on Truth*.
108. Freud, 'Totem and Taboo'.
109. Freud, 'The Uncanny', p. 357.
110. Ibid., p. 356.
111. Ibid., p. 357.
112. Deleuze, *Cinema 2*, p. 58.
113. Deleuze, *Cinema 2*, p. 58.
114. Deleuze and Guattari, *A Thousand Plateaus*, p. 275.
115. Chion, *David Lynch*, p. 157.
116. Ibid.
117. Ibid., p. 186.
118. Ibid., p. 153.
119. Ibid.,,, p. 150.
120. Ibid.
121. Breton, 'Manifesto of Surrealism', pp. 49–110.
122. The ghost is Dale's girlfriend Annie from the TV series.
123. Ibid.
124. Ibid.
125. Ibid., p. 54.
126. Ibid., pp. 58–9.
127. Deleuze, *Cinema 2*, p. 56.
128. Ibid., p. 59.
129. Powell, *Deleuze and Horror Film*, pp. 187–95.
130. Deleuze, *Cinema 2*, p. 46.
131. Ibid.
132. Ibid.
133. Ibid.
134. Ibid., p. 47.
135. Ibid., p. 48.
136. Ibid.

137. Ibid., p. 49.
138. Ibid.
139. Ibid., p. 54.
140. Ibid., p. 48.
141. Ibid., p. 54.
142. Ibid.
143. Deleuze, *Cinema 2*, p. 55
144. Ibid.
145. Ibid., p. 63.
146. Ibid., p. 58.
147. Ibid.
148. Ibid.
149. Ibid., p. 59.
150. Ibid.
151. Ibid.
152. Ibid.
153. Ibid.
154. Ibid.
155. Ibid.
156. Ibid.
157. Ibid.
158. Ibid.
159. Ibid., p. 66.
160. Ibid., p. 60.
161. Ibid.
162. Ibid., p. 61.
163. Ibid.
164. Ibid.
165. Ibid.
166. Ibid., p. 62.
167. Ibid.
168. Ibid.
169. Ibid.
170. Ibid.
171. Ibid.
172. Ibid.
173. Ibid.
174. Ibid., pp. 62–3.
175. Ibid., p. 63.
176. Ibid.
177. Ibid.
178. Ibid.
179. Ibid.
180. Ibid., p. 64.

181. Ibid., p. 54.
182. Ibid., p. 64.
183. Ibid., p. 67.
184. Ibid.
185. Ibid.
186. Ibid.
187. Ibid., p. 66.
188. Deleuze, *Cinema 1*, p. 90.
189. Pisters, *The Matrix of Visual Culture*, p. 188.
190. Ibid.
191. I am grateful to Fiona Price for musical insights.
192. Silverman, *Acoustic Mirror*.
193. Pisters, *The Matrix of the Visible*, p. 197.
194. Ibid., p. 194.
195. Deleuze, 'The Exhausted', p. 159.
196. Ibid., p. 160.
197. Pisters, *The Matrix of the Visible*, p. 198.
198. Deleuze, 'Bartleby', p. 87.
199. Harding, *Jacques Offenbach*, p. 239.
200. Deleuze, *Francis Bacon*, p. 112.
201. Ibid., p. 150.
202. Ibid., p. 152.
203. Ibid., p. 142.
204. Deleuze, *Cinema 1*, p. 106.
205. Ibid., p. 61.
206. Deleuze, *Cinema 2*, p. 67.

CHAPTER 2

Pharmacoanalysis

experimentation with drugs has left its mark on everyone, even nonusers.[1] (Deleuze and Guattari)

a strafing of the surface in order to transmute the stabbing of bodies.[2] (Deleuze)

In *A Thousand Plateaus*, Deleuze and Guattari announce the replacement of psychoanalysis by 'pharmacoanalysis'.[3] The polemical assertion reveals the impact of drugs, or at least drugs-related art, on their project. In this chapter, I make a Deleuzian intersection of drugs and film. My focus is on cinematic images of drug-use as I discover a specifically intoxicant cluster of images, music, editing and other stylistic techniques. By identifying these, I want to interrogate how far each film impacts on us as an agent of becoming by inducing affectively altered states of consciousness.

The film *Altered States* does not just depict Jessup's mental alterations. It literalises alterity as physical transformation. In revisiting Russell's film to explore chemical alterities, I link up a dynamic assemblage of philosophers, artists and psychedelic experimenters alongside Deleuze and Guattari. As well as Bergson, I include Carlos Castaneda, Artaud, Timothy Leary and Russell himself. As part of this chapter's agenda, I theorise and problematise drug-induced altered states.

Russell's film belongs to an intriguing network linking alterity and hallucinogens. This includes the original novel *Altered States* by screenplay writer, Paddy Chayefsky, based on psychologist John Lilly's flotation tank trips chronicled in *The Centre of the Cyclone*.[4] Other works in the cluster are Timothy Leary's writings on LSD and Carlos Castaneda's Don Juan books. In cross-referencing DeleuzeGuattarian philosophy with these sources, I locate it in the context of wider cultural and artistic responses to the impact of psychedelic drugs.

Altered States: The Return of the Repressed

Jessup's alterity passes through several stages in Russell's film. Each 'trip' moves him further back in time until psychological changes manifest in bodily alteration. At the same time, he moves further away from the repressive Oedipal structures colonising his unconscious. I am reading cinematic material here via Deleuze's alignment of brain and screen, a concept that informs the affects and percepts of my encounters. The hallucinatory mental states presented by Russell literalise Deleuze's figure. I start with an aspect of pharmacoanalysis emphasised both in Russell's film and *A Thousand Plateaus*: its anti-Freudian struggle for psychic autonomy.

Jessup's first on-screen hallucinations adopt a Freudian inflection as he struggles against repression imposed by a harshly patriarchal superego. His trip begins with affective facial alteration. His face flattens and stretches into horizontal and the blindfold is edited out to key in an altered mode of vision. Against a back-projection of elemental imagery – floating clouds, fishes and eels – time winds back and he regresses to his earlier self as smiling schoolboy.

Jessup's beatific state is soon wiped by Russell's *grand guignol* scenario of Freudian/Christian guilt as his dying father is aligned with the crucified Christ. Jessup's father appears on his deathbed with his arms outstretched in a crucifixion posture, the fiery cross of suffering on his chest. As he dies, a piece of fabric imprinted with Jesus' face, like St Veronica's veil, falls down over his own and seeks to absorb him into its own image. He pushes this off angrily, refusing to become 'one body' with Jesus, but Jessup himself oscillates between the suffering Christ and his anti-Christ adversary.

An infernal scene features a seven-eyed, apocalyptic Beast against back-projected hellfire. Christ on the cross grinds his hips suggestively as Jessup attempts to throw off religious oppression by blasphemous sexuality. The image recedes to a silhouetted Golgotha fronted by a Romanesque ruin. An ornate book with the apocalyptic Beast and INRI on the cover lies on a sacrificial altar. Here, Jessup re-enacts the Old Testament tale of Abraham and Isaac. He stabs a ram, spilling blood over the cover. This abjection and sacrifice of his own integral animality leads to his later compensatory becoming-animal.

Increasingly sexual hallucinations overlay the ornate pages. Abstracted images of blood, eye and sun gel into a primal scene of sex as sacrifice enacted by Jessup wearing the Beast's head. Jessup's unconscious has been colonised by the Oedipal primal scene, where intercourse appears to the child as a frightening act of violence.[5] This is impounded by religious images of retribution. Together, they produce his guilt-ridden patriarchal elision of father, Jesus and Jehovah internalised in super-egoic form.

For Deleuze and Guattari, Freud's case study of Judge Schreber's schizophrenia maintains 'intact the rights of Oedipus in the God of delirium'.[6] According to Freud, 'we must *necessarily* discover Schreber's daddy beneath his superior God' as Oedipal triangulation limits the analysis of Schreber's visions.[7] Deleuze and Guattari note the disparity between what Schreber experienced and his complicity with 'the whole game' in agreeing with the analyst's suggestion to identify his mother with the Virgin Mary.[8] In actuality, Schreber's visions project 'desimplified' divine forms that complicate as they break through the limited terms and functions of the gendered Oedipal triangle to become autonomous schizzes. As Artaud put it in his celebration of the BWO,

I don't believe in father
                       in mother,
got no
pappamummy.[9]

Likewise linking schizophrenia and experience of the divine, Jessup's first hallucination cuts to a close-up of a schizophrenic patient's visionary stare. Jessup observes her from the apparently detached perspective of a video monitor yet her experience of God clearly connects to his own 'complete transport' of religious ecstasy in youth.[10] Jessup's next trip travels further back, before subjective history into the supposedly 'primitive' consciousness of a Native American tribal people. His regression is induced via the hallucinogenic mix of *sinicuiche* or *hema salicifolia* and *amanita muscaria*.[11]

Castaneda and Becoming-Primitive

Jessup, who had read Castaneda, should have expected something like this.[12] (Chayefsky)

Jessup's participation in a Mexican Native American mushroom ritual is partly motivated by the works of Carlos Castaneda.[13] After the publication of *The Teachings of Don Juan: A Yaqui Way of Knowledge* in 1968, Castaneda's books became central texts of the counter-cultural quest for mystic revelation. Hippies and spiritual seekers sought to imitate the use of hallucinogens as spiritual sacrament by tribal cultures.

The semi-fictional nature of Castaneda's books does not detract Deleuze and Guattari from enthusiastic endorsement. Their assertion that they prefer the books to be 'a syncretism rather than an ethnographic study, and the protocol of an experiment rather than an account of an initiation' places use-value above issues of authenticity.[14] Russell's film is an even looser blend of Castaneda's *Yaqui* with other anthropological sources. The tribe Jessup visits are *Hinchi*, but their *brujo*, or sorcerer, appears to be a *Tarahumara*. Don Juan deploys mescal and psychoactive herbs to stop the disciple's 'internal dialogue' by flooding his mind with information to prepare for new modes of perception.[15] His account directly shapes DeleuzeGuattarian perspectives on intoxicants.

I argue that Castaneda's semi-fictions also influenced Deleuze and Guattari's concepts of alterity more broadly via becoming and lines of flight. Castaneda's training as a sorcerer includes becomings with non-human forms of life, such as the tree, which produces 'a soft, spongy, bouncy feeling, which was outside me and yet was part of me' as it 'invited me to melt with it. It engulfed me or I engulfed it'.[16] Castaneda also describes the sorcerers' lines of flight that enable them to perform 'impossible' feats. Don Genario, one of his mentors, rises up a sheer cliff via 'something that looked or felt like a line or an almost imperceptible thread of light pulling him up', which emanates from his navel.[17] Castaneda later learns to produce his own lines of flight.

When engaging with these forces, humans are no longer focused on a single subjectivity, but experience themselves as more complex: 'luminous beings' as a 'cluster' or multiplicity of fibres.[18] For Deleuze and Guattari Don Juan's teachings evoke a pre-subjective level of autonomy and the genesis of a radical mode of operations prior to imposed structures of signification.

At this point I want to interject Artaud's account of his initiation into the *Ciguri* peyote rituals in a similar kind of subjective dissolution. Seeking to alleviate opium addiction by botanical drugs in a sacred tribal context, Artaud visited the *Tarahumara*s in 1936. His traumatic hallucinations offer insight into Jessup's tortured and blissful visions in *Altered States*.

Although Artaud is a formative influence on Deleuze and Guattari, *The Peyote Dance* is, surprisingly, less often cited in their writing on drugs than Castaneda's tales of ritual ingestion.[19] Importantly, though, it reinforces their philosophical use of the terms 'plane' and 'stratum'. Artaud describes *Ciguri*'s *'plane'* which is 'the very mystery of all poetry', inaccessible to normal consciousness.[20] He contrasts this with the more limited level on which mundane awareness operates.

In the *Tutuguri* ritual, Allen Weiss explains that *Ciguri*, as well as being peyote, the psychoactive plant, is also 'the God himself'.[21] The therapeutic action of the drug demands 'total pillaging of our organism; *Ciguri* is man himself assassinated by God'.[22] Artaud's *Tarahumara* mentor recommends peyote to him as an aid to autopoesis, used to

sew yourself back together in your wholeness, without God who assimilates you and creates you, and as you create yourself out of Nothingness and in spite of Him at every moment.[23]

For Weiss, Artaud desublimates this 'metaphysical homeopathy' into an 'anticultural poetics'.[24] Artaud's powerfully affective work strengthens the schizoanalytic connections I am making between Russell's film, drugs and DeleuzeGuattarian thought.

Castaneda's sorcerer also describes a kind of autopoesis that can 'combat the mechanisms of interpretation and instil in the disciple a presignifying semiotic, or even an asignifying diagram'.[25] Deleuze and Guattari counsel their readers to follow Don Juan's lead, 'find your own places, territorialities, deterritorialisations, regime, line of flight! semioticise yourself instead of rooting around in your prefab childhood and Western semiology!'[26] They recommend Castaneda's books as an inspiration for new becomings.

Don Juan's existential cartography depends on the dynamic interaction of two forces: *tonal and nagual*. The *tonal* is the 'organiser of the world'.[27] The creative force of the *nagual* is found in 'nonordinary reality', the sorcerers' field of operations.[28] In Deleuze and Guattari's interpretation of Castaneda, the *tonal* is the subjective level of signification, while the *nagual* is 'the same everything, but under such conditions that the body-without-organs has replaced the organism and experimentation has replaced all interpretation'.[29] Subjective consciousness is thus transformed into 'flows of intensity, their fluids, their fibres, their continuums and conjunctions of affects, the wind, fine segmentation, microperceptions' in the dynamic flux of material forces.[30]

The destratified *nagual* enables becomings, intensities and the moving forces via which, as Artaud writes, 'personal consciousness has expanded in this process of internal separation and distribution' as peyote strengthens the will to power.[31] Artaud details his schizoid experience of dissolving into component elements, as 'from what was your spleen, your liver, your heart, or your lungs' organs break away and burst in 'this atmosphere which wavers between gas and water'.[32] His response at this stage in his *Ciguri* trip, when 'you no longer feel the body which you have just left and which secured you within its limits, but you feel much happier to belong to the limitless than to yourself' is a euphoric embrace of subjective dissolution.[33]

Yet affect is not a denial of action, but contemplation of the most life-enhancing action in preparation for further motion. Total absorption in dynamic chaos might irrevocably annihilate the schizoid subject, destroying not enhancing *élan vital*. For Deleuze and Guattari, 'a *nagual* that erupts, that destroys the tonal, a body-without-organs that shatters all strata, turns immediately into a body of nothingness, pure self-destruction' with death as its outcome.[34] Don Juan warns the would-be warrior to be a 'customs house', maintaining forces in equilibrium by adapting them to the

demands of the situation, for 'intent is the gate in between. It closes completely behind him when he goes either way'.[35] The ideal, for both Don
Juan and DeleuzeGuattari, is to move freely between planes at will as particular operations demand.

Jessup's quest for revelation exposes the dangers lurking for Westerners
who merely dabble in tribal sacraments. The physical and psychic framework of the *Hinchi* contrasts sharply to Jessup's academic and Christian
training. However rigorous Jessup's scientific discipline might be, though,
it is only a thin veneer on religious fanaticism lacking psychic equilibrium
or genuine strength of will. Such a perspective, leading to what Artaud
calls 'the shameless fantasies of an unhealthy mind',[36] directly opposes the
spiritual autopoesis offered by *Ciguri*, with its Nietzschean self-created
man 'in the space HE was constructing for HIMSELF, when God mur-
dered him' (*sic*).[37]

Russell's thematic leanings are indelibly Freudian. Despite the outdoor
location of Artaud's *Ciguri* rite, Russell's film locates Jessup's ritual in a
womb-like cavern, entered through a crevice of dazzling light. Here, via a
'tearing' and 'agony', he undergoes a torturous and botched attempt at
rebirth, as though 'reversed to the other side of things'.[38] Although they
do not advise undergoing physical traumas, Deleuze and Guattari advocate
a comparable death and rebirth by autopoesis.

Chayefsky's novel and Russell's film depict Jessup's quest for alterity as
temporal regression via 'primitive' human other, through sub-human to
pre-human. In the semi-darkness of the cave, the celebrants crouch by a
fire while musicians play wooden pipes and drums with hollow monotony.
The camera tracks down to a face daubed in white mud as the *Hinchi*
negate their separate human status by melding with the earth, which
Jessup, stiff in his elegant safari suit, is unable to do.

A senior *cunadera* (medicine woman) brews a bubbling cauldron of
lumpy, blood-like liquid. The abject appearance of her sacred potion is
intended to repel by its colour and texture. Jessup's hand is slashed
between his third and fourth finger by the *brujo* so his blood drips into the
brew. His life-force, with its Western genetic makeup, is mixed with
Mexican fungi and herbs in a mystical bonding ritual. This blend is
ingested in a communion like an abject perversion of a Christian Mass.

Jessup leaps up, impelled by the rapid rush when, according to Artaud,
'the idea of matter is volatilised by *Ciguri*'.[39] Divisions between subject and
object are undermined by synaesthetic distortions. Artaud describes being
'an effervescent wave which gives off an incessant crackling in all directions'
and Jessup likewise feels sounds and hears visions in a synaesthetic mix.[40]
Fireworks explode and shower sparks to produce lens flares. With the

sonorous music, they make him stagger and wince, caught up in the 'burn-ings and rendings' of *Ciguri*.[41] The explosions rip into his ego defences, but though his psychic templates are damaged, they are not blown apart.

As the *tonal* and the *nagual* face off, Jessup is the battleground between ego loss and Freudian structuration. Early conditioning combats pre-subjective affective awareness. Hallucinations blend moments from per-sonal history with archetypal imagery accounted typical of mescal and other botanical hallucinogens. For Jung, the psychoanalyst exceeded parental images and 'frequently appeared in the guise of a devil, a god, or a sorcerer', here the *Brujo*, who can 'see though' Jessup.[42] Without the tribal spiritual framework, Jessup undergoes a kind of psychotherapy during which psychic matter surfaces.

The antagonism between Jessup's rigidity and the shifting, molecular plane of affects passes through repressed fantasies of himself and his estranged wife Emily. Despite her demure white Edwardian gown, she is aligned with a lizard by intercutting. Deleuze and Guattari note 'very special becomings–animal traversing human beings and sweeping them away'.[43] Our engagement in becomings-animal potentialises new connec-tions. Later, a sphinx-like Emily melds more closely with the iguana, in a DeleuzeGuattarian becoming-animal projected by Jessup's paranoid sexuality.

As Eve, she tempts Jessup, also in pristine white, with white food: ice-cream, before a python coils around his head to choke him. This recalls the biblical alignment of the phallic snake with the Devil and Eve's sinful quest for knowledge. Artaud notes the phallic rock formations in *Tarahumara* country and Russell's film sports a plethora of phallic mushroom shapes including the tribe's totem. Mescaline users report human heads becom-ing mushrooms, and Emily is similarly transformed.[44]

As well as this heavy-handed symbolism, Russell's imagery is shaped by standard accounts of drug phenomena. Heinrich Klüver, a German phar-macologist, drew up a list of typical mescaline 'form constants' described by his subjects.[45] Among these were rotating jewels, lightnings, comets and explosions. The totemic masks of the gyrating *Hinchi* dancers are similarly intercut with fireworks, coloured lights and flowing forms, as frenetic editing rhythms keep pace with the drumbeats.

Hallucinations peak with a vision of a radically altered Jessup and Emily. Outlined by stars, their sparkling, naked silhouettes dance adoration of the sacred mushroom totem. Drops of golden light emanate from the cut in Jessup's hand as his blood transforms into light. The *nagual* vision turns to *tonal* horror as a nuclear mushroom cloud replaces the totem. Jessup's red-stained clothes implicate him in the abuse of scientific knowledge.

Jessup's uncharacteristically passive posture as he watches a now sphinx-like Emily leads into the molecular erosion of Freudian subjectivity by the *nagual*. Narcotic distortions of time and motion are also conveyed as the couple are covered by mounds of drifting grains. Indistinguishable from sand hills, their obliterated figures are blown into the desert, grain by grain. In a shocking jump cut back to the 'real' of the *tonal*, a lizard lies eviscerated by Jessup's unleashed violence.

Despite Jessup's apparent return to sobriety, changes in his chemical makeup continue to undermine subjective control and lead to further experiments in a Harvard lab still intercut with the Hinchi village. Having sampled psychedelics in a ritual context, Jessup wants to extend their disruption of linear time. In terms of Deleuze's philosophical paradigm, this process engages the insights of Bergson in *Creative Evolution*.

Creative (D)evolution

Using himself as experimental subject, Jessup's next trip starts with a rerun of traditional hellish imagery from *Dante's Inferno* (Harry Lachmann, 1935) as a lightning storm plays over him. His face, distorted by a scream, flattens and tears apart in red ribbons, engulfed by a forest of crimson crucifixes and a sea of fire.[46] Moving beyond this recycled religious iconography, Jessup experiences a cosmic cataclysm both subjective and objective. The eclipse recalls Artaud's 'eternal death of the sun' evoked in his poem *Tutuguri: The Rite of the Black Night*.[47] He experiences the Big Bang and the geological origin of earth. The extremity of his visions is distanced by a reversed tracking shot framing the back of his shuddering head though an observation monitor.

Jessup intensifies the stimulus by combining botanical drugs with sensory deprivation. Re-using an old LSD flotation tank in the basement, he experiences a genetic regression carried over into physical manifestation. He briefly becomes one of his own progenitors, a prehistoric hunter, and emerges with a bloodied mouth and a face daubed with white mud like the *Hinchi* ritual celebrant.

Jessup's temporal reversals produce molecular shifts in his genetic makeup, flamboyantly presented by Russell's cinematography. His body physically alters without the stimulus of drugs or the tank. In the bathroom, his arms and torso buckle into lumps and his feet sprout hair. The empirical nature of this change is undermined by drug flashback insertions of Hell.

Jessup's experiments can be traced to Lilly's accounts of psychoactive regression, in which hallucinations reminiscent of Bergson enabled him to 'literally *project* visual images out of memory'.[48] Lilly overlaid his own face with those of his ancestors, travelling back in time, until a 'hairy anthropoid' then a sabre-toothed tiger appeared in the mirror.[49] His analysis concludes 'an event that had no contemporary model to explain it'.[50] Jessup and his fellow scientists are similarly mystified.

A close-up of Jessup's EEG scan shows consistently non-human patterns. He has achieved physical molecular transformation, emerging from a further trip as a hirsute pre-human creature. In this simian form, his pent-up violence is released at figures of authority: the university security guards. After a fight with a pack of stray dogs, he is drawn to the city zoo, where he kills and devours a hartebeest. Like Jekyll and Hyde, Jessup has little control over his transformations and ends up back in human shape, naked and exhausted by a pond. At this point, I want to connect Jessup's becoming pre-human and Deleuzian alterity via Bergson's work on evolutionary continuity.

To support his theory of duration, Bergson investigated the evolutionary relation of humans to other life-forms. Rather than humans being the Darwinian crown of creation, Bergson argued that our evolutionary status is not predetermined. Like the rest of the universe, homo sapiens are a more random product of durational interaction in 'invention, the creation of forms, the continual elaboration of the absolutely new'.[51] Universal flux can be perceived by a consciousness that has likewise become flexible, as 'life, like conscious activity', is 'continuous creation of unforeseeable form'.[52]

Bergson asserts 'continuity of change, preservation of the past in the present, real duration'.[53] The past is preserved in a virtual time accessible by memory. In a parallel process, the actual past is also preserved. Plants and animals share common features and all forms of life contain 'in a rudimentary state – either latent or potential – the essential characters of most other manifestations'.[54] If this is so, then differences between descendant and ancestor are 'slight'.[55] He compares the evolutionary stages of animal species to formal changes of a human embryo in gestation.

Bergson's belief that nature has 'neither purely internal finality nor absolutely distinct individuality' is central to both Deleuze's Bergsonian conceptualisation of molecular becoming and Jessup's experimentation.[56] In Bergson's terms, the human is both 'one with this primitive ancestor' and 'solidary with all that descends from the ancestor in divergent directions'.[57] Philosophically, Jessup's condition exemplifies the union of individuated forms and 'the totality of living beings by invisible bonds'.[58]

My cross-fertilisation of Deleuze, Bergson and Russell is further elucidated by the insights of psychedelic researchers circulated in the fictional Jessup's actual intellectual milieu. No account of drug experiments in the

1960s and 1970s is unmarked by the input of acid guru Timothy Leary, likewise a lapsed Harvard research scientist. For Leary, who claimed LSD as the herald of a paradigm-shifting 'molecular revolution', the basic unit of consciousness is molecular and radical change occurs at this level.[59] Despite the uneven quality of Leary's work, particular concepts sound remarkably Bergsonian and DeleuzeGuattarian.

Leary's account of narcotic effects is based, like Chayevky's and Russell's, on evolutionary forms 'multiplying in endless diversity – reptile, insect, bird' and becoming Australopithecus.[60] Leary suggests that 'moments of crisis' in which our 'forebears escape from fang, from spear' are most deeply imprinted in 'the neurological memory bank' for their 'life-affirming exultation and exhilaration in the perpetuation and survival of the species'.[61]

Like Bergson, Leary holds that humans carry the genetic memory of earlier evolutionary forms. Instead of deploying this as a philosophical tool to explore temporality, his approach is more literally biological. He claims the existence of a 'protein record' of 'an ancient strand of molecules that possesses memories of every previous organism' contributory to present existence.[62] This, Leary asserts, is 'a living memory of every form of energy transformation on this planet'.[63] He contends that LSD experiences of retrogression and reincarnation are not 'mysterious or supernatural' but 'modern biogenetics'.[64]

Leary advocates the user's active engagement in the mental challenge posed by regression. He pronounces that the tripper's 'duty' is to 'recapitulate personally the entire evolutionary sequence' that is already inherent.[65] Taking Leary's biological rather than Bergson's philosophical method as guide, Jessup undergoes more drastic devolution.

Becoming Anti-matter

Impressed by his results, Jessup ups the stimuli and travels as far back in time as possible. The sound waves of his scream are visualised as wavy green lines like electrical interference across the image. Jessup's face tears and disappears in rainbow light waves as his human subjectivity is ripped away by pure affect and the screen is swamped by primordial chaos. An amorphous shape struggles to manifest itself and splits Jessup's body apart, exploding his head.

Chayefsky's novel and screenplay focus on Jessup's dissolution into anti-matter. Imagery draws on scientific terms to describe 'shuddering bands of radiation' that catch Jessup 'in a pinch of energy waves' that change from the 'burning red of ultra-violet radiation' to 'grays the quality of X-rays'.[66] However extreme Russell's images of raw force become, the film's redemptive plot insists that, sporadically, a recognisably subjective element of Jessup remains.

A smooth semblance of Jessup's head, with a quicksilver colour and texture, appears without a conventional human body, its skull distended by an enormous brain. In Russell's metaphysical version of the story, Jessup, having regressed to the First Cause, returns as a monstrous, post-human *übermensch* with godlike powers of destruction.

Usurping Jessup's place, a cluster of matter writhes across the screen. His ultrasonic yell bends the metal pipes of the lab and explodes them in steam. In DeleuzeGuattarian terms, the sound has passed 'from the howling of animals to the wailing of elements and particles'.[67] The force of transformation is physically conveyed by blinding stroboscopic light and the material substance of the lab violently abstracts into negative footage. A swirling supernova leads into a vortex of anti-matter with Jessup's screaming mouth at its core. To pulsing electronic music and an amplified heartbeat, cosmic and molecular flash-frames are intercut.

According to physics, if a particle could travel back beyond the start of time, its material properties would transform into anti-matter. Returning to the present, it would carry anti-matter back with it. This is what happens to Jessup in the novel, 'dissolving in shimmering vibrations into the pulsating waves of energy penetrating him' and imploding 'as if he were being sucked up into a black hole of his own' and becoming 'shuddering, increasingly shapeless antimatter'.[68] The graininess of Russell's film foregrounds the molecularity of the dissolution process as Jessup becomes anti-matter cell by cell.

The tank explodes in pyrotechnics of light and sound, flash frames of cell clusters and pulsing valves. Deleuze and Guattari note similar images in Castaneda, when everything 'appears supple, with holes in fulness, nebulas in forms, and flutter in lines'.[69] Particular drugs alter the templates of percepts and concepts in 'acts of segmentation that no longer coincide with the rigid segmentarity'.[70] Phenomena include rippling lines, fringes and overlappings.[71] Such 'visual and sonorous microperceptions' reveal 'spaces and voids, like holes in the molar structure'.[72] In this flux of particles, new mental formations are born.

A kind of Creation scene is enacted as water 'rains' and a whirling chaos of steam seeps from the tank. Yet, Russell keeps Jessup insistently human, an X-ray skeleton with breathing lungs, as light streams from his heart region and floods the room. Emily wades into the centre of the vortex, grasps his head between her hands and rebirths her husband back into human form.

Emily is herself later caught up in the conflagration of anti-matter. Her body ignites and splits to reveal burning energy glowing like a coal. As Jessup beats himself against the wall to keep himself together, she maintains grip until he solidifies in her embrace. Their molten bodies cool to a calm blue with rainbow coronas. According to Chayefsky and Russell, they are 'entirely reconstituted'.[73] Safely human, they have driven the affective forces of anti-matter back to their proper place, before time and evolution began.

Russell presents Jessup's altered states as descents into madness and horror. Yet from a DeleuzeGuattarian perspective, the very hallucinations are the site of the film's alterity. The reterritorialisation of the 'happy ending' is thus invalid. For Deleuze and Guattari, experimentation with drugs marked everyone, 'even nonusers', because 'it changed the perceptive coordinates of space-time and introduced us to a universe of microperceptions in which becomings-molecular take over from where becomings-animal leave off'.[74] At the point where Jessup encounters loss of subjectivity in becoming-molecular lies potential for beneficial change.

Between the actual and the virtual, cinematic altered states may catalyse new, productive kinds of perception. At the same time, Deleuze and Guattari's awareness of the partial and flawed nature of drug insights strikingly recalls the images of anti-matter in Russell's film. If the user becomes psychologically or physically reliant on the drug to provide insights, 'deterritorialisations remain relative, compensated for by the most abject reterritorialisations'.[75] Seeking alterity, addicts open themselves up to dissolution from which there may be no return.

Deleuze and Guattari's theoretical lines of flight explore both the insights of intoxicants and the physical and psychic dangers of over-use. Russell's film of *Altered States* is a nexus of productive connections between sources of insight, fictional and theoretical, on the nature of narcotic alterity and its perils. The sensory barrage of cinema is uniquely placed to express both types of experience. The pyrotechnics of the 'good trip', as affectively potent as images of drug damage, are often relegated to early sections of film narratives.

Tuning In, Turning On, Dropping Out: *The Trip* and *Easy Rider*

life is a process of breaking-down.[76] (F. Scott Fitzgerald)

Feel Purple . . . Taste Green . . . Touch the Scream that Crawls Up the Wall! (Poster for *The Trip*)

In a move typical of his image-based lines of flight, Deleuze interweaves intoxicants with art, here Scott Fitzgerald's fictionalised tale of chronic alcoholism *The Crack-Up*. Using the image of the alcohol-induced crack as a philosophical tool, Deleuze addresses the 'plane of immanence' or becoming. For Deleuze alone and with Guattari, consciousness is a virtual plane crossed by shifting, pre-subjective percepts and affects. It has properties of both density and surface and functions on two levels: macro (the plane itself) and micro (molecularity).

In perpetual motion, together but distinct, the virtual plane of images and the human centre of indetermination intersect in 'speed and slowness, floating affects' that 'perceive the imperceptible' and produce desire.[77] A cartography of non-subjective affects crosses the plane's surface, its fluctuating potential actualised in the lived experience of a particular body.

Deleuze speculates that intoxicants produce a 'silent, imperceptible crack' as 'unique surface Event', which is 'imperceptible, incorporeal, and ideational', at least in its early stages.[78] Yet the crack's location is neither internal nor external but 'at the frontier' between, intersecting them in 'complex relations of interference and interfacing, of syncopated junctions – a pattern of corresponding beats over two different rhythms'.[79] Cracks on the virtual plane can be manifest in actual change. It is the nature and scope of this that I investigate in my cinematic examples.

In *Altered States*, Jessup's early experiments happened in the congenial context of late 1960s Harvard marked by Leary's research. Deleuze's essay, 'Porcelain and Volcano', was written in 1969. I want to augment this chronological linkage of Deleuze, Leary and other psychedelic researchers via LSD feature films of the period. In particular, I will consider Leary's claims that the drug offers a 'breakthrough' experience. My readings of two well-known American 'acid' movies *The Trip* (Roger Corman, 1967) and, more briefly, *Easy Rider* (Dennis Hopper, 1968) assess how far they manifest breakthrough or breakdown.

Corman's low-budget 'exploitation' film was made in 1967 at the height of the 'Summer of Love' and targeted youthful audiences. Rather than opting for an action-driven plot where we merely watch characters take drugs, the film is overtly 'about' LSD itself and seeks to express its affective impact directly. Like pornography, setting and characters are an excuse for extended sections of drug 'action' (including two psychedelic sex sessions). Acid visuals, with psychedelic footage, disrupt representational norms.

Corman welds techniques of 'expanded cinema' from light-shows and abstract animations into mainstream narrative to induce hallucinogenic sensation. At their most effective, they might produce a kind of 'contact high', the phenomenon when a non-user is affected by another's intoxication.[80] I argue later that Deleuze also posits the possibility of a 'contact high' as a basic premise in his theorisation of intoxicant-based art.

So what was an acid trip supposed to look like in 1967 and how were its affective properties cinematically conveyed? The light-show sequences in Corman's film draw extensively on accounts of narcotic effects as well as the then current 'cultural capital' of psychedelia. Such conventions inevitably appear dated, inviting the pastiches of nostalgia and parody.[81] At the time, however, hallucinogens were a matter of substantial scientific as well as aesthetic investigation.

In such journals as *The Psychedelic Review*, neurologists, pharmacologists and psychobiologists such as Ronald Seigel and Jolyon West built on Klüver's identification of mescaline form constants to typify images shared by hallucinogens. Saturated colours and displays of light are common.[82] Perceptual distortions of motion and speed favour jerky, automatic movement or rhythmical contraction. Images pulsate as they tunnel in and flow out from a central light. Lattices, geometric forms and kaleidoscope effects are frequent.[83] Images are rarely fixed or static but transform and merge, with abstract patterns overlaying complex imagery. Music intensifies synaesthesia to produce spiralling arabesques.[84] These effects are staples of experimental art and film of the period, simulating LSD by stimulating comparable modes of perception.

In Leary's account, the hallucinating subject does not exist as a personal perspective distinct from phenomena, but is experientially melded with them. At the peak of the trip, subjects recount 'merging with pure (i.e. content free) energy, white light' like *The Trip*'s acid novice Paul Groves (Peter Fonda) who sees 'the light inside'.[85] Users note 'the breakdown of macroscopic objects into vibratory patterns, visual nets, the collapse of external structure into wave patterns'.[86] Leary's scientific paradigm informs his account of a 'dance of particles' in the 'cyclical nature of creation and dissolution' difficult to describe in the 'flimsy inadequacy' of language.[87] Such descriptions of subjective dissolution and becoming imperceptible elaborate Deleuze and Guattari's own intoxicant figurations.

After narrative preliminaries, Paul engages in the film's main business. As he fits a blindfold, the screen fades to black and we share his first LSD images. Darkness glows purple as the screen splashes out contrasting red and blue patterns. The heartbeat soundtrack intensifies the impact of amorphous forms and glowing lights. A favourite device, the kaleidoscope lens, is frequently used and its rapid turns intensify hypnotic effects. Jewelled forms become pulsating dots then flower petals. Concentric rings swirl into paisleys. Shifting meshes overlay an atomic diagram. Purple, masked human figures are superimposed over abstract black and white petals.

I am less concerned with the narrative *representation* of Paul's adventures, with its Freudian gothic *mise-en-scène* of femmes fatales, torture and ritual execution, than with the narcotic properties of cinematic *style*.[88] Corman's ethical dichotomy (or censorship strictures) results in a trip alternatively 'good' and 'bad'.

Despite the staginess of Freudian gothic bogeys, though, Paul's slippage between parallel worlds can be read otherwise, via Deleuze's model of intersecting planes. Along with superimposition and split screen, overlay is a cinematic expression of the intensive 'layering' of planes. Interconnected but distinct realities coexist and we cross between them via the intensive movements of thought. Although both Paul's LSD planes are virtual, one is closer to actuality than the other. I will detail the actual/virtual dynamic further in Chapter 4.

Relocated 'back' to the well-appointed crash-pad owned by drug dealer Max (Dennis Hopper), Paul removes his mask and enters the next stage of his trip as his empirical surroundings, seen through acid-tinted lenses, undergo sensory transformation invisible to the viewer. Deferring an actual walk outside, Paul's exploratory journey happens anyway in the interlinked virtual world. Spatial and temporal cross-cutting validates the virtual plane as more than a simulacrum of actuality. Intercutting opens up perceptions of 'reality' to a multiplicity in which the virtual and actual are equally valid.

Corman follows Leary's advice to the LSD novice, providing Paul not only with a congenial 'set and setting' but also with John (Bruce Dern), an experienced guide, to reassure him. John suggests that Paul should 'let everything flow' and 'float right to the centre' of immanence. On cue, Paul feels like 'everything's alive' and perceives the flow of 'whole energy levels and fields flowing'. The apparently solid material world is radically changed via his new relation to it. He perceives the orange's vital force as a 'cloud of light'. Paul's new awareness of material vibrancy recalls Bergson as well as Castaneda's becomings. His direct experience of the normally invisible flux of forces is, like the Deleuzian virtual plane of consistency, alive with floating affects and percepts.

We saw that one of the 'form constants' of LSD was shifting abstract patterns overlaying complex imagery. This effect is showcased when Paul and his estranged wife Sally (Susan Strasberg) make love. Shimmering concentric circles spread across the room. Their intertwining bodies are tiger-striped with mutating colours and amorphous shapes produced by slides and a shifting lens. As the tempo of pounding electric rock increases, multiple images of the lovers spin by camera rotation. Mirrored lenses give a crystalline quality to the images.

In Deleuze's typography of cinematic affects, the tactile is not an *extensive act* of the hand, but an *intensive sensation* of touch possible if 'the hand relinquishes its prehensile and motor functions to content itself with a pure touching'.[89] Deleuze adds 'tactisigns' to his sensory categories of 'sonsigns' and opsigns. Explored more fully later in relation to eroticism, they reveal 'a touching which is specific to the gaze'.[90] The multiple, extended nature of Sally's arousal is rendered tactile in close-ups of her feet and toes curling and stretching in pleasure. Image content is fragmented into flows of pure colour as her orgasm splits and diffuses figuration. In its double-dosed removal of perceptual barriers, acid-fuelled sex is literally sensational.

Corman's techniques offer an overt version of Deleuzian tactisigns. Synaesthesia, the mixing of different sense modalities, is frequent in hallucinations. The promotional tagline for the film 'Feel Purple . . . Taste Green . . . Touch the Scream that Crawls Up the Wall!' foregrounds the film's acid-fuelled sensory mix. This is also mobilised when Paul's scream is seen not heard. In a visual equivalent to the yell, jagged black shapes stream in a vortex from his mouth.

Paul is transfixed by his own image in the mirror. A spiral of black lines forms a second vortex around the 'third eye' mid-forehead. This spot, the *ajña chakra* associated with the pineal gland system, is the reputed locus of visualisation, psychic perception and creativity. Deleuze describes the effect of the cinematic 'unbearable' as 'inseparable from a revelation or an illumination, as from a third eye'.[91] These mirrored images suggest the deterritorialising potential of affective mutation in socially and subjectively constructed faciality.

Defamiliarised, the face epitomises the 'unextended' affection-image.[92] The intensive qualities of 'the pure affect, the pure expressed' are displayed as a 'complex entity' by the cinematic face.[93] Close-ups magnify modalities, such as 'shadowy and illuminated, dull and shiny, smooth and grainy, jagged and curved'.[94] These interrelated elements interact intensively among themselves or extensively with others, as an internal composition of close-ups produced by framing and montage.

For Deleuze, the desubjectified close-up attains a trans-personal quality as though 'it had torn it away from the co-ordinates from which it was abstracted' and acts 'like a short circuit of the near and far' assembling disparate elements in commonality.[95] In his altered condition, Paul's face is a tiger-striped, shifting mask in red and black. This transmutes into the face of Sally seen through the cobweb mesh typical of LSD vision.

As well as producing haptic distortions, Leary claims that hallucinogens are 'microscopes of internal biology' revealing the neuronal networks and machinic processes of the embodied brain. He advises the user to focus the 'nervous system within' to 'decode the cellular script'.[96] Corman's trip likewise aims to display the mental processes of hallucination. As though in response to Leary's suggestion, Paul exclaims that his mirror visions trigger his ability to see inside his own brain.

In his hallucinated 'trial', Paul's brain is literally and ludicrously externalised as he sits with his head under a device like a pink chrysanthemum. The repetitious turn of a merry-go-round expresses the guilty fixations of a mind stymied by capitalist ideology. Despite his counter-cultural posturing, Paul is complicit in US foreign policy (Vietnam and the Bay of Pigs). Max, as a kind of counter-cultural superego, interrogates Paul by screened images, including one of Leary himself. In a pastiche of Leary-speak, Max advises Paul to be 'one with, and part of an ever-expanding, loving, joyful, glorious and harmonious universe'. Yet Paul, although happy to 'tune in and turn on', refuses the final, anti-capitalist part of Leary's dictum, to 'drop out'.

The film's final shot underlines Paul's failure to incorporate acid insights. Instead of espousing radical praxis, he remains locked in a narcissism lacking motivation and future direction. As he gazes at the sea from the beach house of his liberated (and wealthy) lover Glenn (Salli Sachse), his sun-bathed face is fragmented with cracks like a shattered mirror. Despite the ambiguity of this ending, Paul has certainly begun to crack, whether from the inroads of multiplicity or self-destruction.

If we disregard the tagged-on anti-drugs warning and the negative implications of the closing shots, *The Trip* presents a provisional celebration both of chemical mind expansion and its drop-out aficionados.[97] The film's rhetoric reflects its historical juncture, when the visionary insights of hallucinogens appeared to offer not only personal fulfilment but also libertarian social change. According to *Easy Rider* (Dennis Hopper) made by members of the same cast a year later, the hippie vision became sidelined into the childlike efforts of a remote commune and the LSD sequence is shot through with guilt-ridden angst.

The Camera as Drug: *Easy Rider*

My brief Deleuzian reflection on *Easy Rider* does not reprieve the political implications of this 'ersatz underground film' rigorously argued by James.[98] I will be focusing, rather, on how style works in distinction from narrative content. In thematic terms, the painfully convincing 'bad trip' is a purgatorial journey heavy with symbols of sex, death and religion. In microcosm, it compresses Freudian scenarios of sexual dysfunction and the actual large-scale horrors of the Vietnam War avoided by 'draft-dodgers'. Hopper's cinematic style, however, is both directly engaged in, and tangential to, symbolic content.

Cocaine-dealers Billy (Dennis Hopper) and Wyatt/Captain America (Peter Fonda) wander through the *Mardi Gras* with two brothel workers, Karen (Karen Black) and Mary (Toni Basil). Their bourbon intoxication is visualised by the manic swoops of hand-held, *cine-verité* footage. Deleuze notes that alcohol offers escape from a 'hardened and faded present which alone subsists and signifies death'.[99] Billy and Wyatt drink to cope with their friend, civil rights lawyer George Hanson's literal death. Seeking a more intense high, they try a different drug. A cemetery is a fit setting for their LSD trip and they swallow their tabs as a funerary sacrament.

At this point, the extensive trans-American motorbike trip of the road movie shifts trajectory from extensive to intensive motion. Bodily movement across space becomes the spatially confined yet experientially intensive movement of hallucinogenic affect. Although the trip sequence runs only five minutes, the experience seems longer as the time-distorting properties of the drug are convincingly simulated by cinematic techniques.

The affective onset of the drug begins in the camera itself. Deleuze asserts that the camera is able to act 'like a consciousness'.[100] Of course, it is set up and moved by human agency, but ultimately, its technological apparatus passively records the object before it in a way that exceeds human ocular capacity. Deleuze disregards the role of the operative and argues that the distinct technological properties of camera-consciousness are 'inhuman or superhuman' rather than human.[101] The camera's inhuman automatism, then, free from idealism, perceives matter more directly than the human vision that it challenges.

For Deleuze, camera-consciousness is manifest as the machine moves through space of its own accord, independent of characters. This concept draws on the Bergsonian brain as image, a Spinozan 'spiritual automaton' rather than a Cartesian, humanist 'I'.[102] Here, 'mental relations' are not the analytical investigations of the Hitchcockian camera but remain on the plane of affects and percepts.[103] By disorientating perception as the four trippers in Hopper's film get 'out of their heads', LSD impacts on customary cognitive patterns. As the viewer's embodied brain connects with the film as event, camera shake, blurred focus, abstraction and coloured filters directly affect our mechanisms of perception prior to the search for 'meaning'.

The hallucinating camera is in disjunctive, shifting relation to the perceptions of characters. It does not attempt to record individual hallucinations, but, rather, displays outward behaviour objectively, without explaining enigmatic behaviour or their disjointed speech randomly intercut with the apostles' creed of a funeral party. Skewed camerawork depersonalises characters and group shots are frequent. What we encounter on-screen is a kind of commonly shared collage of hallucinatory 'constants'. The impact of the camera's intoxicated consciousness dominates any responses enacted in front of the lens. Rather than merely representing subjective psychodrama, its spectacle of light, colour and movement operates in tandem with primary affective processes on the virtual plane.

Stripped of both spatial orientation and psychological scaffolding, Billy, Karen, Wyatt and Mary's wanderings are randomly motivated by the material objects they encounter: statues, crucifixes, mourners and each other's bodies. The emotions displayed – weeping, euphoria, lust and despair – are intensive responses rather than extensive actions triggered by particular environmental stimuli. Ostensibly solid objects are not presented as fixed points or clearly bounded material substances. They are, rather, fluctuating force fields that draw or repel characters. Their modus operandi is the swooping camera and the shifting qualities of light.

In this sense, then, camera-consciousness registers the affects induced by the drug. It 'comes up' (experiences the first perceptual changes) literally via inserts of a sunburst lens flare mounting the screen diagonally. In LSD-induced perception, moving objects may leave multiple images or trails. Streaming like a comet's tail, the lens-flare gains momentum in its flight across the tombs until the screen floods with dazzling light. Such blank frames, whether dark or bright, fragment spectatorial continuity and narrative engagement. Blacked out footage invites interactive projection, whereas white inserts dazzle, as in the direct glare of the winter sun here, which over-stimulates the optic nerves and blanks out analytical thought.

Further disorientation techniques are deployed. The camera shoots a 360-degree spin of a web-like mesh of bare branches. This technique corresponds, but is not reducible to, the disturbance of human perception when we spin our bodies. Unlike the blur and inability to focus in human dizziness, the image here is vertical and retains sharp clarity. Nevertheless, camera spin makes us dizzy.

A psychedelic staple, the fish-eye lens, is used to make particular images, like an elderly man with an umbrella, bulge out from centre frame. LSD gives a sense of retinal expansion, of being able to see further than the limits of normal vision. Yet, the expanded and bent fish-eye vision has no human parallel. Rather, it offers a purely technological hallucinatory display disrupting norms of perspective by affective bombardment.

The trip sequence counterpoints randomness and repetition to intensify trance. Rapid-fire editing becomes a flicker of flash-frames too fast to process. These are intermeshed with a more recognisable image series: the flames of a gas jet burner, the textured petals of a purple flower in macro and a dark, grainy shot of Karen's face. The climactic sequence closes as it began, with a diagonal lens-flare. Although the cyclical structure might appear to freeze time, return to the same place is impossible and the dusk-darkened cemetery attests to a trip lasting several hours.

The capacity of the viewer's eye, in assemblage with the light-driven machinery of shooting and projection is thus expanded and the camera itself becomes an ingested drug. How far the experience changed its fictional users is left open, but later, Wyatt's famous statement 'we blew it', as well as articulating personal failure, is renowned for its wider socio-political significance. The film's counter-cultural heroes use drugs as intervals of unfocused hedonism amid capitalistic profiteering rather than as a tool for radically cracking the surface. Now, Wyatt attains a limited self-reflexivity. Continuing the cinematic consideration of the Deleuzian crack, my next example embodies it in the downward spiral of addiction.

The Breakdown: *Trainspotting* and *Requiem for a Dream*

the breakthrough and the breakdown are two different moments. (Deleuze)[104]

drug-induced compounds are usually extraordinarily flaky, unable to preserve themselves, and break up as soon as they are made or looked at. (Deleuze and Guattari)[105]

Deleuze and Guattari do not distinguish between specific drugs. Their account mingles hallucinogens with addictive depressants such as heroin and alcohol in a generalised 'drugs assemblage' with common elements. They enumerate three ways in which Castaneda's pharmacological teachings open up 'a line of perceptive causality', so that '(1) the imperceptible is perceived; (2) perception is molecular; (3) desire directly invests the perception and the perceived'.[106] Their inspiration is the aesthetic expression of narcotic affects in novels, poetry and painting rather than actual usage. In this way, their work moves beyond content to focus instead on stylistic properties to ascertain potential for new thought.

Although in 'Porcelain and Volcano' the two levels of the 'crack' are aligned, its operations on the surface remain distinct from those in the body. They draw closer via drugs, alcohol, suicide or madness.[107] Of these, drugs and alcohol are the 'most perfect, because, rather than bringing the two lines together in a fatal point, they take time'.[108] If 'the crack is no more internal than external' then 'its projection to the outside marks no less the end's approach than does the purest introjection'.[109] The crack progresses silently, though with concomitant 'noise' of actualisation at ever-widening edges, as 'following the lines of least resistance [. . .] sound and silence wed each other intimately and continuously in the shattering and bursting of the end'.[110] The addict's crack is inevitably embodied as subjective disso-lution approaches physical death.

A scene from Danny Boyle's *Trainspotting* (1996) depicts the crack lit-erally, as a gaping hole in the floor. Heroin addict Renton (Ewan McGregor), injecting a shot of 'pure' from his deaier Mother Superior, goes 'down, instead of high'.[111] The hole externalised here is, of course, in the addict's flesh, viscerally expressed by an extreme close-up of pores, hairs and a drop of blood on the skin on Renton's arm.[112] Going inside, the secret exchange of blood and heroin is depicted. A scarlet explosion is fol-lowed by an implosion as the needle presses in then retracts. An insert of a plug pulled out of a plug-hole is an objective correlative of this process, again in extreme close-up, the tiny grains of heroin powder visible in the water. No distinction is made here between body, brain and screen apart from two inserts of Renton's ecstatic face.

Boyle's Francis Bacon-influenced style uses expressionist colour satu-ration. The dense blue of veins, nauseous green and blood red contrast with junkie pallor to potent effect. In this scene, the cracking of boundaries between subjective and objective event deepens as Renton's opiated state is literalised. He falls back diagonally onto the blood-red carpet. Not stopped by the floor, his drop smoothly continues. His body sinks through the floor with the carpet into a rectangular hole that is both bed and grave. The camera glides smoothly, drawing him down. It pauses to tilt up as Renton's point-of-view sees Mother Superior peering in. The carpet screens each side of the frame, rendering his perception vertical. Stain spots on the ceiling make a visual rhyme with the heroin grains. Renton's fall through a hole that is also in him is given ironic aural accompaniment. The 'Perfect Day' of Lou Reed's velvet vocals is the junkie's overdose.

Numb to the pain of being dragged downstairs, Renton's curtained view forms a continuum between Mother Superior's flat and the hospital, where it is reinforced by the blood red of the emergency trolley. He remains in his carpeted hole until injected with a stimulant. Though he leaps out into harsh white light, his mind is far from straight and his upside-down head continues the disorientation. Renton's *élan vital* is sufficiently strong to get him 'off the hook' as the crack shifts from him to the more vulnerable figure

of his friend, AIDS victim Tommy. The humorous tone of the film gravitates against the impact of its tragic events. Darren Aronofsky's *Requiem
for a Dream*, despite its absence of fatality, offers no such relief from the
devastating impact of the embodied crack.

Black Holes and Lines of Death: *Requiem for a Dream*

The film of Hubert Selby's novel *Requiem for a Dream* (1978) could be
approached from two critical angles, the social and the psychoanalytical.[113]
The social realism of Selby's novel is cited by the direct borrowing from
its dialogue and the casting of the novelist himself as prison guard.
Updating the novel by a decade, it retains verisimilitude in the painstaking
authenticity of the Brighton Beach scene and gang culture. The first critical approach might thus produce a 'social problem film'.

The second, Freudian slant would focus instead on the bonding of the
two main addicts, mother Sara Goldfarb (Ellen Burstyn) and son Harry
(Jared Leto). Their tortured relationship could of course be read as a narcotic sublimation of Oedipal relations. Sara escapes her disappointing
present via memories of her young, innocent son or fantasies that Harry
will give her a grandchild. Heroin can be interpreted as mother-substitute
or back-to-the-womb cocoon. Harry's distress at Sara's addiction is
rapidly buffered by a fix that reassures him better than his mother could.

In the repetition-compulsion of Harry and Sara's habits, the pleasure
principle, Eros, competes with Thanatos, the death drive. Their struggle
cracks open ego defences to psychic leakage. Furthermore, heroin releases
Harry's friend Tyrone (Marlon Wayans) from his present anxiety into nostalgia visions of his own dead mother. A blissful memory features him as a
child on her lap. In classical Freudian terms, Tyrone and Harry also use
sex with adult women to offset their Oedipal lack. Both these critical readings could 'explain' the film, but my Deleuzian consideration of the crack
looks elsewhere, to the film's image assemblage.

I want to cite a couple of Aronofsky's observations, not from auteurist
reverence but to augment my discussion of pharmacoanalysis. The director describes how he and Matthew Libatique, his director of photography,
convey emotion via a kind of 'expressionism', using images to evoke ' the
emotion of the characters and the emotion of the themes'.[114]

One component of the film's distinctive affects is the Snorri-Cam,
attached to the actor's body, keeping it in focus while blurring the background. The Snorri-Cam is a 'subjective' device that 'locks' the camera in
centre frame, makes the background shaky and separates character from
environment, being 'the utmost in subjective filmmaking because the

character is frozen in the centre of the frame while the background is moving'.[115] A striking use of this technique is when a blood-soaked Tyrone is chased by the police after a gang shoot-up. Although he remains in sharp focus, the alleyway he runs through blurs as it sways and tilts with dizzying motion.

Aronofsky aims to subjectivise emotion. Yet, as noted by humanist critics such as Peter Bradshaw, the stylistic impact of his cinematography is far from personalisation.[116] Bradshaw reports a sense of alienation and emotional distancing in the 'relentless, almost aesthetic cruelty' of Aronofsky's style.[117] He resents the film's unjustified treatment of a 'nice old lady', and is disappointed that 'evil and horror are not explained; they are just placed before us with sphinx-like calm' without any clear moral lesson.[118] A further distancing of empathy is provided structurally by the film's schematic stylisation, most overt in the device of intertitles (Summer, Fall, Winter) to mark the temporal progress of addiction.

Instead of analysing social or psychological representation, a Deleuzian approach thinks through experiential engagement with the screened event. Rather than revealing personalised emotions, the Snorri-Cam expresses the affects of opiated consciousness, such as the addict's tangential relation to environmental context. In this sense, rather than conveying emotions, Aronofsky's intention to split subject and object is realised, expressing affective disjunction between narcosis and normative perception. The film's visualisation of such skewed perspective relativises relations between actual and virtual.

According to Deleuze, the perception-image has two poles, subjective and objective. Subjective perception can, on a basic level, be the diegetic point-of-view of a character, but his chief focus is on the objective agenda camera-consciousness, closer to the pre-subjective raw material of thought, affects and percepts. In the human 'centre of indetermination', this depersonalised process is located in the 'gap, or interval between a received and an executed, movement'.[119] The perception-image and the action-image occur on each side of this affective gap, their operations inextricably linked.

Despite Deleuze's concern with presubjective awareness, he nevertheless acknowledges an emotional assemblage with on-screen material via 'subjective sympathy for the unbearable, an empathy which permeates what we see'.[120] His use of the subjective here, though, is not bounded by the limits of our individual, historical personalities but is, rather, a more abstract and commonly shared perceptual dynamic. Group subjectivity has the defamiliarising potential to transform the actual if we open the egoic carapace that split us off from others.

So how does Aronofsky's expressionistic cinematography present the cracking of addicted bodies? Parallel intercutting between Sara and Harry is a deliberately intrusive structural device used relentlessly to jar sense-perception. Two distinct sets of visual and aural styles convey the specific qualities of their drugs: heroin, cocaine and amphetamine-based slimming pills. The worlds of Harry and Sara are distinct, yet interlocking, parts of the assemblage of addiction as it relentlessly pursues a line of flight locked on entropy.

The pre-credits sequence keys in the film's assemblage of addiction via TV as drug. The QTV ('quake television') show is hallucinatory in its mantra-like chanting, flashing lights and excited zips between audience and stage. Split-screen shows Sara's attempts to lock Harry out and his equally desperate attempt to hock the TV to score a deal.

By a kind of opening out of the compression of superimposition, split-screen combines the impact of intercutting and overlay. The viewing eye moves from side to side on a rapid horizontal axis between the on-screen interval of images. Harry's struggle sometimes appears on both sides of the split at once. His image is not neatly doubled, but his manic movements are out of synch and shots vary mid-length and extreme close-ups that reveal the perspiration on his skin. When both images of Harry are juxtaposed in the frame, the slight temporal gap in synchronisation produces schizoid disjunction.

The scene closes with a shocking sound: a loud metallic boom like the slam of metal doors. For Bergson, each sense vibrates with its own form of 'real action', linked to its virtual action on objects perceived. We thus associate particular sensations with the corresponding vibrations of connected senses.[121] Loudness and other sound qualities are felt as physical sensation. The ears and head experience loud noise, then the whole body feels shock waves. Such strong sensations are partly dependent on quantity, such as high volume that shakes the aural nerves, as well as sound quality as we briefly lose 'consciousness of our personality'.[122] The frequent jarring slam of Aronofsky's film is a sound punctuation after climaxes to jar the viewer with acute aural discomfort. It induces an ominous sense of powerlessness and intensified suffering. A triad of electronic chords is also used repeatedly as an interval between stages of decline.

Aronofsky and Libatique convey addiction via both structure (quantity of escalation) and style (perceptual quality). As Harry and Tyrone push the TV set around Brighton Beach, the extension of their journey through a lengthy title sequence evokes heroin's own stretching of temporal perception. In contrast, Marion (Jennifer Connelly), Harry's lover, asks her party guests, 'anyone want some time?' then gives out the speed pills expressed in the jumpy editing of party footage. The spatial distortion of drugs is also emphatic. Deep focus photography makes hollowed out, empty space an objective correlative to the emptiness of addicts waiting for their next fix.

Light and reflections are used to express skewed states. Tyrone and Harry overlook the soft gold light quality at Brighton Beach in their urgency to score. Ironically, the afternoon haze offers a visual equivalent to the state of mellowness they seek. The harsh bare bulb in Tyrone's pad contrasts with the glow of sunlight from a window blocked by his back as he faces his electric preference. When Harry and Marion shove open an emergency exit door, it flashes white light like the drug's explosion of pleasure. White light also seeps in and bleaches out the semi-naked image of Marion in the mirror, flooding her in bliss beyond eroticism. Ironically, she ends up selling her neglected body for heroin. Such narcissistic fascination is shared by Tyrone, who plays with mirror images of himself and ignores his waiting lover.

The film repeats stylised shots of heroin, cocaine and their 'works', or paraphernalia for smoking, snorting or injection. Although the editing rhythms are rapid-fire and edgy, the film stresses the repetitive and ritualised nature of 'cooking' and the inevitable rush of the hit. A close-up eye with rapidly enlarging pupil registers the effect. The stark white of the powder melds with the white light state it brings. Addiction is presented not as a machinic but a mechanical act.

Deleuze and Guattari distinguish between the terms mechanical and machinic. Machinic is distinguished sharply from mechanism, which implies closed sets and is used negatively for repetition that reduces energy, causes damage and eventually stops working. Machinic connections, such as of the interlinked bodies of spectator and text, are potentially energising instead. The connection of the viewer with cinematic techniques is further extended in the machinic assemblage of projection and viewing to generate autoproductive desiring machines.

Ecstatic with a drug rush, Tyrone dances to a hip-hop record. The rubbery moves of his legs and body bending with fluid agility might appear as the unrestricted play possible to DeleuzeGuattarian BWO. As a kind of force-field 'traversed by a powerful, nonorganic vitality', however, this is not a body fragmented by addiction like Tyrone's.[123] His euphoric dance only mimics the liberating possibilities of a BWO.

In its 'honeymoon stage' the addictive drug appears to increase *joie de vivre* and motivation. In time, it saps the users' creativity, while their plans, such as running a clothes design business, come to nothing. Tyrone's false sense of security is underlined by the canting of the shot. High angle shots are used frequently to produce the constricted perspective of a trap. They provide a kind of 'point-of-view' shot of the drug as invisible predator biding its time as the prey becomes more trapped.

Up-close images of Harry with Marion offer Deleuzian tactisigns. The smooth warmth of their youthful skin is evoked in soft-focus sepia tones. The use of split-screen here juxtaposes faces in dialogue with fingers caressing skin and recalls the earlier disjunction of Harry and Sara. However close the intimate rapport of these close-ups, the screen remains ominously split. Each lover is trapped by his/her need and mutual betrayal is foreshadowed by composition here. Their enthusiastic conversation is blotted out as the screen floods with blinding light. Despite their avowal of love, a slowly spinning image positions them no longer facing each other but head to head. As they lie suspended in the cool grey light of a heroin plateau, each partner is off on a private high.

From the outset, Sara's addiction runs parallel to Harry's. Her psychological predisposition is evident in compulsive TV viewing. The repetitive ritual of the programme wraps her in the cocoon of predictability as a close-up of her eyes is intercut with the white light that emanates from the set in a visual rhyme to the heroin hit. Sara increases her viewing pleasure by eating chocolates, with their attendant endorphin and serotonin high.[124] In close-up sharp focus, she sensuously caresses each one before popping it into her mouth as the TV audience urge her to 'be excited'. Ironically, an actual telephone call invites her to join a pool of contestants. Around this fact she constructs the fantasy of a slim, glamorous self on the show with her smart, successful son.

There is a genre of heroin films, from Otto Preminger's *The Man with the Golden Arm* (1955) onwards, but no such generic treatment for the more common and less sensational addiction to weight-loss drugs. The invasive cinematography of *Requiem for a Dream* stimulates synaesthetic experience of virtual taste via image and sound. The thing-world of Sara's hallucinations, whether based on material in her apartment or on TV, is insistently concrete. Prior to addiction, Sara attempts to slim by a Spartan diet of egg and grapefruit. Her plate is harshly lit in irritant colours in sharp contrast with the soft-focus chocolates seductively concealed in tissue wrappers. The visualisation of food items and their accompanying sounds effectively conveys gustatory qualities.

Sara's obsession is focused on the refrigerator, with its store of forbidden goodies. In split screen, it shimmers alluringly with a blurred effect like heat haze. Impelled by anorganic vitality at first comic then monstrous, it develops its own persona as a schizoid projection of Sara's hungry stomach. The freezer compartment becomes transparent to reveal the stockpiled food. When she becomes addicted to slimming pills, the resentful fridge makes explosive, angry sounds.

Sara's hallucinations indicate escalating schizophrenia. Plates overloaded with food materialise in anomalous places like the mantelpiece. Offering three eggs, large lumps of beef and burgers garnished with bright green lettuce, they mockingly adorn her furniture. When she is in bed, cakes, biscuits and donuts fly at her from the air vent, repellent in their ersatz plastic texture and lurid colours.

Deleuze and Guattari note that the temporal distortions of drugs stimulate acute awareness of 'speeds and slownesses'.[125] Like a heroin user in withdrawal, Sara's subjective perception of time lengthens out. Her daily schedule centres on mealtimes while the intervals drag in slow motion. An overlay of clock hands painfully stretches time. Stimulants reverse the effect. Like the party scene in Marion's apartment, time is drastically accelerated. Speeded up footage shows Sara drinking copious amounts of coffee and dancing ludicrously fast to Latin music. Her euphoria matches Marion's burst of optimism as she designs and sews clothes while the dealers make profit at breakneck speeds on the pier. A more pessimistic slant on time occurs when their good supply dries up. For Tyrone, now in come-down time, it 'seems like a thousand years ago since last summer'.

As the force of uncreative energy kicks in, Sara's manic housework routine is superimposed by rapidly spinning clocks. The humour of the 'honeymoon' stage palls and she looks haggard and sweats profusely like her addict son. Ironically, Harry disapproves of his mother's habit evident in her jittery movements and teeth grinding. TV watching is still her favourite pastime but jagged jump cuts and repeated shots produce a manic, irritant quality.

Redeploying the concepts of molecular biology to the temporal impact of the moving image, Deleuze suggests that as 'thought is molecular', so 'molecular speeds make up the slow beings that we are'.[126] To express Sara's molecular makeup driven haywire by pharmaceutical toxins, the slow, stately music of a string quartet splits her hectic temporal perception from clock time. Her disjointed spatial motion is given temporal coordinates as she glides around aimlessly with lipstick-daubed face in her favourite red dress. The melting overlaps remove her from the present to an anomalous, schizoid time-zone. The viewer, likewise composed of speeds and slownesses, feels time through the unique properties of editing.

The intertitle 'Fall' has dual significance as the characters' habits take hold. William Burroughs, whose heroin-themed fiction feeds into Deleuze's consideration of drugs, comments wryly that other interests pale into insignificance for the addict as 'life telescopes down to junk, one fix and looking forward to the next, "stashes" and "scripts", "spikes" and "droppers" '.[127] The film section emphasises the escalating alternation of highs and come-downs. With their dealer Brody dead, the friends endure the costly option of increased dosage, ingesting weaker 'stuff' more often.

In the grey objective correlative of morning light, Marion wakes in sweat and cramps, pleading with Harry to 'dip in' to their diluted stash. A small hole in Harry's arm is revealed as he mainlines. Sara likewise has her first come-down. Slouched comatose before her switched-off TV, her expression is blank. The pills have 'normalised' (as the nurse crisply informs her) so she ups the dose to regain her 'pep'.

As Sara swallows tablets, the battery of nerve-grating sounds includes one frequently heard, the loud popping of a plastic cap wrenched off a bottle. She begins to hallucinate svelte images of herself on the Tappy Tibbens Show. The use of fish-eye lens makes the room bulge out to fore-ground her wrinkled neck and fearful blue-tinged face as she runs around in a blurred circle. Fish-eye vision continues in the surgery as her arms are unnaturally stretched in space, gesturing wildly. In a blue light like that of the TV and Marion's cold-turkey, Sara, 'all mixed up', makes her desper-ate plea for help. Although the doctor's cynical speech is speeded up, time between pills still drags too slowly.

Sara's claustrophobic apartment recalls a horror movie. She jumps at the fridge's unnatural thuds and staggers around bathed in a nauseating green or red light. Her figure in low-angle is back-lit, dark in front so that she walks into extending shadow. A gyrating camera and stroboscopic flicker from the neon light reveal a table littered with empty bottles and scattered pills, gulped down by Sara who wants to feel 'normal' again.

Paranoid delusions peak in a grotesque hallucination. Still covered in TV lines, Tappy and his show hostess invade Sara's room, followed by their crew to film her mortification. The intrusive camera and the flicker-ing glare of lights expose her as the crew dance a mocking conga round her chair. In a sepulchral voice, the fridge jumps out and demands 'feed me Sara!', a mantra adopted by the on-screen audience as well as the presences in her room. Now a ravening monster, the fridge splits open to reveal the gaping jaw and dripping fangs that objectivise her hunger.

The 'Winter' sequence relentlessly completes the characters' decline. Rendered powerless in a down-canted roof-top shot, Sara roams the snow-streaked sidewalks. People blur by her in the too-fast motion of temporal dissociation. Harry and Tyrone drive south, impelled by their dream of a Florida drug heaven, leaving Marion to perform in live sex shows paid in drugs. Amid the lush greenery and azure skies of the South, Harry takes his final shot into the festering sore in the crook of his arm and side-steps reality. Tyrone and Harry are imprisoned as addicts. Ignored by the brutal prison warders, they cry for help in their cell. Their agony is unendurably expressed in a synaesthetic image. When the volume of yells rises, the image on screen shakes and shudders as though part of the sound.

The vortex of suffering bottoms out in a final montage of ironic peace. Curled in foetal position, Tyrone dreams himself back with his mother. After a nightmare about losing Marion over the edge of the pier Harry wakes with his arm amputated. Marion smiles in her sleep as she clasps her heroin wages. Given repeated ECT, Sara lives a permanent 'dream' of Tappy Tibbens Show reruns.

Requiem for a Dream inexorably presents a crack-down of the body impelled by the 'tragic will that presides over all ingestions'.[128] The cracking of the surface is limited here to brief, insubstantial euphoria, pitifully small recompense for physical and psychic damage. The film engages us, via percepts and affects, in the vortex of need impelled by the holes of injection and the buccal cavity. Yet the experiential intensity of the event need not be limited to its harrowing subject matter and downward-spiralling narrative. According to Deleuze, the actualised damage of such entropy can be diverted by art as the virtual crack of delirium seeks more viable, virtual paths.

Counter-actualisation: Two Kinds of Death

Deleuze interrogates our problematic engagement in images of delirium as film viewer, fiction reader or 'abstract thinker'. He asks how, if the surface cracks, we might 'prevent deep life from becoming a demolition job'.[129] Even while he probes the issue, he acknowledges that 'all these questions point out the ridiculousness of the thinker'.[130]

Art might appear to offer a 'safe' way for its user to benefit from a crack that remains in a virtual state. Yet how far is it feasible to 'stay at the surface without staying on the shore?'[131] If the 'eternal truth of the event is grasped only if the event is also inscribed in the flesh',[132] how do we avoid 'full actualisation in a corporeal mixture [. . .] in the depth of the body'?[133] We need to find a way by which one process does not inevitably prolong the other.[134] Rather than complete detachment from fictional delirium, we might perhaps engage in it more intensively and 'go a short way further to see for ourselves, be a little alcoholic, a little crazy, a little suicidal [. . .] enough to extend the crack, but not enough to deepen it irredeemably'.[135]

Productive delirium carefully prevents the kind of actualisation which 'characterises the victim or the true patient' by engineering its creative diversion.[136] By becoming 'the mime of what *effectively occurs*', art lets us encounter a virtual double of painful actualisation in a 'counter-actualisation which limits, moves and transfigures it'.[137] Aesthetic 'identification with a distance' can avoid confusing the truth of the event with its inevitable actualisation.[138] The distancing devices of art thus 'give the crack the chance of flying over its own incorporeal surface area, without stopping at the bursting within each body'.[139]

The aesthetics of affect thus offer 'the chance to go further than we could have believed possible'.[140] If the pure event is 'imprisoned forever in its actualisation', art 'liberates it, always for other times'.[141] Deleuze hopes that the 'revelations' of drugs and alcohol might thus be encountered at the surface,

> independently of the use of those substances, provided that the techniques of social alienation which determine this use are reversed into revolutionary means of exploration.[142]

In this way, the potency of intoxication is actualised productively without self-destruction.

For Michael Goddard, Deleuze advocates a non-judgemental form of 'rigorous and unrelenting sobriety'.[143] He provocatively reworks the term's meaning from the opposition to delirium to a rigorous engagement with 'these chaotic and vital forces [. . .] to give them a consistency rather than a stable form'.[144] The aesthetics of sobriety, Goddard suggests, continues and extends the 'event of intoxication' through art.[145] Through affective style, we can follow 'movements already begun in the artwork into new milieus' and thus, he argues, art can engineer fresh 'modes of existence' to become transformed in their turn.[146]

The crack remains a means of fragmentation and destruction. How and what it destroys is crucial. For Deleuze, if it is 'no more internal than external' then 'its projection to the outside marks no less the end's approach than does the purest introjection'.[147] Despite his distinction of surface and bodily crack, they are 'two aspects of death'.[148] One of these is the actual death of the body. The other is the affective 'death of the subject' that leads to replenished life. In order to attain 'true individuality and acquire a proper name' a subjective death must be undergone via the 'harshest exercise in depersonalisation', opening up to multiplicity and its intensities, because 'experimentation on ourself is our only identity'.[149]

Although psychoactive drugs and alcohol may inspire their users' creativity, addiction can lead to the first kind of untimely death. In this, life-energy is imploded and used up, leaving a human husk. For Harry, Sara, Tyrone and Marion, literal death is deferred by their own kinds of living death: imprisonment, dismemberment and a mind wiped by ECT. Instead of such damage, Deleuze extends the crack into 'a creative breakthrough, rather than a psychotic breakdown'.[150] The mental crack made by experimental art is salutary, he argues, demolishing outworn structures of repression that block radical thought and praxis.

Mainstream narratives often gravitate against the energies released by their own experimental forays. Classical realist conventions bracket off and reterritorialise 'trip' sequences or present a grim anti-drugs warning. Nevertheless, I contend that it is possible to retain the force of this special cinematic material and elude reification *despite* limiting narrative conventions. So what kinds of drugs-related film might induce less morbid kinds of perceptual multiplicity in both style and content? In partial answer to my question, I offer two speculative examples, returning to the form that Deleuze pays surprisingly scant attention to: short experimental film.

Inauguration of the Pleasure Dome: Narcotic Multiplicity

Kenneth Anger's early psychedelic film *Inauguration of the Pleasure Dome* (first version 1954) is overtly 'about' delirium. Intoxicant multiplicity is deliberately used to engineer psychic receptivity. The entire film is one densely layered hallucination. I focus on a climactic sequence near the end, 'Lord Shiva's Dream', when overloaded superimpositions tax cognitive grasp and descriptive language.[151]

The source of Deleuze and Guattari's use of 'multiplicity' is German mathematician Bernhard Riemann, who 'uprooted the multiple from its predicate state and made it a noun'.[152] Multiplicities, metric in nature, can also be non–metrically 'anexact yet rigorous'.[153] Unlike magnitudes, multiplicities

> *cannot divide without changing in nature each time.* An intensity, for example, is not composed of addable and displaceable magnitudes: a temperature is not the sum of two smaller temperatures. A speed is not the sum of two smaller speeds.[154]

Bergson uses multiplicity to conceptualise duration. As well as registering sensations bodily, we are conscious of their affects within our 'personality' either by reflex movements or a sense of spatial motion being suspended. He locates our perception of intensity at the junction between 'the idea of extensive magnitude from without' and 'the image of an inner multiplicity' arising from the depths of consciousness.[155] Multiplicity exists in interwoven layers. Intensive states of feeling are fleeting and difficult to pin down, as their becoming is the fluidity of life itself.

Deleuze opposes the stasis of being with the openness of becoming. Multiplicity is 'different in nature from elementary components and collections of them'.[156] It corresponds to the conjunction 'and' which (as in Jean-Luc Godard's cinema) 'upsets being' by bringing in all relations,[157] 'And's line of flight may be hardly perceptible, but along it, 'things come to pass, becomings evolve, revolutions take shape'.[158]

Here, the film's conjunctions are catalysed by a white potion, imbibed by party guests dressed as gods at an occult gathering.[159] Anger, himself an early experimenter with mescal and LSD, calls his cocktail a 'sacred mushroom, *yage*, wormwood brew' provided by the witch goddess Hecate (himself).[160] Citing the long history of film narcotics, the cupbearer is Cesare, the black-clad, drugged somnambulist from *The Cabinet of Dr Caligari* (Robert Wiene, 1926). Cesare pours the potion into goblets like wide-open flower chalices, while Lord Shiva (Samson de Brier) slips a supplementary drug into Pan's glass.

Total intoxication is instant and a visual orgy ensues with the rapid surge of superimposed deities and richly saturated colours. Astarte (Anaïs Nin) swings a shimmering net across the screen to capture the actants in a mesh of shifting light. The loud, hollow drum-beats of Leos Janacek's *Glagolitic Mass* aurally impound delirium.[161]

The shots are composed, or rather, decomposed, by multi-layering. Masks are serially removed to reveal others and faces are overlaid by superimposition.[162] Conventional subjectivity is absent from this disordered pantheon of multiple personae. Even drinking goblets float freely in space, animated by the drug's magical force. The absence of subject/object distinctions opens the spectator more directly to psychic manipulation.

Images are not just overlaid temporally by earlier shots, but occult symbols are also superimposed. A red and purple eye in a triangle overlays a long-shot of intoxicated gods, fixing them in the filmmaker's magickal framework. There are no edges or boundaries to shots edited together in multiplicity rather than linear sequence. The climax of the film was designed for projection on a triple screen that emerged like a pair of wings that 'took off' to transcendence. Without such triptych screening conditions, the superimpositions induce even more overload.

Time is caught in a ritornello as actants repeat earlier movements. Shiva's circular gestures, Astarte's swaying net and Kali (Marjorie Cameron)'s lotus pose appear at different stages in the same frame as well as interlinked frames. Further simultaneity is produced by the concealment of split-screen by ambient darkness that throws figures into relief and moves them out of synch. Sensory bombardment further complicates temporality as intercutting and music speed up. The gods move so rapidly that their images blur in smoke. Linear clock time is suspended in the layering of Anger's occult duration, where the conventional laws of space and time are unhinged.

Shiva's visions climax in a rapid-fire array of intercutting and flash-frame sigils. A many petalled lotus and other psychically charged symbols flash on screen to bypass the cerebral cortex. Frantic drumming crescendos and Janacek's *Mass* climaxes simultaneously with a full-blown orchestral *intrada* before Shiva's image reduces to a single layer, as though the whole film were his sole hallucination.

In Inauguration of the Pleasure Dome, 'images become too full and sounds too strident'.[163] The intoxicating overlay offers a pre-subjective state. Yet the film does not offer us the open-ended possibilities of DeleuzeGuattarian multiplicity. There are two kinds of multiplicitous desire: one is unified in a structure of containment, and the other fundamentally lacks unity. Unity only develops for Deleuze and Guattari when there is a 'power takeover in the multiplicity'.[164] Anger's intoxicating cinematic world is not free of ideological structures or psychic strictures but, rather, 'sells' us an alternative set: a counter-cultural occult system. This underlying power takeover might gravitate against the film's radical aesthetic force.

Rather than encouraging free molecular becoming, Anger's ultimate intent is a molar indoctrination. Ideally, he wanted to dispense with technology and 'project images directly into people's heads'.[165] The film's decadent chaos points the way to a highly structured and disciplined, albeit alternative, system. Thus mapped out by the dictates of the filmmaker's beliefs, it is overtly and covertly manipulative. Although the film depicts the 'wine and strange drugs' of Aleister Crowley's dictum, intoxicants are not ends in themselves but a method of inducing altered states for magickal purposes.[166] If the force of delirium is thus limited, the crack is prevented from spreading freely across the surface. It is, rather, directed by the magickian's controlling agenda.[167]

Nevertheless, the film's encounter need not be bound by Anger's occult paradigm. Even here, he claims not to damage the body in its depths but to raise delirious flesh to metaphysical heights. However manipulative the film's intentions might be, its complexly affective style nevertheless induces a qualitative crack of the surface. Spectators unaware or sceptical of Anger's beliefs might still, of course, experience the film 'straight'.[168] A viewing without prejudice offers a free-floating surface of ecstatic affects and percepts. The pyrotechnics compel the eyes to shift rapidly around the frame, refusing attempts to focus attention and fix meaning.

Anger intoxicates by light. The Scarlet Woman (Marjorie Cameron)'s chalk-white face gives off light as well as reflecting it. Her close-up face spreads to fill the frame with autonomous force as its turquoise and gold tones bleach out. As well as Leary's 'white light', Anger's psychedelic peer, Aldous Huxley, describes the 'mind's antipodes' as 'brilliantly lit, and seems to shine from within'.[169] My final example of narcotic light turns to a more recently popular drug and a mainstream film, Justin Kerrigan's *Human Traffic* (1999). I want to explore that extended plateau on the dance floor in the Cardiff Asylum club when Ecstasy and dancing peak together as the realist conventions of British sit-com film are transformed.

Dancing in the Light: Ecstasy in *Human Traffic*

Kerrigan's cinematography sets out to convey the visual equivalent of 'E'.[170] Ecstasy (MDMA), an empathogen, diffuses subjectivity and increases sensory receptivity.[171] Ecstasy stimulates 'serenity and calm, emotional closeness' and a sense of rapport with others.[172] Although autonomous hallucinations are rare, the drug's slowing down of time perception is common.[173]

In this state, ego boundaries and haptic body maps become more fluid in a semblance of Deleuzian BWOs. Dance music is perceived as flowing through the permeable body in assemblage with it. Ecstasy induces an autoerotic quality not limited to sexual sensation. Rather than localised organs, 'Lov'dup' (high) bodies develop 'a thousand sexes'. In infinitely extendible orgasm, the body experiences a supplementary *jouissance* not limited to Lacan's genital strictures.[174]

Kerrigan's 'E' fuelled alterity is expressed through slow motion, low image resolution and a mix of monochrome with colour footage. Purple and pink glow with the warm quality of flesh. Alterity is predominantly manifested in the bright yet hazy, soft-focus light, which Sadie Plant describes as Ecstasy's 'pixillated haze'.[175]

Cinematic light is always in motion. The film medium works in light always, already moving, while shooting and projection add technological motion. Our eyes are drawn to light, which impels the reflex adjustments of our irises. Extreme lighting dazzles or dulls vision and refocuses awareness of other senses, shifting from extensive, action-based movement to intensive vibrations. Some affective light modulations are characterised by Deleuze as 'intensive movement par excellence'.[176]

The 'luminous principle' is a fulcrum of Deleuze's metaphysics. Light impels matter-images themselves. It reflects and refracts off objects, enabling us to see them, but affective impact exceeds use-value or expressive function. Light physically permeates us in its passage through our (semi-transparent) bodies. It enters our brain cells by the transmutation of light waves into electrical charges by optic nerves. In a biological sense, then, we see nothing *but* light. Of seminal philosophical significance, we also *think* in images of light.

Deleuze's film-philosophy explores cinematic light *as* movement-image, asserting them as 'two facets of the same appearing'.[177] When light insists on its own materiality, it accesses a quality of the affection-image with profound implications. In Dreyer or Bresson, for example, 'pure, immanent or spiritual light' has 'a physics (or a metaphysics)'.[178] This lucent quality suffuses the screen with a spiritual force in which fixed objects and significations lose their limits.

Although Deleuze's examples of metaphysical light belong to an art-house canon, they can also be discovered in mainstream, popular movies. I am arguing that the dance floor plateau in Kerrigan's film has comparable properties. The dancers' flow of *élan vital* is visualised in light. Strobe flicker is synchronised with the heartbeat rhythms of the music's bass line. Camera, *mise-en-scène* and editing rhythms work together to convey the drug's perceptual distortions as a contact high.

Light flickering onto the dancers gives them an intermittently luminous quality. The euphoric faces of Jip, Moff, Nina, Koop and Lulu 'bleach out into the white background'.[179] This intensifies in a diffused brightness that blends figures with their ground in a condition of becoming-light. Faces are abstracted by close-up, yet encapsulate the broader multiplicity in ecstatic miniature. Abstraction does not distance engagement here and we share the trans-personal empathy encouraged by the drug.

For Deleuze, the defamiliarised face of close-up conveys power qualities directly. The faces of the dancers are 'blissed-out' as they drop their egoic guards. Controlled expressions become spontaneously fluid and open to fleeting affects. Glittering eyes and widened pupils serve to increase the perceiver's rapport. Pink lighting stimulates synaesthetic sensations of warmth. Koop (Shaun Parkes)'s skin, seen in close-up, glistens with sweat from the heat of the dance-floor. The term 'off your face' is literalised as personal boundaries lower to 'embrace an overwhelming feeling of love'.[180]

As consciousness expands, body outlines lose definition to fuse with an already amorphous surrounding space. The properties of blur make the edges of the frame less insistent, removed or extended. Fades into black are used between sections to create a rhythmical pulse like the ebb and flow of respiration. The up and down, rising and falling of the dance performs similar moves on the vertical axis.

Light floods the dance floor with soft, misty brightness compounded by smoke machine and strobes. These mechanical effects transform into machinic affects in our experiential encounter with the screen. Luxuriously sensual as well as light and floating, dance movements and the camera's own motion become increasingly fluid as though performed under water. The blur of slow motion and overlap, as heads develop 'stepped movements', causes a melting sensation.[181]

Music and ambient sounds fade out to faint chords in the background. Jip (John Simon)'s stream of consciousness voice-over is only intermittently subjective. In his own E-fuelled account, he has become 'wide-open', 'fluctuating' and 'in rhythm' as everyone 'flows in unison'. Despite the comic inadequacy of language to anchor affective quality, his terms here can still suggest Deleuzian concepts.[182] By replacing clock time by temporal suspension and action-driven movement by intensive motion on the spot, Kerrigan effectively produces a cinematic taste of drug-induced alterity.

Yet body maps, deterritorialised by affective multiplicity, can easily reterritorialise the morning after. Although Ecstasy-like techniques offer insight into Deleuze's aesthetics, 'recreational' or weekend-only drug use is far from his agenda of delirium. The artists Deleuze engages with include Burroughs, Fitzgerald, André Micheaux and Malcolm Lowry. For them, intoxication, as well as intensifying awareness and relieving existential angst, led to radical defamiliarisation and subjective fragmentation. By auto-experiment, they sought to augment creativity, partaking in a kind of secular sacrament according to their 'own manner of being pious'.[183] Although Deleuze's critique is marked by traces of this modernist aesthetic, his contribution opens up a distinct conceptual model.

Conclusions: Pharmacoanalysis and the Great Health

For Deleuze and Guattari, pharmacoanalysis refers not to particular drugs, or even to drugs per se, because 'many things can be drugs'.[184] They use the term, rather, to articulate a molecular perception permeated with desire. In the mescaline-driven automatic art of Micheaux, Deleuze and Guattari discover 'a whole rhizomatic perception, the moment when desire and perception meld' that enables the imperceptible to be perceived.[185] Drugs in art are one way to give the unconscious the affective 'immanence and the plane that psychoanalysis has continually botched' by Oedipal fixations.[186]

As we have seen, the delirious 'microperceptions' of cinema shift spatio-temporal coordinates in a 'floating time that is no longer our time' and modify speed and slowness.[187] Colours and sounds may be artificially intensified, while faces and landscapes are shredded. Read in this way, such techniques enable us to perceive beyond themselves to possible 'lines of flight'. By thinking through their specificity, we discover how each one is also a thinking otherwise via 'haecceities that are no longer of this world'.[188]

Despite Deleuze and Guattari's welcoming of such radical deterritorialisations in art, they emphasise that drug-induced insights are 'all the more artificial for being based on chemical substances, hallucinatory forms, and phantasy subjectification'.[189] Apparent deterritorialisation can rebound into abject reterritorialisation as 'the imperceptible and perception continually pursue or run after each other without ever truly coupling'.[190] Each benefit identified is outweighed by its harmful double, so that 'the plane itself engenders dangers of its own, by which it is dismantled at the same time that it is constructed'.[191] They depict such dangers, when 'lines of flight coil and start to swirl in black holes', in harrowing terms.[192] Indeed, they assert that the molecular microperceptions of drugs are

> overlaid in advance, depending on the drug, by hallucinations, delusions, false perceptions, phantasies, or paranoid outbursts; they restore forms and subjects every instant, like so many phantoms or doubles blocking construction of the plane.[193]

Deleuze and Guattari advocate a virtual, not the actual, 'dismantling of the organism'.[194] It is imperative to avoid 'organic disintegration', and to keep back 'enough of the organism for it to reform each dawn'.[195] Entrance into a pre-subjective state should not block ability to act from a subjective position when necessary, and it is vital to maintain 'small supplies of significance and subjectification if only to turn them against their own systems'.[196]

So how might harmful effects be turned into health-giving affects that energise thought and stimulate creative becomings? Deleuze acknowledges Burroughs as his 'strange' mentor here. When Burroughs counsels his readers to ' "imagine that everything that can be attained by chemical means is accessible by other paths" ', he suggests a 'quest for the great Health'.[197] Developing this figure, Deleuze contends that many artists have 'irresistible and delicate health', which stems from their hypersensitivity to 'suffocating things whose passage exhausts' necessary to their work.[198]

Yet handling such dangers can achieve the greater Health of society. In analysing their own 'pathology', writers become 'attuned' to 'the world as a set of symptoms or signs' while accessing and describing 'becomings that a dominant and substantial health would render impossible'.[199] It is the ethical 'duty' of artists and philosophers to perform a 'symptomatology', or 'discernment of the sensations that traverse the body' and express 'not merely an individual but a social pathology'.[200]

Art is, then, for Deleuze, both 'an enterprise of health' and a beneficial kind of consciousness-altering drug.[201] Its expressive delirium operates a virtual catalyst for future actualisations. The drug of art does not require users to 'come down' depleted. Not an end in itself, it is a springboard to further lines of flight. If drugs have 'sufficiently changed the general conditions of space and time perception', former users and non-users can also

> succeed in passing through the holes in the world and following the lines of flight at the very place where means other than drugs become necessary. Drugs do not guarantee immanence; rather, the immanence of drugs allows one to forgo them.[202]

Deleuze and Guattari consider drugs to be 'too unwieldy' a tool to grasp the imperceptible and its becomings. Users mistakenly believe that drugs grant them the plane, whereas it 'must distil its own drugs, remaining master of speeds and proximities'.[203] They inquire, 'what good does it do to perceive as fast as a quick-flying bird if speed and movement continue to escape somewhere else?' In actuality, drugs can irrecoverably reduce health and strength. Yet in the virtual form of cinematic expression, subjective annihilation can potentially radicalise even if the narrative gravitates against this.

This chapter has tested pharmacoanalysis on cinematic techniques.[204] I have been inquiring how far drugs-based films head towards breakdown or mobilise breakthrough via the Deleuzian assertion that energies released by fragmentation and disintegration can be used to produce more energy. Films that 'open thresholds and doors where becoming itself becomes' offer a specialised plane for the operations of alterity.[205]

This exploration of drugs in art is motivated neither by voyeurism nor nostalgia. Instead of the image of the self-destructive artist as decadent aesthete, Deleuze deploys the figure of a guerrilla, a member of an irregular armed force that fights a stronger force by sabotage and harassment.[206] He seeks not to encourage ivory-tower aestheticism but activism, and leaves us to decide how this will be attained.[207] My next chapter explores how cinematic corporeality uses the affectively expanded sensorium to make new body maps that challenge corporeal structures and erotic strictures.

Notes

1. Deleuze and Guattari, *A Thousand Plateaus*, p. 248.
2. Deleuze, 'Porcelain and Volcano', p. 161.
3. *A Thousand Plateaus*, p. 283.
4. Chayefsky, *Altered States* (hereafter referred to as *Altered States* novel); Lilly, *The Centre of the Cyclone*.
5. Freud [1990] 'From the History of an Infantile Neurosis', pp. 227–366.

6. Deleuze and Guattari, *Anti-Oedipus*, p. 13.
7. Ibid., p. 14.
8. Ibid.
9. Ibid.
10. Chayefsky, *Altered States* novel, p. 25.
11. Ibid., p. 56.
12. Ibid., p. 59.
13. Castaneda, *The Teachings of Don Juan, A Separate Reality and Tales of Power*.
14. Deleuze and Guattari, *A Thousand Plateaus*, p. 162.
15. Castaneda, *Tales of Power*, p. 236.
16. Ibid., p. 197.
17. Ibid., p. 218.
18. Ibid., p. 225.
19. Artaud, *Les Tarahumaras*.
20. Deleuze and Guattari, *A Thousand Plateaus*, p. 160. The quotation is from *The Peyote Dance*, pp. 38–9. Weaver's translation modified by Massumi.
21. Weiss, 'Pressures of the Sun', p. 3.
22. Ibid.
23. Artaud, *The Peyote Dance*, p. 20.
24. Ibid.
25. Deleuze and Guattari, *A Thousand Plateaus*, p. 138.
26. Ibid.
27. Castaneda, *Tales of Power*, p. 120.
28. Ibid., pp. 138–9.
29. Deleuze and Guattari, *A Thousand Plateaus*, p. 162.
30. Ibid.
31. Artaud, *The Peyote Dance*, p. 24.
32. Ibid., p. 36.
33. Ibid.
34. *A Thousand Plateaus*, p. 162.
35. Castaneda, *Tales of Power*, p. 170.
36. Artaud, *The Peyote Dance*, p. 39.
37. Ibid., p. 31.
38. Ibid.
39. Ibid., p. 31.
40. Ibid., p. 36.
41. Ibid., p. 37.
42. Deleuze and Guattari, *Anti-Oedipus*, p. 48.
43. Deleuze and Guattari, *A Thousand Plateaus*, p. 237.
44. Ibid., pp. 17–18.
45. Klüver, *Mescal and the Mechanisms of Hallucinations*.
46. Russell may have borrowed this (already recycled) footage from Kenneth Anger's *Inauguration of the Pleasure Dome* (1954).
47. Artaud, *The Peyote Dance*, p. 100.

48. Lilly, *The Centre of the Cyclone*, p. 26.
49. Ibid.
50. Ibid.
51. Bergson, *Creative Evolution*, p. 11.
52. Ibid., p. 23.
53. Ibid.
54. Ibid., p. 60.
55. Ibid., p. 23.
56. Ibid., p. 42.
57. Ibid., p. 43.
58. Ibid.
59. Leary, *The Politics of Ecstasy*, p. 83.
60. Ibid., p. 23.
61. Ibid., p. 116.
62. Ibid., p. 115.
63. Ibid.
64. Ibid.
65. Ibid., p. 290.
66. Chayefsky, *Altered States* screenplay, p. 318.
67. Deleuze and Guattari, *A Thousand Plateaus*, p. 249.
68. Chayevsky, *Altered States* screenplay, pp. 182–3.
69. Deleuze and Guattari, *A Thousand Plateaus*, p. 227/8.
70. Ibid., p. 228.
71. Ibid.
72. Ibid.
73. Chayevsky, *Altered States* novel, p. 318.
74. Deleuze and Guattari, *A Thousand Plateaus*, p. 248.
75. Ibid., p. 284.
76. Fitzgerald, *The Crack-Up*, p. 69.
77. Deleuze and Guattari, *A Thousand Plateaus*, p. 267.
78. Deleuze, 'Porcelain and Volcano', p. 155.
79. Ibid., p. 155.
80. Plant, *Writing on Drugs*, p. 198.
81. Such as Jay Roach, *Austin Powers: International Man of Mystery*, 1997.
82. Klüver, *Mescal*, p. 22.
83. Ibid., p. 67.
84. Ibid.
85. Leary, *The Politics of Ecstasy*, p. 22.
86. Ibid.
87. Ibid.
88. Possible out-takes from Corman's Poe Cycle.
89. Deleuze, *Cinema 1*, p. 12.
90. Ibid.
91. Ibid., p. 18.

92. Ibid., p. 66.
93. Ibid., p. 103.
94. Ibid., p. 103.
95. Ibid., p. 104.
96. Leary, *The Politics of Ecstasy*, p. 290.
97. The preface is a moral warning on the dangers of LSD obviously tacked on to appease censors.
98. James, *Allegories of Cinema*, p. 14.
99. Deleuze, 'Porcelain and Volcano', p. 160.
100. Deleuze, *Cinema 1*, p. 20.
101. Ibid., p. 20.
102. Ibid., p. 262.
103. Deleuze, *Cinema 2*, p. 23.
104. Deleuze, *Desert Islands and Other Texts*, p. 240.
105. Deleuze and Guattari, *What is Philosophy?*, p. 165.
106. Deleuze and Guattari, *A Thousand Plateaus*, p. 282.
107. Deleuze, 'Porcelain and Volcano', p. 156.
108. Ibid., p. 156.
109. Ibid., p. 155.
110. Ibid.
111. Deleuze and Guattari, *A Thousand Plateaus*, p. 285.
112. The 'arm' was a remarkably convincing model.
113. Selby, *Requiem for a Dream*.
114. Aronofsky interview, 'Before tackling Batman'.
115. Ibid.
116. Bradshaw, 'Living in Oblivion'.
117. Ibid.
118. Ibid.
119. Ibid., p. 62.
120. Ibid., p. 18.
121. Bergson, *Time and Free Will*, pp. 72–3.
122. Ibid., p. 40.
123. Ibid.
124. Chocolate contains phenylethylamine, the 'love-chemical', and releases endorphins, the body's endogenous opiates. See http://www.chocolate.org/.
125. Deleuze and Guattari, *A Thousand Plateaus*, p. 283.
126. Deleuze, 'The Brain is the Screen', p. 366.
127. Burroughs, *Junky*, p. 23.
128. Deleuze, 'The Brain is the Screen', p. 157.
129. Deleuze, 'Porcelain and Volcano'.
130. Ibid.
131. Ibid., p. 158.
132. Ibid., p. 161.

133. Ibid., p. 157.
134. Ibid., p. 156.
135. Ibid., p. 158.
136. Ibid., p. 157.
137. Ibid., p. 161.
138. Ibid.
139. Ibid.
140. Ibid.
141. Ibid.
142. Ibid.
143. Goddard, 'The Surface, the Fold and the Subversion of Form, p. 5.
144. Ibid.
145. Ibid.
146. Ibid., p. 11.
147. Ibid., p. 155.
148. Ibid., p. 156.
149. Deleuze, *Negotiations*, p. 6.
150. Goddard, The Surface the Fold and the Subversion of Form', p. 8.
151. Kenneth Anger's notes in Hunter, *Moonchild*, p. 110.
152. Deleuze and Guattari, *A Thousand Plateaus*, pp. 482–3.
153. http://www-groups.dcs.st-and.ac.uk/~history/Mathematicians/ Riemann.html (accessed 6 February 2006).
154. Deleuze and Guattari, *A Thousand Plateaus*, p. 483.
155. Bergson, *Time and Free Will*, p. 73.
156. Ibid., p. 45.
157. Deleuze, *Negotiations*, p. 44.
158. Ibid.
159. The white liquid corresponds to ejaculate in sex magick.
160. Hunter, *Moonchild*, p. 110.
161. Leos Janacek, *Glagolitic Mass*, conducted by Simon Rattle, EMI digital CD, 1982, sleeve notes by Robin Golding.
162. Anger deploys number for magical ends.
163. Deleuze, *Negotiations*, p. 45.
164. Deleuze and Guattari, *A Thousand Plateaus*, p. 7.
165. Sitney, *Visionary Film*, p. 123.
166. Crowley, *The Book of the Law*, p. 10.
167. Youngblood, *Expanded Cinema*, p. 87.
168. Audiences in late 1960s Haight-Ashbury were invited to take an 'acid break'.
169. Huxley, *The Doors of Perception, Heaven and Hell*, p. 65.
170. Kerrigan, *Human Traffic*, p. 107.
171. Chemist and drugs researcher Alexander Shulgin rediscovered MDMA in the 1960s. See his account in *PIHKAL*.
172. Ibid.

173. http://www.release.org.uk/html/~drug_menu/ecstasy.php (accessed 6 January 2006).
174. Lacan, 'Encore: le Seminaire XX.
175. Plant, Writing on Drugs, p. 114.
176. Deleuze, Cinema 1, p. 49.
177. Ibid.
178. Ibid., p. 117.
179. Kerrigan, Human Traffic, p. 108.
180. Ibid.
181. Ibid.
182. Ibid.
183. Deleuze, 'Porcelain and Volcano', p. 161
184. Deleuze and Guattari, A Thousand Plateaus, p. 227
185. Ibid., p. 283.
186. Ibid., p. 284.
187. Ibid., p. 283.
188. Ibid.
189. Ibid.
190. Ibid., pp. 284–5.
191. Ibid., p. 285.
192. Ibid.
193. Ibid.
194. Goddard, 'The Surface, the Fold and the Subversion of Form', p. 22.
195. Deleuze and Guattari, A Thousand Plateaus, p. 61.
196. Ibid.
197. Deleuze and Guattari, 'Porcelain and Volcano', p. 161.
198. Deleuze and Guattari, 'Literature and Life', p. 3.
199. Ibid.
200. Goddard, 'The Surface, the Fold and the Subversion of Form', p. 11.
201. Deleuze, 'Literature and Life', p. 3.
202. Deleuze and Guattari, A Thousand Plateaus, p. 286.
203. Ibid.
204. Deleuze and Guattari, A Thousand Plateaus, p. 284.
205. Ibid., p. 249.
206. http://www.wordnet.Princeton.edu/perl/webwn (accessed 13 February 2006).
207. Deleuze, 'Porcelain and Volcano', p. 158.

CHAPTER 3

Altered Body Maps and the Cinematic Sensorium

a pure perception, as it is in things or in matter, to the point to which molecular inter-actions extend.[1] (Deleuze)

a world alive with incomprehensible objects and shimmering with an endless variety of movement and innumerable gradations of colour.[2] (Stan Brakhage)

Sensational Cinema

Glittering fabric from a 1920s ball gown fills the screen, replaced by others in close-up as the camera riffles through an entire wardrobe. Though framing remains static, the dresses dance across the screen by themselves, shimmying from side to side without human agency, not to a Charleston but the rocking rhythm of a bass guitar riff. Gliding closer in to one gown, texture sharpens focus, an invitation to touch, before sequins blur into glinting stars of light on a black ground.

The close-up face of an unnamed Star (Yvonne Marquis) appears, with a blissed-out expression. Heavily made up flapper-style, she flutters her false eyelashes and swings her earrings. She selects the black dress and raises it up to the camera. Her wide eyes look up, down and off screen, her voluptuous smile heightened by lip-gloss. Laughing, she lowers the dress over her naked flesh, as, by a series of melting cuts, it becomes semi-transparent. A deliciously tactile close-up contrasts her bare feet to the fabric's texture and to the blue high-heeled pumps she slips on from their blue cushion before sashaying off.

In her boudoir, rich velvet drapes are made even plusher by soft focus. They enshrine an art deco dressing table laden with cosmetics. The Star's fingers linger over each one in close-up, before selecting a cut-glass black bottle of perfume. As she sprays herself with scent, a pale reflection in a cheval glass softens and blurs her image further as she melts into pure sensation. Uncorking the outsize bottle, she inhales deeply, throwing her head back in ecstasy as she dabs scent on her neck.

The Star reclines in a chaise longue and breathes heavily. Throwing her head back and turning up her eyes, she enters reverie. The camera glides past her into darkness as though slipping out of consciousness itself. The screen darkens on her close-up face. As her shuddering body shakes the couch, one hand is visible on the pillow. Her moist, open lips and disarrayed dress express her autoerotic arousal. A series of facial close-ups and fade-outs work to arouse her further as the rhythm guitar crescendos.

The rocking motion of the Star's erotic pleasure extends the swinging dresses in the wardrobe and her swaying sashay. The whole of this six-minute film is driven by a shimmying vibration that continues until, with her five saluki dogs elegantly fanned, she walks out into the pale light of morning on the Hollywood Hills. Her image fades into camera like an art deco statuette.

The clip from *Puce Moment* (Kenneth Anger, first released 1949) sets in motion this chapter's aim, to remap the body via a DeleuzeGuattarian and Deleuzian approach to the cinematic sensorium. For them, the BWO is not 'fundamentally organs without bodies, or the fragmented body'.[3] Animated by intensive movements, the BWO, predominantly inorganic and affective, is not limited by physical properties. It is, rather, a body of affective force, an 'intensive, anarchist body that consists solely of poles, zones, thresholds and gradients'.[4] It is this body that Deleuze intends when he asserts that 'it is through the body (and no longer through the intermediary of the body) that cinema forms an alliance with spirit, with thought.[5]

I have used the affective impact of Anger's short experimental film (a highly condensed collage of rushes from a longer, unrealised project) to open up the body's potential as a BWO. The range of its sensory palette includes sound, vision, smell and touch, excluding only the sense of taste. Its focus on sensual pleasure also serves to key in my chapter's second aim, to explore altered states of eroticism.

Pleasure for Deleuze and Guattari is materially immanent and desire exceeds fixed sexual limits. Rather than being the product of lack, it is itself productive as 'the nuptial celebration of a new alliance, a new birth, a radiant ecstasy, as though the eroticism of the machine liberated other unlimited forces'.[6] Here, from a molar perspective, a gay male filmmaker ostensibly becomes-woman via the camp subterfuge of period nostalgia, imaging the world via the desiring sensorium of a 1920s movie star alone in her Hollywood mansion. For me, the film is deliciously erotic, a heady cocktail of sensory stimuli. Its force frees up my positioning as a viewer gendered female by setting in motion a flow of becoming-molecular that problematises any such molar labelling (heterosexual, homosexual) that seeks to limit the desiring body.

Deleuze and Guattari's concept of 'becoming-woman' belongs to a wider range of molecular becomings and affective possibilities. Although I use this term to open my discussion of eroticism and the gendered body, I will not detail familiar debates generated by the supposed essentialism of this term.[7] Deleuze and Guattari insist that their usage of 'woman' is free from the traditional, molar associations fixed by biological or subjective identity. Becoming-woman is not achievable via men's imitation of molar women but is, rather, a process of 'emitting particles that enter the relation of movement and rest, or the zone of proximity, of a micro-femininity'.[8] The molecular woman forms a new BWO of fluid forces.

The suggestion remains, though, that actual women might be potentially closer to 'becoming-woman' than men. Despite their radical rejection of molar gendering, Deleuze and Guattari acknowledge the value of imitating women by particular male homosexuals as well as transformations of male transvestites.[9] They argue that these imitative assemblages enter a more molecular condition. For Deleuze and Guattari, '*sexuality proceeds by way of the becoming-woman of the man*' not by mimicry, but by the emission of particles between shifting male and female gender positions.[10] Rather than gender binaries, Anger's camp cinematic sensibility uses opulent colour stock, soft focus, camera glide and intimate close-ups to trace a cinematic sensorium in process, an erotic BWO assemblage with multiple entrances.[11]

Deleuze and Guattari, then, use becoming-woman and becoming-girl (its even more fluid and vibrant extension), not as essentialist labels, but as an inspirational model for all becomings.[12] Although they do so differently, both men and women can become woman and also become girl as non-genitalised and minoritarian processes. The molecular flux of sexuality motivates an endless diversity of potential 'conjugations'. They offer 'n' or 'a thousand sexes, which are so many uncontrollable becomings'.[13] Thus diversified, sexuality can release a libidinal force with the potential to fragment, not reinforce, essentialist gendering.

The altered states of film are ideally suited to unravel molar body maps. Cinematography is itself a transformational body of techniques to rethink incorporation. As well as drawing more extensively on the joint work of Deleuze and Guattari to elucidate the erotic body of film, this chapter deploys Deleuze's speculations on cinematic signs as manifest in *mise-en-scène*, camera movements and editing. I will now move in closer to cinema's altered sensorium.

Images of Sensation

Deleuzian opsigns, sonsigns and tactisigns are unextended images that do not depend on any role they might be given as narrative components. The spectator's perceptions, struggling to process their undiluted affects, slide into a molecular assemblage with the body of the film. Such mimesis is an encounter that is not a simple copying of on-screen behaviours. Both the spectator and the screen are part of the wider material flux. Moving images on screen hook into the BWO to generate affects as the film literally gets 'under our skin'. Impacting on the brain as well as the senses, the cinematic event continues to reverberate as memories and thoughts.

Film viewing involves much more than the eye as a mere machine for optical processing. It is a mental encounter made through the viscera. On-screen images are, in one sense, non-material simulacra, yet the viewer encounters them corporeally as well as conceptually. They stimulate neuronal networks and produce biologically quantifiable effects such as increased pace of heartbeat and breathing, genital arousal and goosebumps on the surface of the skin. But affects and percepts are not limited to our organic bodies. Slumped in our cinema seat or at home in front of the television for DVD and video replay, our sensory-motor extensions are suspended as we become potential BWOs.

Filmmakers maximise their medium's sensational impact by key tools of sight and sound that simulate the haptic response of other senses. By watching characters touch objects and each other on screen, we 'touch' them ourselves, with consequent affective responses. This is not just a fantasy projection. Engaged in the film, spectators recall their own memories of tactility and, via this recollection, virtually recreate the corresponding corporeal effect and 'feel' it.

Yet Deleuze and Guattari clarify that art does more than merely replicate a sensory response in its corresponding organ, however convincing this might feel. The BWO is not bounded by the sensation of particular organs. As a dynamic molecular assemblage, the body of film and the BWO of the viewer meld in 'a being of the sensory, a being of sensation, on an anorganic plane of composition that is able to restore the infinite'.[14] So corporeal becoming is part of a larger responsive reverberation engaging anorganic forces of mind and spirit.

So what part does the eye play in this continuum? Work with the cinematic gaze has dominated film studies over the past thirty years since Laura Mulvey's paradigm shift. For some of a Deleuzian inclination, the reaction against this psychoanalytically informed perspective might render interest in optical dynamics suspect. The eye is regarded as a precision instrument for recording and regulating perception of the environment. In the West, shaped by a renaissance perspective and power structures of the 'scopic regime', optical power relations have been used for sadistic enforcement of surveillance and control. Yet they eye is also a 'soft machine', a conduit between inside and out both organic and anorganic. Via Deleuze, I want to revaluate the eye and its affective possibilities for the BWO.

Stan Brakhage and the Art of Vision

film, like America, has not been discovered yet [. . .] it is something becoming.[15]
(Stan Brakhage)

Independent filmmaker Stan Brakhage refused to have his vision corrected by spectacles. Intrigued by the range of visual variations if 'normal' vision is altered, he developed a substantial visual aesthetic. He foregrounds the affective capacities of the eye, largely unexplored in film theories that assume a standardised image perception focused on representational content. Just as the camera lens extends the capacities of the human eye, Brakhage explores the organ's possibilities as a physical extension of the 'mind's eye' and a tool for the conceptualisation of affects and percepts.

I find significant links between Deleuze's film-philosophy and Brakhage's theory and practice. Both were influenced by modernism and expressionism, stream-of-consciousness literature and Francis Bacon's painting. Like Deleuze, Brakhage's poetic prose style expresses meaning via word play, image clusters and alliteration to stir the reader affectively as well as engage them intellectually. More particularly, Deleuze had encountered Brakhage's work before writing *Cinema 1*.

Discussing the American experimental cinema of 'pure perception', Deleuze references Brakhage's 'Cézannian world before man, a dawn of ourselves, by filming all the shades of green seen by a baby in the prairie'.[16] The pristine quality of an infant's vision is one of Brakhage's aims. In order to see phenomena afresh, he urges his readers to recall their earliest affective perceptions. Such recollection could generate a visionary perspective capable of seeing the world, through 'an eye unruled by manmade laws of perspective, an eye unprejudiced by compositional logic'.[17]

The immediacy of direct apprehension bypasses the capacity of words to fix phenomenal meaning. Brakhage argues vehemently that Renaissance perspective works in tandem with logocentric classification. Like Deleuze, he repudiates epistemologies of stasis that seek to possess the object and to freeze the perpetual flow of matter. To counter this, he seeks an affective eye which 'does not respond to the name of everything but which must know each object encountered in life through an adventure of perception'.[18]

Fixed perspectives, in constraining the eye, drain the perceiver's *élan vital* and 'mirrors the movement [. . .] towards death by its increasing inability to see'.[19] To counter such entropy, Brakhage offers visual self-reflexivity via a 'mind's eye awareness of all addressing vibrations' in terminology that recalls Bergson.[20] He seeks the sensory immediacy of a world 'alive with incomprehensible objects and shimmering with an endless variety of movement and innumerable gradations of colour'.[21] These affects and percepts are linked to the formation of concepts in the mind's eye.

As a filmmaker, Brakhage is committed to the practical expression of these precepts, using celluloid's powers of material capture to re-present immanence. A dynamic mode of vision requires special cinematic techniques. Seeking to induce trance himself while shooting and editing his films, Brakhage advocates deliberately induced altered states without drugs, which he regards as too intrusive. He aimed to maximise his sensibilities to become a fitter vehicle for creation, so that his films 'arise out of some total area of being or full life'.[22]

Brahkage developed direct physical engagement with the medium as a bodily extension, both in shooting and post-production. His hands-on method required taking risks with the machinically aware camera to attain particular visual qualities:

> by deliberately spitting on the lens or wrecking its focal intention, one can achieve the early stages of impressionism [. . .] hand-hold the camera and inherit worlds of space – over or under expose film filters [. . .] unbalanced lights, neons with neurotic colour temperatures.[23]

He relished the camera's capacity to extend the physical limits of the eye by devices like infrared, prismatic and telephoto lenses, anamorphosis and micro close-ups.

To perceive material produced in this way, a more flexible and receptive vision is required. Brakhage's advice to 'allow so-called hallucination to enter the realm of perception' and to accept 'dream visions, day-dreams or night dreams, as you would so-called real scenes' offered visual de-programming exercises.[24] One method of seeing differently involves 'closed-eye vision'.[25] Pressing lightly on the closed eyelids is one way of experimenting with the underused 'internal ability to produce prismatic sensation directly, without extraneous instruments'.[26]

If we exercise neglected optical capacities by such 'eye adventures',[27] they become 'an instrument for striking sparks' not an imposer of control on the material flux.[28] Clearly, this agenda is aimed at a broader range of readers than just would-be experimental filmmakers. Brakhage's theoretical writings have the wider didactic intent to encourage the investigation of the nature of perception in order to enable more fluid connections between decentred subject and phenomenal flux.

For Deleuze, American experimental film sought to express direct perception 'as it is in things, or in matter' rather than being limited to the constraints of a disciplined and sensory-motor subjective vision.[29] Brakhage likewise wanted to remove obstacles to the free flow of vision between extensive and intensive worlds and to record this process. Film thus becomes a form of revelation both sensory and spiritual. Brakhage's magnum opus is *Dog Star Man*, a 78-minute film shot between 1961 and 1964.[30]

Dog Star Man: Connection to the Cosmos

The eye for Brakhage operates as 'visible brain matter, as surface sense of brain' to mobilise concepts as well as registering sensorial data.[31] Here, there is a distinction from Deleuze's image of brain as screen, which, although it similarly evokes immanence, elides the role of the eye as processual organ to model an image continuum not dependent on interface or intermediary stages.

Brakhage's work is a powerful visual encounter. To further stretch the eye's capacities *Dog Star Man* is silent, so that the 'interference' of soundtrack does not detract from, or even counterpoint, the image dynamic. Preferring poetry to more mundane language, he is particularly opposed to both soundtrack dialogue and intertitles. Despite this silence, Brakhage reflects that his films are 'inspired-by-music', so musical qualities are present, although not actually heard.[32] His cinematography and editing mobilise a 'coming-into-being of the physiological relationship' between hearing and seeing that extends beyond the actual organs involved in the process.[33]

'The Prelude' is an intense 25-minute condensation of the whole film. Some sections, random-edited from rushes, are intermixed with more consciously shaped sequences, so chaotic staccato alternates with smoother formal structures.[34] The overall rhythmical pace is rapid-fire and the direction of its flow is unpredictable. With few images occupying the screen for more than a few seconds, symbolic templates intent on fixing meaning are undermined.

The textured and tactile quality of 'The Prelude' asserts the ability of Brakhage's cinematic images to evoke other senses. The sequence combines the vein-like meshes of 'closed-eye vision' with external locale. In tandem, they create the impression of 'moving as if in memory' in an image-based process of recollection.[35] In a Bergsonian sense, intensive affects form the ground for the 'shining points' of memory to crystallise, such as Brakhage's contemplative image of a solitary tree on the horizon. The static shot underlines the artifice of the photograph as it freezes the flux of matter at a moment of identificatory capture. In contrast to this, water drops in close-up slide in and out of focus to exercise the unused possibilities of eyes trained to sharpen and fix focus. The grainy quality conveys molecular shifts in texture as liquefied perception becomes freefloating molecules of vapour. 'Shining points' appear as temporary sharpening of focus within the more abstract blur of material flux.

In this partial account of the film's images and rhythms, I have inevitably had to still the flux of movement into distinct shots in order to analyse them. As with other experimental films I write about, its affective impact as experiential process is only fleetingly expressed by language as analogue. Their distance from both language and recognisable images might be a further reason why Deleuze chooses not to analyse them substantially as film-philosophical case studies.

Yet Deleuze, discussing this structural absence of image in abstract film, cites Brakhage's short film *Reflections on Black*.[36] Brakhage maximises the viewer's awareness of the gradations of colour quality. Black leader is not opaque to light but tinged with other colours and even clear leader is not actually clear but marked by 'dust motes, scratches, imperfections dot its surface'.[37] 'The Prelude' opens with a section of black leader with a greenish-grey tint. This unsettles expectations of signification and invites reflexivity on those very expectations.

A flash of light bursts into a fluctuating world of opsigns and sonsigns as the swirling camera captures indistinguishable red shapes and patches of brightness. Flames flicker and blur. Cracks and scratches on the emulsion of the film's celluloid mimic sun-baked mud or cell walls lined with minutely branching veins. Insistently textural, cracked mud itself recalls the lens scratches that imitate it. A rapid series of superimpositions make a barrage of flicker. Light quality shifts as a silhouetted sunburst becomes jewelled points of light, revealed by a longer shot as glistening snow. Trails made by slow-motion street lamps glow on a reflective surface like sparks of frost.

The film unfolds a series of connections between material macrocosm and human microcosm. The linkages of these internal and external worlds run like threads through the film's image assemblage. The ventricle of a beating heart is superimposed on a cloud, in turn overlaid on a magnified shot of blood pumping through arteries. A rapid run of bright amorphous shapes precedes the blur of the camera's vertical drop. A close-up of organic tissue is linked to street lamps.

The restless camera-eye responds quickly to such affective shifts. Liquid sunshine pours in slow motion. Sunset glow on snow causes lens flare as the material body of the film is touched by varied intensities of light. Rocks, bubbles and cells are threaded together by editing. The use of grey/green leader here offers respite to the eyes from the rapid bombardment, and also acts as a screen for the after-image projection produced by staccato flicker on the retina. The viewer's eye here projects pre-given stimuli back onto the screen's blank space and thus participates directly in the film's flow.

Simultaneity replaces alternating montage by superimposition. A static moon is overlaid on a rush of images too fast for the eye/mind to grasp. For Deleuze, superimposition enables the mutual interactive becoming of its simultaneous images. It conveys the quality of Bergson's melting states of duration or dreams where images are overlaid.[38] Layering bonds images more closely than the montage that keeps them distinct, however brief their time on screen. The film's overlays are not always pictorial. For example, a close-up beating heart and cells under a microscope are intermittently superimposed by the flicker of light.

Images of a naked man (Brakhage) in a snowbound forest are intermeshed with the non-human universe. His hair and face, defamiliarised by extreme close-up, become the moon, clouds and shimmering light and his arms splay out like branches. A sunburst, a woman (Jane Brakhage)'s pubis and a fire are cut together. The fiery sun, viewed through a hexagonal prismatic lens, pulses at heartbeat pace. The camera's slides in and out are dizzying. As the horizon tilts away, its swirls are reflected in circular scratches on the film emulsion, as circuitry permeates all components of the machinic assemblage.

Brakhage wanted to remap the body's geography. Intermittent shots of naked lovers meld flesh with broader flows of force. In part three of *Dog Star Man*, there is a DeleuzeGuattarian meld of genders. Molar bodies are exchanged for a fluctuating assemblage in which 'penises replace breasts in flashes of images [. . .] or male hair will suddenly move across the whole scape of the female body'.[39] After briefly becoming each other, the writhing 'mound of male-female flesh' pulls apart and separates back into distinct genders.[40]

The camera's tilts and swirls culminate in a 360-degree spin as the inner world of human perception and outer world of matter peak in unison. The man's face is filmed in reverse footage through a mesh, his horizontal flight impelled by ecstasy. A sunburst fills the screen and pulses like a heart before bursting orgasmically from the sun's centre. Scratches on the film's surface imitate the sunburst's path as the filmmaker marks the celluloid with traces of cosmic phenomena.

As befits the closed eye's imperviousness to perspective, superimposition has a two-dimensional, flat-plane quality. The surface of the film is painted and scratched on each layer. Their tandem effect is the simultaneity of conscious vision and spontaneous surges of affect. In a holistic montage, abstract lines of light are manifest like the frozen energy of tree trunks and human hair resembles grass. The natural pace of a sunset is speeded up. Although conditioned vision might be too slow to capture natural fluxes the machinic camera-eye is able to keep pace. Black leader slows for reflection before the sunrise heralds a new mode of vision.

The life-affirming epiphanies of Brakhage's work are clearly modernist-inflected. Yet his plethora of shining points far exceeds the quest for rare moments of perfection crystallised by the visionary artist out of chaos. Rather than freezing the flux into transcendent moments by an act of subjective will, the film fuses the flow of matter and human perception as a unified immanence.

The aesthetics of Charles Olson, expressed in his influential manifesto, *Projective Verse* (1950), shaped Brakhage's belief that art has privileged access to a holistic vision that it is the artist's duty to convey. Rather than focusing on syntax and logical structure, Olson called for a poetic metre 'based on the breath of the poet and an open construction based on sound and the linking of perceptions'.[41] Brakhage cites Olson's Deleuzian-sounding 'third term, so that movement or action is home' with approval.[42]

According to James, Brakhage's immanentism seeks to convey 'the dynamic experience of what is phenomenally present', in order to reach 'unmediated perception where consciousness and nature are in direct contact'.[43] James then tries to fix the filmmaker within the postmodern moment of Romantic poetics. For ideologically informed structuralism, Brakhage's 'inarticulate empiricism' is anathema.[44] According to James, by mistakenly operating outside language, Brakhage's perspective is rendered 'ideologically complicit'.[45]

Yet if we reposition Brakhage in Deleuzian terms, it appears that the filmmaker bypasses the Romantic ego via a sensational flux closer to abstract expressionism than postmodernism. In his film, the eyes are not the controlling gaze of cinepsychoanalysis but act liminally, conjoining interior and exterior. The human eyes and the monocular, but technologically more extensive, camera-eye make direct contact with the flux of matter through their ability to process the force of light. Their affective ability to connect physical and mental worlds is also highly self-reflexive and enables conceptual insight into new ways of living.

Brakhage' s images are compounded not for dramatic effect but are in Youngblood's words a 'matrix for psychic exercise on the part of the viewer'.[46] The spectator is invited to push off the grip of signification so that denotation and connotation become 'subsumed in the sensual play of light', a prospect that unsurprisingly disturbs the structuralist James.[47] The more celebratory Sitney locates the film in the 'mythopoeic' phase of American avant-garde film along with Deren.[48] For him, Brakhage's inter-linked planes convey both 'the birth of the universe and the formation of the individual consciousness'.[49]

Brakhage's project subverts perceptual conventions and Western ontology. By melding the camera-eye, the phenomenal world and human consciousness, he offers a fluid univocity as 'one image constantly manifesting'.[50] Away from such modernist epiphanies linking human consciousness with cosmic flux, some filmmakers were experimenting with a more mechanical and mathematical method to fragment norms of vision and alter consciousness: flicker. Of course, some films already analysed deploy rapid-fire editing at flicker pace. What I focus on next is the specificity of flicker/strobe films of the 1960s produced by filmmakers aligned with structuralism in their methods, though not in their aim to induce altered states.

Flicker

With little or nothing of representation, flicker film works by mainlining light into the brain via the eyes in short bursts that alternate with darkness. Fragmenting optical norms and preventing smooth retinal adjustment, flicker film is the image become imperceptible. Of course, flicker is an integral component in the cinematic machine's optical percepts and affects. The flicker on the screen, reflected backwards by the stimulated rods and cones of our optical apparatus, can literally act to enlighten us. In the dynamic motion of these circuits, film becomes thought as well as feeling.

Film viewing demands two optic mechanisms: persistence of vision and the *phi* phenomenon. Persistence of vision is the inability of the retina to follow rapidly changing intensities. A light flashing at a rate greater than fifty flashes per second appears steady. Cinema projects at twenty-four frames per second (fps), but a three-bladed shutter can raise the flicker rate to seventy-two, three for each frame. In the *phi* phenomenon, apparent movement occurs because the intermittent stimulus is adequate to stimulate retinal movement if the gaps are not too long. The image/retina system can tolerate gaps, to maintain continuity, as objects are hidden briefly behind obstructions or retinal images behind blood vessels.

In a medical context, flicker is used for diagnosing symptoms such as epilepsy (hence the strobe public health warnings in mainstream film). Low-frequency flicker at rates of five to ten flashes per second can produce hallucinatory effects like brilliant colours and vivid shapes. These arise from the direct disturbance of the visual system, massive repeated bursts of retinal activity overloading the brain with stimuli and altering perception.

The adoption of stroboscopes during the 1960s at rock concerts and discos clearly aimed to replicate such psychedelic distortion. Experimental filmmakers like Tony and Beverly Conrad and Paul Sharits worked with flicker's effects on the eyes and minds of audiences. Strobe films are aligned with 'structural cinema'.[51] This new formalism moved away from the romantic exploration of psychological subjectivity to mount a minimalist and mathematically deliberate challenge to perception. Without figurative images, flicker films like Sharits's colour piece *Ray Gun Virus* (1966), for example, aims at 'the (pre-) conceptual nervous system of the viewer'.[52]

The Flicker: Stroboscopic Film

Conrad's own commentary elucidates the aim of his working methods.[53] He began experimenting with strobe in 1962, producing 'semi-hallucinatory and hypnotic effects' with flicker from a modified 16 mm projector.[54] Concerned with 'the ambiguous outer limits of human sensation', he nevertheless seeks to produce the 'impression of serenity and repose'.[55] Minimalist sensory content enables the spectator's own input in a 'hallucinatory trip through unplumbed grottos of pure sensory disruption'.[56] His sparse optical and sound style, although it aims to induce alterity, is at the opposite pole to psychedelic extravagance.

In *The Flicker* (1965) the 30-minute montage of black and white leader progresses from twenty-four frames per second down to four then back up to twenty-four. The crescendo/diminuendo structure is accompanied by a varying electronic buzz on the soundtrack. Conrad's sound combines tonal pitch in the 'lower ranges of audibility' and rapid rhythms.[57] He claims that this 'confusion' of pitch and rhythm 'gives unexpected birth to a sense of aural vastness and spaciousness'.[58] The sound thus offers an aural correlative to the harmonic structures of light.

These are opsigns and sonsigns becoming-imperceptible, purified of both imagery and melody. Conrad suggests that the lack of 'contamination with imagery will be the fulcrum to lever the audience directly towards full receptiveness', whereas, when images are lit by intermittent flicker, as in

Sharits's *Piece Mandala: End War* (1966) in which images of a couple who 'make love not war' are presented in coloured strobe flicker, eye motion will perceive the image as representational.[59]

But how might the flicker effect on the cinematic sensorium produce altered states of consciousness? Conrad advised fixing the eye on one point for maximum effect as he researched audience responses. His account reports 'strange things' that occur in the range of six to eighteen fps when the film moves in then out of the flicker range. The first noticeable effect can be

> a whirling and shattering array of intangible and diffused colour patterns, probably a retinal after-image type of effect. Vision extends into the peripheral areas and actual images may be hallucinated. Then a hypnotic state commences, and the images become more intense.[60]

The alpha–rhythm brain–wave frequency lies in the range of eight to sixteen cycles per second, so the central nervous system itself must be operating more directly here.

The bigger the screen, the stronger the flicker effect will be. There are obvious diminutions of impact on domestic DVD or video playback. At a full-sized screening I experienced the structural phenomena of two–eyed vision: a doubling then quadrupling of the screen.[61] Effects become more complex as monochrome shifts into overlaid colours – 'floaters', starbursts, zigzags and coronas similar to those of closed eye vision. Other viewers report complete visual images that appeared over the screen.[62] Unfortunately, the public experience of these films is rare but many people are familiar with the phenomena of strobe lighting in the more diffuse environment at dance clubs and rock concerts. Mainstream feature film such as *Jacob's Ladder* (Adrian Lyne, 1993) showcase flicker within more conventional narrative parameters.[63]

Attempts have been made by film theorists with a structuralist bent to fix what these films, with their rapidly alternating frames, are 'about'. For James, they set out to analyse cinema's 'constitutive condition' by fore-grounding frame-speed and its alternating rhythms of light and dark.[64] Such experiments with perception mobilise cinematic light, he asserts, to 'question the form and function of film as a medium of expression' and 'artistically explore the photo-chemistry of seeing'.[65] Despite its mechanical and mathematically precise structure, though, the fundamental energy unleashed by flickering light is machinic in a DeleuzeGuattarian sense. Yet such structural film experiments are given scant attention in Deleuze's cinema books, perhaps because of his broader ideological distrust of structuralism.

Encounters of the cinematic sensorium with the pure dynamics of light raise interesting questions about whether the perceiver can engage more fully in becoming if given fewer stimuli. Such becoming-imperceptible might make us work harder with the film and with the mind, expanding existing gaps and exploring them. The hallucinated images these films produce could also be used to explore the time-image further. They foreground how mechanical means can be used to stimulate memory-images, an area I will consider more fully in relation to the feature film *Strange Days*.

Flicker film of the 1960s disrupts customary eye/brain relations by the structural repetition of content-free shots of light and dark. Contemporaneously, a more stylistically molecular kind of film was seeking to induce altered states of consciousness in order to access the dimension of spirit through the affects of pure opsigns and sonsigns.

Yantra and Lapis: Analogue Trance

The work of Ken Jacobs and that of his colleague Belson is cited in Deleuze's discussion of the furthest pole of the perception-image. UK critic of experimental films David Curtis suggested that the 'flooding rhythms' of sound and visual patterns in Belson's work released 'basic physiological and psychological phenomena' repressed by the conscious mind.[66] In 1970, Youngblood's description of Belson's films coins phrases later borrowed by Deleuze in his 'gaseous cinema' category of the American experimental film. For Youngblood, 'in their amorphous, gaseous, cloudlike imagery' it is 'colour, not line, which defines the forms that ebb and flow across the frame' and this, he claims, citing Castaneda's terms, induces a 'state of *nonordinary reality*'.[67]

According to Deleuze, the 'material, energic element' of this type of film extends the liquid mode of perception by moving closer to the fluid dynamic of matter itself.[68] Its free molecular movement induces a correspondingly gaseous state of perception. Gaseous cinema's 'machine assemblage of matter-images' does more than extend the liquid mode by stylistic condensation.[69] It expresses perception's *'genetic element'* per se.[70] Deleuze compares its ability to suspend space-time and sensory-motor action to drug-induced awareness. Like hallucinogens, these films mobilise pure auditory and optical images that make intervals perceptible to the senses. For Deleuze, they 'trace coloured forms and movements back to molecular or atomic forces'.[71]

A further reason for the brevity of Deleuze's focus on experimental shorts may be his interest in the broader temporal and ideational sweep of stylistically adventurous art-house feature films. Although the limited availability of Belson's work might well have reduced Deleuze's opportunity to work with it, the films deserve further circulation and exploration for practitioners as well as theorists, which is one motivation for my current study.

Belson and James Whitney designed their films as an aid to meditation. The traditional use of abstract graphic film as 'visual music' in the USA by Oskar Fischinger, Douglas Crockwell and Mary Ellen Bute was adapted to spiritual use in a West Coast countercultural context. Attraction to 'Eastern' religions, particularly Buddhism, flourished in the area with its cultural links with China and Japan. Of course, the 'hippie trail' to India further augmented this fascination.

Buddhism's emphasis on vision and colour in meditation offered ample scope for filmic interpretation. The *Bardo Thodol* (*Tibetan Book of the Dead*) was particularly influential at this time. In his introduction, Trungpa Rinpoche emphasises the centrality of colour, light and visual spectacle in the Bardo state: the interval between death and rebirth. He describes 'brilliant colours and sounds' that instead of being a tangible situation of form' are rather 'an intangible state of quality' in intriguingly Deleuzian or Bergsonian terms.[72] Inner light is a goal of meditation. Yet, however diffuse the egoic subject might become when 'absorbed into the state of luminosity', consciousness is not lost, but retains 'intelligence operating, sharp and precise, with a dazzling quality'.[73] The book offers precise descriptions of the light and colour qualities operant on metaphysical planes, such as *Dharmata*'s mirage-like shimmer[74] or the 'soft smoky light of the hell-beings'.[75]

Of particular relevance to the visual content of these cinematic aids to meditation, the 'Four Wisdoms' manifest themselves as an intersecting formation of light-reflecting coloured discs, as

> in this cloth of light rays a sparkling white disc will appear, very clear and bright, like a mirror facing downwards, adorned with five discs like itself, ornamented with discs and smaller discs, so that it has no centre or circumference – turquoise, yellow and red.[76]

Sounds, like a 'great roar of thunder' emanating from the light, are integral to *Bardo Thodol* visions.[77] The visionary content of the films were partly shaped by devotional texts such as these, which could almost be a description of them as we will see.

Influenced by Duchamp and Mondrian, James Whitney and his brother John worked with digital rather than photographic aspects of cinematography in a method stressing the operations of chance. Following Einsteinian relativity, they wanted to use film to convey 'conceptual simultaneity of space-time'.[78] John Whitney was among the first to explore the graphic potential of both analogue and digital computers.[79] He devised a method of graphically composing and recording synthetic sound as analogy to visuals, so that the films are 'unified bi-sensorially'.[80] The 'ebb and flow' patterns of pendulums generated tones on the soundtrack in the projector.[81]

James Whitney developed a series of films designed as meditational aids. He acknowledges the difficulty of representing spirituality in concrete images and seeks to 'go beyond any language' in his techniques.[82] In *Yantra* (1955) and *Lapis* (1966) he conveys a potent visual and aural affect by a rhythmical abstraction that aims to induce trance. According to Youngblood the techniques of these films 'attempt to approximate mind-forms'.[83] In James's film *Yantra*, for example, he deploys a *yantra* as a 'machine to stimulate inner visualisations, meditations, and experiences' an instrument designed to focus psychic forces by concentrating them on a pattern.[84] Its complex abstract motion acts as a focus to absorb attention while freeing the mind from preoccupation and association.

Yantra was made by hand-drawing a series of basic dot structures on cards. These were multiplied, coloured and spun into patterns in an optical printer. James Whitney approximated the breaking up of forms in meditation by a method which 'reduced the structural mode to dot patterns' in order to evoke '*Akasha* or ether, a subtle element before creation' which 'permeates the universe before it begins to break down into the more finite world'.[85] This terminology recalls the Deleuzian 'plane of immanence' moved by non-subjective affects.

From the outset of *Yantra*, shimmering coloured dots hypnotise by stimulating the retina. Spiralling points of light radiate outward from a central nodal point to become shifting, vaporous patterns of floating particles. They form concentric circles and spirals that explode outwards. Bubbles fizz and burst, leaving trails of light. Strands of opulent colours pulsate in red and turquoise, gold, orange and purple. When experiencing the film, the mind abandons fleeting associations (fireworks, sunbursts) to the immanent purity of the patterns and colours themselves.

Cellular coloured dots form patterns that flicker and disperse. Apparently random chaos moves around two invisible centres, loose clusters that become circles magnetising floating molecules to them. Rather than these centres being fixed points at the hub of a wheel, they are rather holes for the dots drawn in and emanating out to eventually disappear off frame. Saturated colours, purples and pinks alternate with minimalist black and white sequences.

Compositions sporadically gravitate into rectangular formations, but these burst apart as though they cannot contain the circling momentum within linear borders. A mirroring that doubles the dot formations creates further formal balance. Other compositional elements draw attention. In a rapidly intercut section of blue and red dots with a rhythmical pulse, a horizontal line forms in centre-screen and vertical lines pulsate randomly.

Deleuze's aesthetics emphasises the vibrant materiality of film, body and mind, intermeshed in the film event as molecular assemblage. Gaseous cinema's foregrounding of molecularity offers a vision of the vibrant flux of material force. Its multiple, rhizomatic connections link the human mind, itself a matrix of molecular particles of thought, with other material networks.[86] The alternations of randomness and focus in Whitney's dot-matrix films enable Deleuzian 'microperceptions' to become manifest.

Sonsigns as scintillating electronic chords and trills also make up the shifting fabric of the film's formations. The synchronised notes swell as visual variety and pace increases. The shimmering climax features five crystalline shapes with high-pitched electronic notes as aural counterpart. Only eight minutes long by clock-time, the intense affective stimuli of Whitney's film extends its temporal impact into the plane of spirit. The sensory impact of *Yantra*, then, is immanent surface chaos with an underlying durational cohesion.

Lapis extends *Yantra* by the recently developed analogue computer. The *lapis*, or alchemical philosopher's stone, a gateway to mystical revelation, is the meditative focus, though it does not function as a fixed symbol. For the Gnostics, the power of the *lapis* lay at the centre of a spiral or maze. In expressing this figure, the film's intricately programmed dot patterns form a mandala-like structure of interwoven circuitry. It shifts and revolves to the complex rhythms of a tabla and the flexible, high-pitched vibrations of sitar strings.

A pure white frame is the ground for a ring of tiny particles round a central sphere of light. This spreads until a dazzling flicker blanks out the screen. The sphere glows scarlet and forms geometric green patterns inside crystalline modules. The particles disintegrate and re-form as the title: *Lapis*. The word bursts apart as the first beats of the tabla begin the parallel aural hypnotism of a raga. Belson, too, synthesises sound or electronically enhances existing music. It becomes integral to the impact of the image, so that 'you don't know if you're seeing it or hearing it'.[87]

The entire composition, including the edges of the frame, is in continuous flux. The concentric dynamics of *Lapis* cause the fascinated iris to contract and expand as it scans between centre and periphery. Vision shifts around the on-screen space as it registers micro-movements even when the centre-screen 'event' with its meshing of interlocking circles demands special attention. The rings tunnel in and burst out in rapid alternation as the minute networks of forces flow together. Their insistent circling gravitates against the constraints of rectangle and border.

The dots are not quantifiable in *Lapis*, being replaced by others that flow smoothly from the centre, enter from the off-screen elsewhere or are replaced by editing cuts. Despite the compositional tendencies visible in the force-field, each dot vibrates along a random path. Overall shimmer induces a sensation of melting out from a focal point, as cognitive recognition gives way to amorphous and fluid affects in the shifting dance of pure light and colour.

Their sensational affect can be thought via Deleuze's use of Brownian motion to discuss cinematic movement of random velocity and direction. The British botanist Robert Brown observed in 1827 that magnified pollen grains in water 'danced continuously and erratically around' and that 'movement arose from the particle itself' or possibly from a 'vital force' imbuing matter.[88] His theory was adopted by Albert Einstein to provide direct evidence of the existence of atoms and molecules as part of what developed into the 'kinetic' theory of matter and perhaps indirectly to Bergson's philosophy of material flux.[89]

As an effect of colliding molecules, Brownian movement produces equal motion in all directions. The average position of each particle remains the same as the centre of all movement. Anomalously, the volume of the space occupied increases over time. Within the molecular flux, the multiplicity of particles and fibres adopt specific formations as they conjoin with others. In Deleuze's own fractal-like cinematic world, a force is a-centred because of its inseparable relation to other forces. This kind of cinematic 'world-movement' is at the opposite pole to the fixed shot as 'a to-and-fro, a multiplicity of movements on different scales'.[90]

The gaseous molecules in *Lapis* elude representational templates, such as the 'cosmic eye'. In some shots, areas of darkness surround the moving edges of the circle. When the camera glides in closer, it extends the centre outwards towards the viewer before moving in like systole and diastole. As the camera-eye nears the centre, overlapping circles of dots shift their shades and tones as they intermesh. Each circle contains others, so that when the centre glides back out into long-shot, the process resumes an endless outpouring of affects, mental and spiritual in their impact.

The film closes with a more frenetic phenomenal display as the reappearance of a white globe cues in a speeded-up recap of formations. Two translucent globes with a shimmering centre of white light stretch apart diagonally until black leader ends the film. According to Whitney, this incomplete, suspended image marked the limits of film's ability to express 'inner imagery' and he abandoned filmmaking for a fuller engagement with Buddhism.[91]

Lapis aims to dissolve the centre of egoic subjectivity by absorption in its increasingly consistent yet ever changing rhythms. Whitney stressed the film's attack on Western egocentrism that splits the self from the universe and endorses the Buddhist phrase *Tat-Swam-Asi* (That art Thou).[92] For Amos Vogel, the film's 'governing visual rhythm [is] as vital as that of human breathing'.[93] He suggests that it can engineer the radical change of consciousness necessary for human becoming.[94]

So how far might Deleuze's perspectives on religion throw light on Whitney's use of film as spiritual catalyst and how might cinema relate more broadly to spirituality? Deleuze does not address religion per se in the cinema books, although he refers to the expression of spirit and spirituality in aesthetic terms as the metaphysical immanence of pure cinematic light.[95]

Via devices such as the out-of-field implied by the closed frame, Deleuze also endorses Bergson's identification of spirit with duration. One function of the closed frame is to introduce 'the transpatial and the spiritual into the system which is never perfectly closed'.[96] The more closed the framings appear, the more open they are to duration as a fourth dimension, and further to 'a fifth which is Spirit'.[97] The out-of-field implies the metaphysical presence of the radical elsewhere beyond measurable space and time.[98] Certainly in Whitney's dot-matrix films, the out-of-field is evident, not through the human gaze off-screen, but from the disappearance of dots out of frame and the influx of a seemingly endless variety of new ones.

In *A Thousand Plateaus*, Deleuze and Guattari discuss religion's power-relations. For them, organised religion generally acts as a force of territorialisation that 'organises the forces of chaos'.[99] Yet, however much *'territorialising marks simultaneously develop into motifs and counterpoints, and reorganise functions and regroup forces'* (*sic*) there is always an unrecuperable element as 'the territory already unleashes something that will surpass it'.[100]

This potential 'moment' of subversive counterpoint, however 'fictional or raw', depends on stylistic qualities, such as 'the becoming-expressive of rhythm, the emergence of expressive proper qualities, the formation of matters of expression that develop into motifs and counterpoints'.[101] Each milieu has a specific code, yet a territory retains decoding possibilities as 'milieus continually pass into one another'.[102] Expression thus enables disjunction between territory and code, because 'the territory arises in the free margins of the code', not as indeterminate, but rather 'determined differently'.[103]

The expressive purity of opsigns and sonsigns in *Yantra* and *Lapis*, then, function primarily as deterritorialisation. Religion, however broad-based and eclectic it might be, as in various orders of Buddhism, has the potential to develop yet more free-floating spiritually oriented practices, such as the use of aesthetic absorption to trigger meditative trance here. Intensive states might not, of course, be located under a spiritual aegis at all. I would now like to turn from the eye and ear to other parts of the cinematic body and consider the operations of eroticism from a Deleuzian perspective. In the next section, I move across the map from spirit to flesh as I engage the erotic sensorium, surely one of the pivotal cogs in the cinematic machine.

Sensational Sex

Sexuality, any sexuality, is a becoming-woman.[104] (Deleuze and Guattari)

Explicit sexual encounters might at first seem outside the remit of a Deleuzian approach to film. Sexuality does not appear as a thematic focus per se in the cinema books. Yet, sexual pathologies analysed by Freud and problematised by Deleuze and Guattari are seminal to *Anti-Oedipus* and Deleuze wrote significant studies of masochism. In Deleuze's usage of literature and film, style takes predominance over plot and theme. In more adventurous forms of cinema, the former is foregrounded and the latter may disappear altogether as in abstract animations. In this section, I aim to express sexualities of flux and becoming. To supplement Deleuze's lack of specific engagement with erotic material in the cinema books, I import relevant concepts from elsewhere in his solo and joint work.

Pleasure for Deleuze and Guattari is materially based in immanent sensation. Desire exceeds the sexual or, rather, it unleashes affective forces of which sexuality is only one among many. It is not, as Lacan and others would have it, the negative product of lack, but has productive potential as an autonomous force in its own right. Freed from Oedipal constraints, machinic desire can mobilise new forms of production and a new politics. Such ecstasies are not experienced subjectively, but via the potent states of 'haecceities' or 'things in themselves', and afford an 'intense feeling of *transition*' rather than the static finalities of psychoanalysis.[105]

Deleuze adapts the masochistic dynamic of Sacher-Masoch's fiction to map a psychosexual shift that will be developed with Guattari as the BWO. His analysis looks elsewhere than sexual arousal and refutes interpretations that limit masochism to a binary dialectic with sadism. For him, masochism's intent is anti-Oedipal as it 'disavows the mother and abolishes the father' and operates a different political dynamic to 'institutional' sadism by being 'contractual'.[106]

Masochism foregrounds the romantic ego's idealisation of the erotic object. For Deleuze, the 'aestheticism' of delayed gratification in masochistic fantasies is preferable to Sade's assault of his reader by a mathematically exact escalation of the libertine's tortures and victims. The effect of Sade's tales depends on the brutal explicitness of his descriptive language as cruelty operates through the manner of the telling. In Masoch's novels, on the other hand, intensive periods of suspense keep fulfilment at a distance, so that delay itself becomes eroticised in 'suspense as a plenitude, as a physical and spiritual intensity'.[107] Fetishisation is pivotal to masochistic scenarios. The fetishisation of fur in Masoch, for example, enables humans to extend their boundaries by forming assemblages with animals. They engage in become-animal via 'zones of indetermination or proximity in which woman and animal, animal and man, have become indiscernible'.[108]

Steven Shaviro made a pioneering application of Deleuzian concepts to the active and affirmative operations of masochism in the spectatorship of extreme cinema. For Shaviro, horror and pornography bombard the spectator's sensorium to produce immanence outside the psychoanalytic realms of subjective fantasy.[109] Via their mimesis of erotic tension, they offer a 'technology for intensifying and renewing experiences of passivity and abjection'.[110] Like Deleuze, Shaviro claims that the aesthetic experience can transform consciousness, as the agitated body, overloaded by affect, 'desires its own extremity, its own transmutation'.[111]

Deleuze writes that the erotic descriptions in Sade and Masoch attain maximum impact when they act on the senses directly as 'words are at their most powerful when they compel the body to repeat the movements they suggest'.[112] This 'pornological' language subverts the symbolic order and its restrictive codes by using a style that 'confronts language with its own limits'.[113]

More than any significatory content in the description, the sensory forces of style determine erotic affects. This position is developed further when Deleuze and Guattari present art as the language of sensations. As a living 'monument', art 'undergoes the triple organisation of perceptions, affections, and opinions in order to substitute a monument composed of percepts, affects, and blocs of sensation that take the place of language'.[114] By this apparent refutation of art's ideological content, they advocate looking elsewhere than representational equations or Oedipal symbolism.

Deleuze and Guattari offer a very different perspective on aesthetic dynamics than structuralist approaches such as that of Wolfgang Iser.[115] Iser applies psychoanalytic accounts of subjectivity and the role of projection in object-relations to the process of reading. According to him, we use imaginative projection and introjection to 'animate the meaning of the text as a reality' and thus incorporate it into our consciousness.[116] The 'irrealisation' of the real by fiction thus serves to strengthen subjectivity as the reader constitutes themselves by 'constituting a reality' that is unfamiliar.[117]

In this interaction, Iser's reader is both 'textual structure' and 'structured act' as textual repertoires are transmuted into personal experience through ideation.[118] As Iser himself admits, though, such work with readerly response is both limited and partial. The reader's subjectivity retains a degree of impenetrable opacity (for him, the unconscious) not easily amenable to discourse. His attempt to constrain the reader to textual structures and psychoanalytic subjectivity is as limiting as auteurism or the Leavisite close reading of texts that he strongly repudiates.

The language of sensations offers a more fruitful concept with which to conceptualise the moving images of cinema. Although Deleuze focuses on masochism's literary pornology rather than the erotics of heterosexual sex on film, his critique of Masoch still raises points applicable to the films I discuss here, despite its absence of the 'imperatives' of sadistic possession and domination or the masochistic pact. Although fetishism operates in one of my examples and both might be accused of foregrounding exhibitionism, their overall emphasis is on mutual pleasuring and female erotic agency. I will approach these examples via the erotics of the work that problematises normative sex most closely: *Anti-Oedipus*.

Deleuze and Guattari stress libido as an omnipresent force of 'machine energy' not reducible to the phallus posited by the 'anthropomorphic representation' of sex in psychoanalysis.[119] They endorse D. H. Lawrence's 'passional' use of erotic forces in his fiction and poetry to combat this imposition of 'reason' on the sexual sphere.[120] In Lawrence's work, the desiring potency of the unconscious escapes the psychoanalytic prison of human sex 'unified and identified in the molar constellation'.[121]

Deleuze and Guattari follow Wilhelm Reich in regarding Freud's concept of Thanatos, the Death Drive, as inimical to desire.[122] By establishing a binary dynamic between Eros and Thanatos, Freud deprived sexuality of its generative role to make it instead into 'the autonomous cause of sexual repression'.[123] Like Reich, Deleuze and Guattari regard the libido as socio-political as well as personal. If the entropy of the Death Drive is inimical, as in Freud's model, however much energy libidinal forces might generate, they are inevitably stymied so that 'sexuality as desire no longer animates a social critique of civilisation'.[124]

Despite the blockage of libidinal forces in contemporary culture, Deleuze and Guattari posit more fulfilling and productive erotic possibilities. They begin by mobilising Melanie Klein's theory of part-objects to rethink the gendered body. Klein's work foregrounded the primacy of object relations with the maternal breast, split into good and bad part-objects in a cluster of infantile fantasies. As the bad breast is subject to sadistic fantasies, the good one is over-invested and idealised. According to Klein, the schizophrenic denies the existence of the bad object and in repudiation of psychic reality develops 'strong feelings of omnipotence'.[125] Deleuze and Guattari develop a fresh take on part-objects as 'discovered' by Klein, who, according to them, worked 'to water oedipus down, to miniaturise it, to find it everywhere' (sic).[126]

The agenda that drives Deleuze and Guattari's work with part-objects is radically different from Klein's. From the outset they repudiate her splitting of the same entity into good and bad. They assert that part-objects should not be 'the differentiations of a single being, such as the masculine and the feminine in the human sex', but, rather, they are 'different or really-distinct things, distinct "beings", as found in the dispersion of the nonhuman sex (the clover and the bee)'.[127] Whether they are linked to a particular organ or not, partial objects do not belong to 'any organism that would function phantasmatically as a lost unity or a totality to come'.[128]

Rather than being structured by Freudian Oedipality like Klein's work, Deleuze and Guattari give part-objects a more pivotal role in the new molecular machine of the unconscious where,

> with every structure dislodged, every memory abolished, every organism set aside, every link undone, they function as raw partial objects, dispersed working parts of a machine that is itself dispersed. In short, *partial objects are the molecular functions of the unconscious.*[129]

So libidinal partial objects as 'micromolecules' and the 'giant molecule' of the BWO function together as a continuity in the schizophrenic desiring-machine.[130] They manifest the 'direct powers' of the BWO, which in turn forms the 'raw material' of partial objects.[131]

Unlike Klein's binary split of good and bad objects, Deleuze and Guattari's partial objects operate in a fluctuating field of force. Again, Lawrence's image of sexuality as 'an infinity of different and even contrary flows' inspires their thought.[132] Each partial object is linked with others in a fluid multiplicity. It emits a libidinal flow that defines the 'potential field of presence' of the other as a multiplicity.[133] Yet the syntheses that inter-link partial objects remain indirect. One of the partial objects inevitably breaks the flow emitted by another in a field of 'two-headed' flows.[134]

If flows evade being broken by the 'uniform figures' of territorialisation, they reconnect into 'chains of decoding' by 'mobile and nonfigurative points (the flows-schizzes)'.[135] The aim of schizoanalysis, whether applied to abstract or concrete material, is to produce a 'nonfigurative and nonsymbolic' unconscious.[136] Although Deleuze and Guattari mention painting here, their evocation recalls the gaseous flux of abstract animation films. The non-symbolic unconscious is 'a pure abstract figural dimension ("abstract" in the sense of abstract painting) flows-schizzes or real-desire', apprehended 'below the minimum conditions' of egoic identity.[137]

Although materially grounded, the BWO is also an abstract machine that does not operate within distinct representational, semiotic or structural systems. In the Deleuzian abstract machine of cinema, style and content are one for the spectator's embodied consciousness. At this point, I bring in Carolee Schneemann's *Fuses*, which operates its own flows-schizzes in a radical deterritorialisation of sexual desire that extends from actual organs to a pure figural dimension influenced by abstract expressionism.

Fuses

[in] the libidinal investments of the social field [. . .] it is sexuality that constitutes the indices.[138] (Deleuze and Guattari).

tactile material, palpably aroused.[139] (James)

Schneemann's *Fuses* expresses the plane of immanence accessed by the BWO of intense states of erotic arousal. As a riposte to her friend Brakhage's masculinist interpretation of her own sexuality in two of his films *Loving* (1957) and *Cat's Cradle* (1959) she produced a 'polemically female' erotic vision of herself and partner James Tenney.[140] *Fuses* makes tangible both the vibrations in the intensive body and their extended assemblage with fields of force. Stimulated by touch, erotic energies connect sensorially with those of the environment via waves of light and colour.

In the twenty-five minutes of *Fuses*, the camera itself, held or set up by the filmmaker/actor, is a direct participant in sexual action. Schneemann's working methods involved direct excitation of the physical body of the film, using celluloid as what James suggestively calls 'tactile material, palpably aroused'.[141] Like Brakhage, Schneemann uses artisanal techniques such as scratching and baking the footage in a human/film becoming.

Sprocket holes are intermittently visible in *Fuses*. This moderates the fictional intensity of the profilmic diegesis by highlighting the materiality of the medium and its constructed nature. At the same time, it authenticates its hands-on, independent status. It is without soundtrack for reasons similar to Brakhage's own: to maintain a more direct engagement with opsigns and tactisigns.

The affective flows of colour and light are mobilised from the outset. Abstract coloured forms alternate with black leader. Amorphous swirls solidify into extreme close-ups of body parts shot through coloured filters that slip back in turn from identifiable partial objects to become schizzes of pure light and colour. The subsequent footage resembles flashes of recollected sensation, more like the partial flows of pure affect than Bergson's crystalline 'shining points' of specific memories.

Black leader becomes white light interspersed with shots of Schneemann running along a beach. Intimate images of the couple in their bedroom shift to the window curtains as subjective and objective viewpoints alternate in a complicated and fluid perspective. The cellular texture of curtain lace is highlighted in contrast to the dark exterior. Editing pace increases as its rapid flicker at times reaches strobe speed. The flickering motion of light impregnates the coloured images to meld subject/object together in a superimposition not of one distinct image over another but of two kinds of intensive motion, light and colour, engaged in a mutual vibration.

Perspectives shift between long-shots and close-ups of faces and body parts as the lovers are overlaid by light and darkness like a patterned veil. Shots taken from the bed as they shift in and out of more intense levels of arousal travel round the room in intermittent fragments. As ecstasy mounts, alternating shot lengths become a close-up inserted into a long-shot by split screen.

The film's tactisigns express the affective impact of images beyond their visual content. Tactility is expressed by the haptic sensation of skin being stroked in extreme close-up. This action is shot upside down then side-on to evoke a variety of responses and positions. The heat of passion is coloured fiery red as bodies burst into light. A scarlet filter intensifies arousal in a close-up of fellatio, while a blue filter overlaid with stars expresses the distinct sensory quality of extended cunnilingus. The screen is flooded with turquoise light at a peak of pleasure and a swirl of coloured oils leads into an erect nipple frosted in black that sharpens sensation.

According to Deleuze and Guattari, the libido freed from imposed Oedipal fixations without 'even the most undifferentiated ego of narcissism' becomes free to engage in 'molecular desiring-production'.[142] Libidinal investments have thus entered the pre-personal regime 'of partial objects, of singularities, of intensities, of gears and parts of machines of desire'.[143] In *Fuses*, bright light and dense colour filters defamiliarise body parts as desire welds separate subjectivities together. Bleach-out and flicker abstracts and spreads physical sensation. Although shots of faces and intercut (unheard) dialogue develop more subjective elements, these are overlaid with intensive facial close-ups blurred by soft focus as faces, distorted by sexual bliss, melt into each other.

Machinic waves of erotic energy ripple out to draw a nearby cat into their assemblage. Silhouetted against the window's light the cat is lit in red and gold as though charged by the affective waves of arousal itself, shifting to solid black with eyes of light. The restless cat indicates the becoming-animal of ever-spreading libidinal force on the plane of immanence. Sporadic inserts of waving grass and the sea recall Brakhage's nature mysticism and open the intensive domestic space to more extensive assemblages.

Black-and-white footage is overlaid with meshes that float a shifting web of sensations across the lovers. They cool the heat of saturated colour and spill over the lovemaking by superimposition. A close up penis-shot is intercut twice in the simultaneous collage of intimacy that renders affective sensations timeless. The blur of streetlamps is interlinked with fast-motion rays of golden light in the bedroom window as temporal linearity is compressed into ecstatic time. Thus the qualitative impact of the film at any one moment engages a structural overlay of temporal planes at once experienced immanently and recollected as matter melds with memory.

Erotic intensity subsumes distinction. The material actuality of bodies is diffused by the flux of unlocalised sensation as colour, texture and form blend into a moving collage of images. Visual phenomena play over bodies linked in sexual contact but also emanate from them as a physical wave of sensational arousal. Figures melt into ground and images into medium. The material properties of the film are likewise eroticised and carry an affective charge equal to that of profilmic events.

For Schneemann, *Fuses* is 'free in a process that liberates our intentions from our conceptions' while Youngblood notes its 'overall mosaic simultaneity of flesh and textures and passionate embraces'.[144] Schneemann's desiring machines, with their partial object components, express an ' "erogenous body" ', Leclaire's term cited by Deleuze and Guattari to describe 'an emission of preindividual and prepersonal singularities, a pure dispersed and anarchic multiplicity, without unity or totality'.[145] In the flowing forcefield of part objects, permutations are possible, via 'fringes of interference on the edge of each field of presence' to form 'residual conjunctive syntheses' that guide the passage of mutual becoming.[146]

Deleuze and Guattari use the biological concept of genetic code to consider complex expressive images. According to genetic coding, if codes form a chain 'inasmuch as it folds into exclusive molar configurations, it undoes the codes by unfolding along a molecular fibre that includes all the possible figures'.[147] However far into molecularity *Fuses*' abstraction travels, one level of operations still retains a signifying chain, with molar components 'composed of signs of desire'.[148] Despite periodically recognisable images of breasts, penis, mouth, hand and vagina, the schizzes/flows of Schneemann's abstracted part-objects remain able to 'pass through the signifying wall, thereby undoing the codes'.[149]

Fuses uses explicit genital sex to exceed the limits of the gendered body. It deploys a haptic melding of sight with touch, colour with movement and light that refutes any simple 'copycat' model of pornographic arousal. In Schneemann's film, not only do part-objects meld into abstraction, but also images of erotic sensation mobilise synaesthesia. Overall, the film expresses the schizoid becomings of the BWO. It mobilises diffused and immanent affects by 'bands of intensity, potentials, thresholds, and gradients'.[150]

I will move on to compare Schneemann's artisanal work to a big budget feature film that also thematises female erotic pleasure. By this move, I want to interrogate libertarian sexual agendas though a Deleuzian prism. Although again featuring a camera-wielding woman as sexual agent, *Performance* was shot in the ostensibly open sexual milieu of 'Swinging London' in 1968 by two male filmmakers.

Performance: Erotic Home Movie

you're perverted! (Chas in *Performance*)

it is as deplorable to miniaturise, internalise the binary machine as it is to exacerbate it; it does not extract us from it.[151] (Deleuze and Guattari)

Performance (Donald Cammell and Nic Roeg, 1970) explores extreme and fluid states of consciousness. Although it presents both drugs and violence as cinematically altered states, I am interested here in the film's third alterity: gendered sexuality. To explore this, I look at a sex scene between three lovers, two female and one male. Pherber (Anita Pallenberg) manipulates the film's events by psychological games. Here, performing both as filmmaker and lover, she shoots footage of her own encounter with Turner (Mick Jagger), a 'resting' rock star, and Lucy (Michele Breton), their young acolyte.[152]

Chas (James Fox), a gangster on the run, intrudes into the household to hide out in its 'bohemian atmosphere'. The sex scene here functions to consolidate the group prior to further confrontation with their interloper. The emphasis here is on mutual pleasuring and polymorphous play in contrast to the controlled violence of the rituals of Chas and his lover Dana earlier.

The erotic sequence superficially seems to be an anti-Oedipal Deleuzian 'permutation' involving '3, 2, *n* organs; deformable abstract polygons' that 'make game of the figurative Oedipal triangle' and deploy 'binarity, over-lapping, or permutation' in order to destabilise it.[153] So let us examine its sensory terrain rather more closely to ascertain how this apparently radical 'engineering of desire' operates.[154]

Harsh sunlight from the outside world contrasts with the diffuse light-ing of a Moroccan globe lamp in Turner's artificial paradise. Pherber caresses her camera before wielding it at a more phallic angle like Chas's gun with which she toys later. Pherber's mimicking of Chas's speech mixes mockery with the growing fascination she attempts to counteract by focus-ing on her own mirror image. Pherber masquerades in various personae in the film. Here, her image is temporarily captured by its mirror reflection and by her capture of herself on film. By pointing her camera at a mirror, it includes the spectator in self-reflexive perspectival duplicity.

As Pherber enters the boudoir, a tinkling keyboard run makes an aural parallel to the shimmering light. In keeping with Turner's orientalist fantasy world of kaftans, hashish and 'arabesque' décor, the bed recalls a sultan's divan. Its white gauze drapes both conceal and reveal, offering the camera-eye multiple entrance points. Pherber approaches it through elab-orate, wrought gold décor, admiring her passing image in a further mirror suspended in air by its solid black ground. Gliding towards the bed, she retreats deeper into the diegetic series of interlocking worlds, one of which is driven by erotic affects she sets in motion.

A fish-eye lens distorts Pherber at the foot of the bed as though it were a skewed point of view from the pillows. Her features adopt a sinister, feral cast, lit from below as she steadies the camera with her arm to shoot. Part of this soft-porn sequence is actually filmed on a 16 mm Bolex home-movie camera like the one wielded here by Pherber herself. A sudden switch in gauge from 35 mm to 16 mm introduces a grainy effect as a glimpse of the camera's viewfinder again foregrounds a multiplicity of viewpoints.

The pillow space next to Turner is highlighted in visual anticipation of Pherber's presence. With his lipsticked pout, the androgynous Turner in repose mixes innocence and decadence. The film's celebration of gender subversion could be read as reflecting the permissive pretensions of the 'swinging' sexual scene. Freud suggested that sexual identity was funda-mentally bisexual. For Deleuze, however, bisexuality is not necessarily lib-erating. Without abolishing the foundational concept of two sexes, he argues, 'it is as deplorable to miniaturise, internalise the binary machine as it is to exacerbate it; it does not extract us from it'.[155]

Pherber's camera shifts to the sleeping Lucy, as an androgynous twin of Turner. In order (as he said) to 'get the viewer under the sheets', Roeg shot the lovers with the Rolex as Cammell directed them from the other side of the bed.[156] The roving camera explores and suggests sexual action. Pherber's voyeurism turns to narcissism as she exchanges recording for participation and leaves the camera to shoot the scene itself. Touching Lucy's nipple leads in a rush of abstracted body parts and flesh compositions bathed in a warm pink glow. When Lucy stirs in response, Pherber steps back to her roles of filmmaker and erotic controller.

The music of a *santur* (a Persian plucked string instrument) played by Nasser Rastigar[157] adds to the film's array of 'psychedelic drones and pulses'.[158] The ethereal delicacy of its tones intensifies the mood of erotic aestheticism. Pherber's hand, laden with talismanic rings, arranges the sleepers' limbs to expose their genitals for the camera, although Turner's hand covers his penis (marking the jump-cut of censorship).

Erotic intensity mounts as the motion of the lovers synchronises and Pherber finally abandons her controlling position to lie down. Golden light streams over them, manifesting erotic energy that transfigures their bodies as becoming-light. Turner's features fade out in the blur of extreme close-up as pleasure deletes egoic consciousness. Pherber enters a comparably melting state, depersonalised by the grainy affect induced by a kiss. The light forms a halo round Turner's head and reflects off his lip-gloss to emphasise his voluptuous mouth. Pherber's tongue leads the kissing and directs his response as she slips her tongue, lit like a bar of gold, between his lips. Like Schneemann's filming of actual sex with her lover Tenney, these love-scenes were apparently played with conviction because of the 'double personal' involvement of the actors.[159]

Alternating with the 35 mm camera, the scene's qualities vary soft and sharp focus. As Pherber slips off her robe, the soft luminescence of a smoky candle flame enhances the flickering quality of the light. Lucy wakes and the three bodies are enmeshed in an anonymous tangle of limbs as the affective force of 'a thousand sexes' temporarily subsumes their individuation. Themes on strings and piano meld with the visual images. Turner lifts the sheet until the fabric's pattern and colours fill the screen, but the camera slips beneath, into a greenish light that envelops the lovers, blurring outlines further and making flesh luminous. The screen briefly blanks out in a mutual erotic climax, to return to recognisable images tinted with the pink glow of flesh.

The hand-held camera is overwhelmed by the profilmic plethora of writhing flesh. As it roves restlessly around, its own pace becomes increasingly frenzied like an excited sexual partner demanding action. The lifted sheet exposes thrusting buttocks and an anonymous hand strokes anonymous skin. From above, the sheets undulate and Pherber's hair falls in a slow motion that holds back linear time. Pherber mounts Turner but at the onset of her orgasm, a rapid switch of camera set-up shifts to a long-shot at ceiling level. Wooden banisters intrude and screen off the action below.

Both films were accused of being pornographic, *Performance* by the BBFC and *Fuses* by some feminist critics. Both *Performance* and *Fuses* deploy sexual organs in close-up as part-objects fragmented from bodily wholeness. Tenney's penis is shown erect and Jagger's has clearly been edited out. Schneemann's vagina is overtly featured in the cunnilingus scene and more explicit genital details that do not appear were obviously shot by Cammell and Roeg.[160]

Unlike much generic porn, though, both films aim to use cinematography experimentally to extend bodily sexual sensation beyond gender limits and to combine the physical with the metaphysical. *Fuses* does this by stylistic density and affective intensity whereas *Performance* links sex with other kinds of altered states via a complex chain of image series that cross the film. Nevertheless, the alternation of binaries is its most obvious dynamic via its technique of 'vice and versa' role exchange.[161]

Androgyny is pivotal to *Performance*. Chas insists to the sexually dominant Pherber that he is 'all man', while Pherber describes Turner as a hybrid 'male and female man'. She suggests Chas's own potential for 'a change' by holding a half mirror reflection of him to her own half face to form a complete whole. Clearly in denial of his own homosexuality, he adapts to the gender modifications of a 'feminised' disguise of long wig and robes after a hallucinogenic trip. Lucy is 'like a boy' to Chas's predominantly homoerotic tastes, whereas Turner is feminised. Although Pherber is a sexual controller, her energy is stymied by narcissism and heroin.

Like the experimental work of Schneemann, eroticism in *Performance* insists on its status as an altered state of awareness. So what are Deleuze and Guattari's views on the ostensibly liberating effects of non-normative sexual practices? According to them, if perversion and even sexual emancipation remain marginal to the existing Oedipal-narcissistic system, they cannot offer genuine liberation. Deleuze and Guattari assert that deviant and transgressive practices, if 'confined within the framework of the [Lawrentian] "dirty little secret"', will continue to be 'cynical, shameful and mortified'.[162]

The Oedipal system asserts repression on both externalised societal and internalised subjective planes. Even if more permissive censorship laws allowed the publication of the sexual 'secret', repression would continue to keep 'the corresponding flows within the limits of the Oedipal code' and continue to 'impose a familialist and masturbatory form or motivation on it that makes any perspective of liberation futile in advance'.[163]

The sexual interactions of *Performance* are ultimately far from DeleuzeGuattarian liberation. However fluid they might appear, these 'polymorphously perverse' couplings remain narcissistic and exhibitionist performances to (diegetic) camera and (extra-diegetic) controlling film-makers. Allon White, in his contrast of the medieval carnival with modern subcultural bohemias, describes the latter's 'long night's festival – interiorised, privatised, ultimately linked to the individual psyche structured around transgressive thrill'.[164] The adult chamber games in Turner's artificial paradise, cut off from further social connection, are unlikely to form assemblages of becoming outside its hermetically sealed world. Chas's own altered gender image is not able to survive outside when dramatically confronted by his former gangster role. The visceral passion and molecular connections of erotic play are undercut by Pherber's direction of the scene to make her home movie. A comparable mechanism that seeks to direct erotic passion and replay it as memory works differently in Kathryn Bigelow's *Strange Days*.

Strange Days: Sex in the Head[165]

Lost in playback memory bliss.[166] (James Cameron)

so alive it's like red hot and cold at the same time.[167] (Lenny Nero)

transverse communication in the decoded flows of desire.[168] (Deleuze and Guattari)

Lenny Nero (Ralph Fiennes), an ex-cop, lies in his bedroom-cum-living room, the windows foiled over to make a private movie theatre. A shot of strong vodka eases the stress of the LA streets. The mirror by the bed positioned to reflect his image and a box of video clips at his groin keys in his autoerotic interests. Yet, as he riffles through them, he chooses the clip marked with the most personalised traces of another: a doodled sketch of a woman's eyes, promising home-made material with personally known performers rather than mass produced porn.

He puts a device like a technological crown of thorns on his head. This is the SQUID (superconducting quantum interference device) originally developed by federal intelligence agencies as a tool for espionage and available to the public via the black market economy that Lenny works like a drug dealer. He sells not only virtual sex, but also adrenalin-fuelled footage of robbery and other crimes, while drawing the line at 'blackjacks' or snuff material. The SQUID bypasses the visual cortex to mainline data into the viewer's central nervous system.

A rapid whoosh, like audio overload, shifts Lenny into a virtual reality. Once the blur of pixels solidifies into a recognisable image, part-objects appear at the edge of his vision. Feet on roller skates and hands holding other hands intrude into and lead out of the frame, disrupting its rectangular equilibrium and insisting on the off-screen space of the camera operator. This elsewhere operates in the Deleuzian sense of being temporal as well as spatial in nature and depends on Lenny's subsequent 'completion' of the clip in replay. The warmth of his smile as the woman skater laughs into the camera suggests that the material feeds emotional as well as sexual needs. Yet after setting up the mood of the scenario he fast-forwards like a porn user to a more explicit section.[169]

Faith (Juliette Lewis) mounts the stairs into a flesh-tinted apartment. The images are hazy with pixel blur, the grainy quality of video distinguished from sharper 35 mm cine shooting, in a similar effect to the 16 mm gauge of *Performance*. Like Pherber, too, Faith is an experienced erotic performer conscious of the camera. Faith is fully aware of Lenny's voyeuristic intent to re-use the footage and plays up to it directly by her teasing words, 'I love your eyes, Lenny; I love the way they see' and asking him 'How do you feel?' Visual/tactile connections are foregrounded in this futuristic form of 'teledildonics', or virtual reality sex.

The cameraman's identity is revealed by a brief shot of Lenny himself in the mirror, but the sequence's main interest lies in playback as direct event rather than the activity of filmmaking. This of course enables any other user to take his place more easily thus the viewer is directly implicated in the pornographic voyeurism problematised by Bigelow.

Faith blurs into large pixels as she leans over to kiss Lenny. In a cut back to him in his room, as though the present were a flashback of the past, he caresses his own lips, moaning for Faith and putting his hand out in the air to 'touch' her as he relives the tactility of the experience. As Lenny experiences an orgasm both virtual and actual, he 'exhales sharply behind a wave of electronically recorded pleasure', having become 'lost on the swirl of sensation'.[170] The disturbingly close intimacy of the scene compels direct sensorial engagement and challenges theories of the distanced gaze in cinepsychoanalysis. The apparent male control of this material is undermined by the vulnerability revealed in his responsive reactions to an invisible lover's presence as exposed to the movie camera in close-up.

I am not the first film theorist to test out the Deleuzian implications of *Strange Days* and I must acknowledge a degree of overlap between my own response and two earlier ones. Barbara Kennedy's expressive reading was first to focus on the sensational becoming-woman in the film. For Kennedy, the haptic impact of colour and tactility in Faith's performances, particularly in the Retinal Fetish Club numbers, expresses a 'scintillatingly erotic' vitalism.[171] Kennedy describes the film as a Deleuzian haecceity, an event of 'intensity that vitally courses through the diegetic veins and body'.[172] As well as acknowledging their molar currency as representational symbols, she stresses how the film's images impact on us sensorially as they 'perform across the synaesthetic scopic matrix'.[173]

In a later reading of *Strange Days*, Patricia Pisters draws out other Deleuzian possibilities in the film's style, particularly in its disorienting spatial perspective. She notes Bigelow's 'spatial abundance' and endless rooms that have 'always an opening on to another connecting space'.[174] Her comment is informed by Deleuze's description of 'electronic automatism' in the imagery of new technology. This emphasises distortion and stretch in on-screen spaces that 'no longer have any outside' and create 'omnidirectional space, which constantly varies its angles and co-ordinates'.[175] Yet Deleuze is far from celebrating these effects if they operate without the 'cerebral creation' of the 'will to art'.[176] He thus opposes the serious ethical intent of modernist aesthetics to postmodernist fascination with styles as surface effervescence.

Pisters underlines the film's literalisation of Deleuze's concept of the brain as screen. She notes that Lenny's 'digital drugs' replace the distancing devices of traditional cinema by their directly physical engagement of both body and brain, thus the film 'necessitates an immanent conception of the image'.[177] Yet the embodied brain's functions are only partly driven by the perceptual effects of sensory stimuli. I will explore this issue further in my conclusion to the book.

Pisters argues the film's 'flexible and nomadic' conceptualisation of desire and selfhood.[178] Certainly, Lenny offers clients a choice of both virtual sexual partners and their own gender. Keith, a Hollywood accountant, tests out a perverse form of becoming-girl via a mainlined clip of a teenager taking a shower. Revelling in his re-incorporation as a young woman, he 'puts his hands on his body and "feels" it wonderingly'.[179] Yet the film's fantasies of erotic and gender flexibility, however convincing they might be, are mixed with, and appear to depend on, actual physical and psychological brutality that is chiefly male authored. Bigelow's sensorially insistent camera compels us to relive the degradation and murder of the hooker Iris, when the intensity of the killer's sadism and her terror is doubled by the shared SQUID playback looping between murderer and victim.

Faith's erotic agenda involves a more ambivalent play with gender and power. As well as wanting to further her career as a singer by sleeping with her manager, Philo Gant, her choice of him as a more domineering partner seems partly fuelled by over-familiarity with Lenny's adoring yet voyeuristic turn-on. Ironically, Gant, too, becomes an addicted 'wire-head' whose resultant paranoia leads him to murder suspects and includes Faith herself on his hit-list.

The film's erotic implications can be explored more broadly than their immediate impact on the sensorium. I want to ascertain how far they evince Pisters' more celebratory application of Deleuze and Guattari's 'transverse communication in the decoded flows of desire' as an epithet to the film.[180] As Deleuze and Guattari remind us, desiring machines are pre-eminently social, whether they be 'agglutinated or dispersed', and the social plane is permeated by the erotic motive.[181] Love and sexuality motivate the social field's unconscious libidinal investments. But erotic object-choices and practices can follow either 'lines of escape or integration'.[182]

The social context of the diegetic pornography market and its voyeuristic clients wages war with the apparently unbounded erotic and gendered possibilities offered by the chips' virtual worlds. Lenny's trade depends on his customers' taste for 'forbidden fruit', the very metaphor implying the pornographer's dependence on a psychic economy of transgression and perversion as well as more 'liberated' forms of sexual encounter and gender assemblage.[183]

In his sales spiel to Keith, Lenny asserts that 'the brain is the most important sexual organ'.[184] This claim certainly validates the pornographer's business and could also be read as anti-Cartesian. Yet, it downgrades both the extensive and interactive actual in favour of the solo intensiveness of the virtual. For Deleuze and Guattari, desire should be extended as 'a force to love, a virtue that gives and produces, that engineers'.[185] Both by their methods of production and consumption and their content, the SQUID clips limit the power of erotic energy in the wider socius.

The force of desire cannot be inherently revolutionary or reactionary, but is, rather, an index of the libidinal investments of the social. By their emphasis on the 'directly social character' of the libido and its sexual investments, Deleuze and Guattari follow Reich in endorsing the release of a 'nonsublimated' desire into the social field.[186] If unleashed, this desire has the revolutionary potential to invest both the sexual and the social plane together.

Pisters usefully flags up the operations of Bergson's 'ethics of memory' in this intriguing 'metafilm'.[187] She points out that Lenny, lost in recollection playback and unable to act, conveys the dangers of Bergson's circuit of dreaming. If memory is overdeveloped, according to Bergson, it is at the expense of action-oriented decision-making in the present.[188] An example of this occurs at the start of the scene, when Lenny just misses a desperate phone-call from Iris, one of his performers in fear of her life. In the morning, he is too preoccupied to focus for long on the thematically crucial news of the death of Afro-American militant Jericho 2.

So how far do Lenny's playback memories correspond to those of the Deleuzian time-image? In one sense, Lenny is able to access virtual memory and actualise it in a Bergsonian way by replaying the sensory (in his case tactile as well as visible and audible) memory of the originary experience. Pisters notes that, although memories are a necessary and automatic adjunct to perception, they should only be actualised if they helpfully illumine the present.[189] In an attempt to move Lenny on from his fixation with Faith, his driver Mace (Angela Bassett) reminds him that 'memories are designed to fade away'.

SQUID playback chips speed up and compress the interlinked layers of duration in Bergson's model. The intoxication they produce actually only travels in one direction of Bergsonian time. It operates by a back-tracking that can be addictive rather than returning to take present action informed by recollection and move on. Lenny's replayed memories of Faith are reliably the same every time. Temporally frozen, they are unable to impact on the present and shape the future. They hold Lenny back from being fully alive and stymie his potential to develop.

As well as advising against the dreamer's use of memory as opiate, Bergson's durational time raises further problems for the actualisation of the virtual in *Strange Days*. Bergson's memories are personal experiences that extend beyond their immediate perceptive and affective impact to join the infinitely large circuits of duration. Unlike Lenny who makes his own clips, the usual user of SQUID tapes jacks in to another person's experiences and actualises their potency as viscerally experienced events. Their impact on the central nervous system bypasses the brain but feels actual enough. The ethical implications of any actual actions involved remain largely unanalysed by the characters, yet Bigelow's film offers the process of conceptual reflection as well as visceral engagement to the viewer.

The discussion of Bergsonian time I have opened up here in relation to the erotic sensorium and memory leads in to the focus of my final chapter. Bergson's duration becomes central to my exploration of altered states of temporal perception in the Deleuzian time-image.

Notes

1. Deleuze, *Cinema 1*, p. 84.
2. Brakhage, 'The Camera-Eye', p. 211.
3. Deleuze and Guattari, *A Thousand Plateaus*, p. 171.
4. Deleuze, 'To Be Done with Judgement', p. 131.
5. Deleuze, *Cinema 2*, p. 189.
6. Ibid., p. 18.
7. For Deleuze and feminist politics, see *A Thousand Plateaus*, p. 276 and *Dialogues*, p. 2. For feminist discussions of 'becoming-woman' see Buchanan

and Colebrook, *Deleuze and Feminist Theory*; Grosz, 'A Thousand Tiny Sexes', p. 207.

8. Deleuze and Guattari, *A Thousand Plateaus*, p. 275.
9. Ibid.
10. Ibid.
11. Ibid., p. 278.
12. Ibid., p. 276.
13. Ibid., p. 278.
14. Deleuze and Guattari, *What Is Philosophy?*, p. 302.
15. Brakhage, 'The Camera-Eye', p. 212.
16. Deleuze, *Cinema 1*, p. 84.
17. Brakhage, 'The Camera-Eye', p. 211.
18. Ibid.
19. Ibid.
20. Ibid., p. 221.
21. Ibid., p. 211.
22. Brakhage, in James, *Allegories of Cinema*, p. 39.
23. Brakhage, 'The Camera-Eye', p. 215.
24. Ibid., p. 212.
25. Brakhage, in Sitney, *Visionary Film*, p. 174.
26. Brakhage, 'The Camera-Eye', p. 223.
27. Ibid.
28. Ibid., p. 222.
29. Deleuze, *Cinema 1*, p. 84.
30. The prelude and four other sections were edited over the next four years. There is an extended form of the film called *The Art of Vision* (1961–65).
31. Brakhage, *Brakhage Scrapbook*, p. 13.
32. Ibid., p. 49.
33. Ibid.
34. Sitney, *Visionary Film*, p. 181.
35. Brakhage, *Brakhage Scrapbook*, p. 175.
36. Deleuze, *Cinema 2*, p. 200.
37. Brakhage, *Brakhage Scrapbook*, p. 54.
38. Bergson, *Time and Free Will*, p. 136.
39. Brakhage, in Sitney, *Visionary Film*, p. 175.
40. Ibid.
41. http://www.english.uiuc.edu/maps/poets/m_r/olson/life.html (accessed 12 September 2006).
42. Charles Olson cited without source in Brakhage, *Scrapbook*, p. 16.
43. James, *Allegories of Cinema*, p. 38.
44. Ibid., p. 51.
45. Ibid.
46. Ibid.
47. James, *Allegories of Cinema*, p. 44.

48. Sitney, *Visionary Film*, p. 195.
49. Ibid., p. 179.
50. Youngblood, *Expanded Cinema*, p. 87.
51. Curtis, *Experimental Cinema*, p. 155.
52. Ibid., p. 157.
53. Russett, 'Contemporary Imagists', pp. 150–3.
54. Conrad, in Russett and Starr, *Experimental Animation*, p. 152.
55. Ibid., p. 151.
56. Ibid.
57. Ibid.
58. Ibid.
59. Ibid., p. 153.
60. Ibid., p. 152.
61. In the Psychedelic Film section of Manchester Kino Experimental Film Festival I curated in September 2000.
62. Post-screening discussion.
63. Powell, *Deleuze and Horror Film*, pp. 174–8.
64. James, *Allegories of Cinema*, p. 243.
65. Ibid.
66. Curtis, *Experimental Cinema*, p. 58.
67. Youngblood, *Expanded Cinema*, p. 156.
68. Deleuze, *Cinema 1*, p. 84.
69. Ibid., p. 83.
70. Ibid.
71. Ibid.
72. Rinpoche, commentary to *Bardo Thodol/The Tibetan Book of the Dead*, p. 15.
73. Ibid.
74. Ibid., p. 41.
75. Ibid., p. 43.
76. Ibid., p. 51.
77. Ibid., p. 43.
78. Whitney and Whitney, 'Audio-Visual Music', p. 85.
79. John became IBM's first artist in residence and developed 'a whole new area of conceptual form' with computer graphics. See 'Interview with John Whitney', In Youngblood, *Expanded Cinema*, p. 214.
80. Whitney and Whitney, 'Audio-Visual Music', p. 84.
81. Ibid.
82. James Whitney, in Youngblood, *Expanded Cinema*, p. 228.
83. Youngblood, *Expanded Cinema*, p. 222.
84. Zimmer, *Myths and Symbols*, pp. 141–2.
85. James Whitney in Youngblood, *Expanded Cinema*, p. 223.
86. Deleuze and Guattari, *A Thousand Plateaus*, p. 275.
87. Belson, in Youngblood, *Expanded Cinema*, p. 158.
88. Ibid.

89. http://www.bbc.co.uk/dna/h2g2/A6083633 (accessed 14 May 2006).
90. Deleuze, *Cinema 1*, p. 128.
91. James Whitney, in Youngblood, *Expanded Cinema*, pp. 227–8.
92. Vogel, *Film as Subversive Art*, p. 323.
93. Ibid.
94. Ibid.
95. Deleuze, *Cinema 1*, p. 117.
96. Ibid., p. 17.
97. Ibid.
98. Ibid.
99. Deleuze and Guattari, *A Thousand Plateaus*, p. 322.
100. Ibid.
101. Ibid.
102. Ibid.
103. Ibid.
104. Ibid., p. 277.
105. Deleuze and Guattari, *Anti-Oedipus*, p. 18.
106. Deleuze, 'Coldness and Cruelty', p. 134.
107. Deleuze, 'Re-presentation of Masoch', in *Essays Critical and Clinical*, p. 54.
108. Ibid.
109. Shaviro, *The Cinematic Body*, p. 65.
110. Ibid.
111. Ibid., p. 60.
112. Deleuze, 'Coldness and Cruelty', p. 18.
113. Ibid., p. 22.
114. Deleuze and Guattari, *What Is Philosophy?*, p. 176.
115. Iser, *The Act of Reading*.
116. Ibid., p. 129.
117. Ibid., p. 151.
118. Ibid., p. 35.
119. Deleuze and Guattari, *Anti-Oedipus*, p. 323.
120. Ibid.
121. Ibid.
122. Ibid., p. 331.
123. Ibid., p. 332.
124. Ibid., p. 333.
125. Klein, 'Notes on Some Schizoid Mechanisms', in *Envy and Gratitude*, p. 2.
126. Deleuze and Guattari, *Anti-Oedipus*, p. 45.
127. Ibid., p. 323.
128. Ibid., p. 324.
129. Ibid.
130. Ibid., p. 327.
131. Ibid., p. 326.
132. Ibid., p. 351.

133. Ibid., p. 324.
134. Ibid., p. 325.
135. Ibid., p. 251.
136. Ibid.
137. Ibid., p. 351.
138. Ibid., p. 350.
139. Ibid., p. 320.
140. James, *Allegories of Cinema*, p. 217.
141. Ibid., p. 320.
142. Deleuze and Guattari, *Anti-Oedipus*, p. 358.
143. Ibid.
144. Youngblood, *Expanded Cinema*, p. 119.
145. Ibid., p. 324.
146. Ibid., p. 325.
147. Ibid.
148. Ibid., p. 328.
149. Ibid.
150. Deleuze and Guattari, *Anti-Oedipus*, p. 19.
151. Deleuze and Guattari, *A Thousand Plateaus*, p. 276.
152. For the actual relationships underlying the fiction, see McCabe, *Performance*, pp. 45–6.
153. Deleuze and Guattari, *Anti-Oedipus*, p. 325.
154. Ibid.
155. Deleuze and Guattari, *A Thousand Plateaus*, p. 276.
156. McCabe, *Performance*, p. 56.
157. I am grateful to Peter Playdon for this detail.
158. Savage, 'Snapshots of the 60s', p. 17.
159. McCabe, *Performance*, p. 73.
160. Neville, *Hippie Hippie Shake*, p. 240. The offcut footage won a prize in an Amsterdam Pornography Festival in 1970 and Neville stole a frame for an *Oz* back cover.
161. Film poster caption beneath a split screen still of Fox and Jagger.
162. Deleuze and Guattari, *Anti-Oedipus*, p. 350.
163. Ibid.
164. White, 'Pigs and Pierrots', p. 62.
165. This Lawrentian phrase was used in, Williams, *Sex in the Head*.
166. Cameron, *Strange Days*, p. 32.
167. Ibid., p. 38.
168. Deleuze and Guattari, *Anti-Oedipus*, p. 350.
169. Ibid., p. 333.
170. Cameron, *Strange Days*, p. 32.
171. Kennedy, *Deleuze and Cinema*, p. 188.
172. Ibid., p. 180.
173. Ibid., p. 187.

174. Pisters, *The Matrix of Visual Culture*, p. 42.
175. Deleuze, *Cinema 2*, p. 265.
176. Ibid., p. 266.
177. Pisters, *The Matrix of Visual Culture*, p. 44.
178. Ibid., p. 43.
179. Cameron, *Strange Days*, p. 40.
180. Deleuze and Guattari, *Anti-Oedipus*, p. 350.
181. Ibid., p. 357.
182. Ibid.
183. Cameron, *Strange Days*, p. 38.
184. Ibid.
185. Deleuze and Guattari, *Anti-Oedipus*, p. 333.
186. Ibid., p. 113.
187. Pisters, *The Matrix of Visual Culture*, p. 43.
188. Ibid., p. 40.
189. Ibid., p. 41.

CHAPTER 4

Altered States of Time

that Deleuze is a philosopher of time means that he is a philosopher of life: an inventor of concepts that affirm life and its untimely forces of creation.[1] (Daniel W. Smith)

Sculpting in Time: Deleuze, Tarkovsky and *Stalker*

In Tarkovsky's *Stalker* (1979) three travellers enter a mysterious 'Zone' where alien activity is reported. At such a climactic moment, we might well expect clear signs of alien presence or a dramatic encounter. Despite the science-fiction promise of the plot, however, very little appears to be happening in terms of on-screen events. Instead of exciting action, we have long, slow shots that focus in close-up on the care-worn faces of three travellers deep in contemplation. They ride in silence on a rail-cart through a blurred landscape that looks like a back projection. Yet, there *is* something moving profoundly in this sequence: time itself.

The travellers' heads are depersonalised and defamiliarised by the camera's obsessive scrutiny. The influence of Eisenstein's Marxist theory of typage, by which actors were cast not as psychologically complex individuals but as representatives of a class type, can be seen here in Tarkovsky's use of the Writer (Nikolai Grinko) and the Professor (Anatoli Solonitsyn), as typical of artists and scientists. The subjective identity of the travellers is further abstracted by camera set-ups that film the backs of their heads or their profiles. These techniques make it easier for the viewer to 'become' the characters, not in a psychological sense of identification but by entering into a machinic assemblage with the camera-eye.

The camera pans slowly along the row of silent men from right to left before gliding back. Its rhythmical motion is replicated within shots too, as the three heads move in unison with the panning camera as part of its mechanism. As Deleuze suggests in his concept of the brain/screen assemblage, the viewer's own mind is implicated in such cinematic motion via the intensive movement of thought.

The moving images in Tarkovsky's film are not extensive and action-oriented, but rather they impact on and alter our awareness of time via their overt stretching out of the affective interval between action and perception in which, even in the more extensive movement-image, a 'perception of self by self' occurs.[2] In *Stalker*, external action and character interaction are suspended at times almost to zero as the movement-image is displaced by the time-image. The viewer's expectations of dramatic engagement and familiar narrative templates are likewise challenged. Like the travellers, we peer into an opaque landscape via a slowly tracking survey without clues to help us decipher it. As well as the Stalker (Aleksadr Kajdanovsky) leading the two newcomers into the Zone, viewers have their own, supplementary guide. We share affectively in the intensive movements on-screen as we input speculative mental activity in place of dramatic action.

Deleuze's 'inorganic' cinema of the time-image explores more abstract, 'philosophical and logical' film work like that of Godard which foregrounds pure description.[3] The very 'restraint' or 'thinness' of this kind of cinema reveals the object's singularity as 'inexhaustible, endlessly referring to other descriptions'.[4] It is in this self-reflexive, temporal sense that the less 'dramatic' cinema of pure optical images is richer than that of sensory-motor images.

Tarkovsky, whose theoretical writing on film influenced Deleuze's own, described his work as 'sculpting in time' and the events of *Stalker* are temporal rather than spatial.[5] Time slows down and narrative pace is suspended as the viewer also enters a different zone of time and space. The use of sepia film stock in alternation with washed-out colour further confuses the shifts between past and present. We thus travel in an interior realm of the mind, cut off from organic matter in a silent and contemplative passage through space and into duration. Without the familiar temporal or spatial landmarks of cinema, we are led into the anomalies of a time-zone and a state of consciousness that is alien indeed.

While we watch, the Writer's curiosity exhausts and he falls asleep without further information having been given to us. We have no choice but relax the tension of our own suspense and wait out his sleep. In the interim, we become aware of time's stretching out and fill in the gap with speculative thought of an affective kind. The Writer's weary face is deeply lined with the marks of time itself. The film heightens our awareness of temporal properties via such physical markers. In the cinema of the time-image, Deleuze tells us, the body is 'the developer of time, it shows time through its tirednesses and waitings'.[6] When the Writer eventually wakes and renews his curiosity, we likewise re-engage more extensively with the world.

The travellers enter the Zone almost imperceptibly, without dramatic break or special signifiers apart from an anticlimactic shift of sepia into subtle colour. Yet all is far from normal. Despite the scarcity of dramatic action or visual diversity, anomalies appear, such as the long-shot of a ship stuck in trees after a flood. These markers are not singled out for their narrative impact, but passed over once they have been subtly used to disorientate.

In the Zone, human norms are likewise suspended in the slowly moving medium of time and natural forces. Motion here is intensive rather than extensive: swaying grasses, wild flowers stirred by wind and darting insects. Sensory deprivation is a characteristic of the Zone – it is utterly silent and even the flowers lack scent, although Stalker claims that it had 'lingered for many years'. This intensive quality makes the Zone an interior plane rather than an exterior place.

The Zone is alive with the intensive, self-reflexive forces of the mind itself. A shot of the three men from behind suggests that the Zone, or a presence in it, watches them unawares, as 'the moment someone shows up, everything comes into motion'. This process parallels that of the viewer attracted to the moving images of cinema that affect us intensively. As Zone and viewer, screen and brain intersect, we are the visitors on which it depends. Together, brain and screen make an unformed hiatus of waiting, with potential for unexpected change. The onus is on us here to engage the movements of our thoughts. Leaving the movement-image behind, we enter the realm of the time-image. Having opened up altered states of cinematic time via this brief clip from *Stalker*, I will return to it later in the chapter when discussing the crystal-image.

Time is the central cog driving both the operations of the movies and the spectator's interlocked consciousness. Reels of film unwind temporally through the projector and we give up time to watching them. In return for ticket money, rather than merely using films to 'pass' time, we expect them to engineer a special temporal experience. Cinema that alters states of time can shift the gears of the mind into anomalous activity, replacing outworn patterns of thought. Deleuze and Bergson's cartography of time opens up the interior workings of temporal alterity, giving us a new set of tools to think a typology of the time-image.

For psychoanalytic models of the subject, the unconscious is a time-free zone, but its contents remain fixed by significant family events from our early life. The time of psychoanalysis is the personal history of desire, taboo and repression. When the unconscious 'speaks' to us in displaced forms, its 'messages' may sometimes be uncanny, but they have an identifiable, deep structure that can be dredged up into the present and acknowledged: by the 'talking cure' of a competent analyst (or the writing of a psychoanalytic film theorist).

Rejecting Freud in favour of Bergson and Nietzsche, Deleuze replaces the static deep structure of personal time with a dynamic, open-ended and universally applicable model. Instead of traditional scientific paradigms of solid bodies in motion, Bergson posits a relativistic universal flux. As Bogue notes, he elides movement and time by avoiding 'the visual image of bodies and the concomitant and inevitable abstraction of movement (i.e. time) from that which moves'.[7]

Bergson's view of time was a response to contemporary theories of relativity in physics. Despite his disagreement with Einstein on the nature of duration, the physicist's own theory of space-time, with time as the fourth dimension, was the pivotal ground for Bergson's distinct concept. His model of the cone, in which the present is the peak of the cone as it penetrates the 'moving plane' of images and the layers are 'sheets' of past, clearly reflects Einstein's use of cones to model the speed of light.[8]

A new map of human consciousness emerges from this major philosophical paradigm shift. Bergson's human 'living image' is a specialised part of the perpetual flow of images, a centre of indetermination with the ability to process the material flux to which it is integral. Our inherent ability to perceive the flowing dynamic of duration has the potential to empower free will.

Creative artists deploy their media's techniques to express the operations of time and crystallise them in sensuous form. Cinematic movement has a unique capacity to mimic temporal processes. It enables us think their implications via perceptual and conceptual interaction with moving images of light and colour. Basing his own cinematic explorations on Bergson's theory, Deleuze interrogates what happens on film when time is not measurable by the close translation of movement into action.

Deleuze distinguishes two kinds of time. Chronos – actual, spatialised time – is both measured and produced by the humanly invented clock. Aeon is the virtual existence of duration itself. Its transpersonal force is powered by the *élan vital* of evolving life. Chronos organises on the present moment as basic unit and measures out the action of bodies and causes. Aeon is the unlimited flow of past into future. The present instant is *never* fully present because it becomes past even as we try to grasp it.[9] Aeon, which is 'always already passed and eternally yet to come' is the '*pure empty form of time*'.[10] We travel through the layers of duration each time we seek to recall past events.

The temporal process, unseen in ordinary perception, is expressed when cinema self-reflexively foregrounds its own mechanisms, such as the synthesis of shots by editing and the rhythms set in motion by the resulting sequence. Cinema does, of course, *depict* time in one sense: the fictionalised 'present' of its diegesis. Unlike the instantaneity of televisual images, though, the film image can never actually be *in* the present moment because it never stops moving. Although what each shot *represents* can be considered as in the 'present', then, the motion in each shot is perpetual and eludes any attempt to measure it or hold it still.

This is exemplified by the use of the freeze-frame button on playback machines. In using this tool to analyse composition, *mise-en-scène* and framing, we have abstracted them from their context to produce an artificially static image. Deleuze asserts the cinematic image as 'ensemble of time relations from the present which merely flows', and argues that it makes temporal relations 'sensible and visible'.[11] Movies enable us to become consciousness of duration in ourselves as part of the film assemblage.

Cinema uniquely catalyses altered states of time. For Deleuze, the self-reflexive films of such directors as Tarkovsky, Herzog and Yasujiro Ozu offer powerful versions of the 'direct' time-image. In his philosophical version of cinema history, the movement-image has long been the dominant form, whereas the time-image is still emergent. Historically, it appears post–Second World War in the stylistic experiments of Italian neo-realism. Deleuze is less concerned with neo-realism *as* a style than with its desire to move beyond the replication of the 'real' into the thought processes stimulated *by* the style. His concern is to 'turn from exteriority or extensiveness in space toward a genesis in mental relations or time'.[12] His examples exhibit the workings of time by defamiliarisation techniques that challenge temporal expectations.

The newer cinema disrupts the conventional relationship of sound and vision so that the soundtrack no longer arises naturally from the image content. In such films as Alain Resnais's *Hiroshima, Mon Amour* (1959) and *Last Year at Marienbad* (1960) the movement-image is superseded by a cinema that expresses time. No longer derived from movement, time now 'appears in itself and gives rise to *false movements*'.[13] In *Last Year at Marienbad*, although several virtual pasts coexist, none of them might have ever actually happened. The effect of this is to refute conventional plot linearity. In films like these, a mystery is not gradually solved en route to a neatly tied-up ending, but the film's world remains mysteriously opaque.

Deleuze asserts that particular films offer a more contemplative cinematic experience. Despite his distinction of two main types of cinematic image, *all* film images inevitably work in the medium of time in motion. The interface of the movement-image and the time-image is permeable and fluid. Movement is *always* in time, and one force does not function without the other. All film images inherently destabilise time by their modulations of past, present and future. While accepting that some films foreground the workings of time more self-consciously, I contend that many types of film, including more mainstream generic examples excluded from Deleuze's canon, reveal and reflect on temporality. Deleuze's time-image evolved from Bergson's duration-based theories, which I consider more closely at this point.

Bergson's Time: Movement and Duration

The multifaceted concept of duration develops across Bergson's work. It is manifest as the free act in *Time and Free Will*, memory and the virtual past in *Matter and Memory* and the evolving vital impetus of *élan vital* in *Creative Evolution*.[14] In *Matter and Memory*, Bergson explicates duration by comparison with the familiar impact of sensation on consciousness.

We are powerless to resist the impact of intense sensory stimuli. Producing 'irresistible' physical reflex movements, they can briefly dissolve our subjective personality. Reflecting on such experience, we perceive an inner multiplicity of quality, not quantity. Multiple states of consciousness interpenetrate. Even in the simplest, 'the whole soul can be reflected'.[15] To conscious perception, then, inner duration appears as a 'melting of states of consciousness into one another, and the gradual growth of the ego'.[16]

States of consciousness, being intensive rather than extensive, are not external to each other. If we locate them spatially rather than temporally, they have mistakenly been externalised. From this process, Bergson draws his frequently made distinction between duration and spatialised time. To reflect on, and communicate about, the fluid process of consciousness, we are inevitably compelled to freeze its intensive flux into discrete thoughts socially extended into language.

By distinguishing and separating its intermeshed states, we make time into a kind of space, which leads to its outward extension. States are thus laid out side by side to help us perceive them simultaneously. In this way, we 'project time into space' and erroneously extend duration so that succession becomes 'a continuous line or a chain, the parts of which touch without penetrating one another'.[17] In order to give symbolic form to our mental states, this method shifts duration into the false simultaneity of spatialised time.

The fluid nature of duration eludes the freezing, splitting and structuring processes of the very language we need to communicate about it to others. Duration thus appears as 'confused, ever changing, and inexpressible, because language cannot get hold of it without arresting its mobility or fit it into its commonplace forms'.[18] Adapting duration to socio–linguistic demands, the self is 'refracted and thereby broken to pieces'.[19] The linguistic version of duration is limited to 'the shadow of the self projected into homogenous space'.[20] By adapting consciousness to fit everyday frameworks, then, we lose contact with its more intensive levels.

A similar illusion is produced if we perceive movement by confusing it with space. By falsely eliding motion with the divisibility of the space it passes through, we forget that we can 'divide an *object*, but not an *act*'.[21] This error is a kind of 'endosmosis, an intermingling of the purely intensive sensation of mobility with the extensive representation of the space traversed'.[22] Duration cannot be sliced, partitioned or cut up into pieces because it partakes of indivisible, universal flux. Mixing past and future, the moment passes even as we try to grasp it. Making way for a new present, it is already past.

For Deleuze, the past 'does not follow the present that it is no longer, it coexists with the present it was'.[23] This coexistence shapes his insistence that the cinematic image is never actually present.[24] Between perception and action, the affective, temporal interval remains. Despite footage being chopped into discrete shots and edited together, no shot, even a freeze-frame, can ever be still. All cinematic images share the perpetual motion of images in duration. Deleuze uses the properties of the cinema to think the unison of movement and time, augmenting his case by citing Tarkovsky's own intent to reveal the 'pressure of time' in each shot.[25]

So how can we perceive the nature of duration more effectively? Bergson argues that by stepping outside everyday modes of thought, the 'deeper' self intuits fluid and multiple states of consciousness in duration's flow. He asserts that the insights of 'immediate intuition' show us 'motion within duration, and duration outside space'.[26] By intensive focus on these states, we will, in Bergson's lyrical simile, see them 'melt into one another like the crystals of a snowflake when touched for some time with the finger'.[27] Distinction disguises underlying cohesion. Duration is seamless, the continuum of past, present and future. If we turn time into space, then, we impose an illusory division on its unity.

For Bergson, the nature of duration is revealed most effectively by art. Aesthetic absorption triggers intensive affective vibrations in consciousness. Duration, like music, is 'an indivisible multiplicity changing qualitatively in an ongoing movement'.[28] It conjoins in an organic whole, as 'when we recall the notes of a tune, melting, so to speak, into one another'.[29] Although linguistic limitations offer only the 'shadow' of duration, a skilled novelist such as Marcel Proust is able to shape language to reflect something of its quality. Bergson cites his potent evocations of memory's 'search for lost times'. Describing an 'infinite permeation of a thousand different impressions which have already ceased to exist the instant they are named', writers like Proust can bring us 'back into our own presence' to enable recollection of the enduring past.[30]

In order to *endure*, consciousness is not entirely absorbed in the passing moment and retains awareness of its former states. Time passes, but time continues. Memory, by returning the past to the present of consciousness, allows the ego to experience 'full, living, potential' in the 'pure hetero-geneity'.[31] Pure duration is 'the form which the succession of our conscious states assumes when our ego lets itself *live*, when it refrains from separating its present state from its former states'.[32] The reanimated past is not an escape route from the demands of the present. Alive to the rich complexity of time, we can access the affirmative potential of becoming.

Memory, like the flux of matter and our own perception, is image-dependent. Experiences and perceptions are shot through with memory. Outstanding memories form 'shining points round which the others form a vague nebulosity'.[33] If we actualise these virtual focal points, they can reproduce their corresponding affects in us. A powerful sense impression once experienced is thus reanimated in the virtual reality of a 'coloured and living image' that reveals it to memory.[34] Although memory 'imitates' perception as it returns from duration 'like a condensing cloud', its 'original virtuality' distinguishes it from the present.[35] To experience the potency of duration, we must 'frankly place ourselves within it'.[36]

Despite psychoanalysis's very different paradigm of personal psychic history, I find some commonality between Bergson's account here and Lacan's concept of barred plentitude.[37] Bergson likewise seems to consider duration as a primal state of fulfilment 'lost' to us via linguistic articulation. Despite the presence of such idealising tendencies, Bergson's duration offers both founding concepts and motivation to Deleuze's thinking about time and movement in cinema.

Deleuze's Time-Image

Deleuze applies Bergson's distinction of linear time and duration to the cinematic process. Working in time as its basic medium, it reveals temporal relations to the senses and mind as intensive movements within and between shots. Although the time-image foregrounds temporality, the movement-image also offers each shot as a 'mobile section' of time. A shot, as 'temporal perspective or a modulation', is edited with others in the 'variable, continuous, temporal mould' of a sequence.[38]

A movement-image sequence can also express 'time itself as perspective or relief' and thus 'takes on the power to contract or dilate, as movement takes on the power to slow down or accelerate'.[39] In the movement-image, Deleuze identifies two temporal types: 'time as a whole, as a great circle or spiral, which draws together the set of movement in the universe'[40] is distinct from 'time as an interval, which indicates the smallest movement or action'.[41]

Nietzsche's eternal return combines with Bergson's duration here in Deleuze's 'spiral open at both ends, the immensity of past and future'.[42] If 'infinitely dilated, the present would become the whole itself. Infinitely contracted, the whole would happen in the interval'.[43] The accelerated, variable present lies in the interval, the impact of which exceeds the gap between shots edited together, or the longer temporal ellipse used to exemplify it.

In Dreyer's *The Passion of Joan of Arc* (1927) Joan's 'internal' spiritual time is distinct both from the historical time taken by her trial and the running time of the film. The present moment is a fluid amalgam of past, present and future. Dreyer uses extreme facial close-ups to convey the distinct qualities of Joan's dual physical and metaphysical time. Two presents, one established and the other perpetually arriving, compound 'the same event but one part of it is profoundly realised in a state of things, while the other is all the more irreducible to all realisation'.[44] Deleuze's interpretation recalls Bergson's elusive present and everlasting duration.

Although some films in the movement-image category use framing, lighting and temporal overlay to make time qualitative, they are still driven by sensory-motor action-images and a broadly linear plot. Their temporal scheme thus remains dual, with the two kinds of time in conflict. Postwar art cinema moved further away from the action image to work 'beyond' movement via the pure opsigns, sonsigns and tactisigns of the time-image.

Pivotal to cinema's philosophical resonance, the time-image provides a more metaphysical experience of duration. Rejecting cliché, this challenging cinema makes 'powerful and direct revelations' via the time-image (chronosigns), the readable image (lectosigns) and the thinking image (noosigns) equivalent to narration, description and thought.[45]

We can 'read' the impact of these innovative images. The work of American semiologist Charles Sanders Pierce informs Deleuze's concept of reading a film, and the term 'lectosign' is derived from the Stoic use of *lekton*: what the image expresses. This is distinct from the film semiology that identifies the cultural and symbolic meaning of representational signs and their codes.[46] Deleuze's reading refers not to the semantic template of linguistics as inappropriately applied to film, but to conceptualisation via the encounter with visual and sound images.

In a film reading, lectosigns are inseparable from chronosigns, which force us to read so many symptoms in the image, that is, to treat the optical and sound image like something that is also readable. Not only the optical and the sound, but also the present and the past, and the here and the elsewhere, constitute internal elements and relations which must be deciphered, and can be understood only in a progression analogous to a reading.[47]

The lectosign makes the descriptive content of the image multifaceted or 'crystalline' by adding supplementary dimensions.

The chronosign is a 'purer' form of image, gravitating away from its referent towards a pure optical and sound situation. Via their distance from sensory-motor actions, chronosigns produce a more transcendent temporal perception. In their direct presentation of time, rather than its indirect implication in the gaps and fissures of the movement-image, they are closer to Bergsonian duration. Chronosigns form three types: 'points of present', 'sheets of past' and the series. In Rodowick's definition, the series is the 'transformation of states, qualities, concepts, or identities' across a series of images.[48]

Noosigns appear when movement undergoes the qualitative shift from spatial extension to intensive thought. They are located in the autonomous motion of camera-consciousness, independent of characters. The 'mental connections' of the independent camera include 'questioning, responding, objecting, provoking, theorematising, hypothesising, experimenting, in accordance with the open list of logical conjunctions ("or", "therefore", "if", "because", "actually", "although . . .") or in accordance with the functions of thought'.[49] Hitchcock's autonomous camera expresses, stimulates and extends human mental processes.

Rather than being the Cartesian 'I' who thinks as a subjective mind superior to externalised objects of thought, the brain as 'spiritual automaton' is itself an image. The 'organic' or 'kinetic' movement-image prefers a linear, sensory-motor and 'naturalised' diegesis. In its more self-conscious forms, the movement-image can shock us into thought. In Eisenstein's montage, for example, the dynamic collision of two disparate images produces a revolutionary idea as their third term (thesis – antithesis=synthesis). Truth and falsehood are clearly distinguished as binaries in order to produce a more profound understanding of the truth. Rather than this being limited by the film's ending, it continues to work in the brain.

Thought processes in the time-image are distinct from those of the movement-image, which retain sensory-motor extension. In seeking to 'augment our powers of thought through assisting our knowledge of these powers', the time-image is overtly and self-consciously cerebral.[50] In Deleuze's Bergsonian scheme, brain is not distinct from world, but a specialised, yet integral part of the universal flux of images. Corresponding more closely to mental processes than the movement-image, the time-image is multifaceted and open-ended, with a contingent and provisional perspective on truth.

Rather than seeking to capture a profilmic, objective world in order to 'tell' us a story, the time-image is more interested in foregrounding stylistic techniques to challenge familiar patterns of thought. By a deliberate use of opsigns and sonsigns, shifts of consciousness are engineered in us. Whether 'chronic' or 'crystalline', then, the time-image produces a more self-consciously philosophical type of cinema. The polarities of the crystal image are expressed with particular force in Werner Herzog's film *Heart of Glass* (1977).

Entrancing Time: The Crystal-Image and Altered States in *Heart of Glass*

Film is not analysis, it is the agitation of the mind. (Werner Herzog)[51]

The search for the alchemical heart and secret, for the red crystal, is inseparable from the search for cosmic limits. (Gilles Deleuze)[52]

It is hypnosis that reveals thought to itself. (Gilles Deleuze)[53]

Werner Herzog literally wanted to entrance the audience of his film *Heart of Glass*. The director originally planned to appear in a prologue, make hypnotic passes to put viewers in a trance state, then reappear at the end to bring them back to waking consciousness. Rejecting this as 'unethical', he limited his actual trance-induction to the actors. They all performed under hypnosis, apart from Hias (Josef Bierbichler), the Bavarian herdsman/seer, and the glassblowers filmed at their work. Even without his literally hypnotic prologue, I will argue that the aesthetic techniques of Herzog's film and their manipulation of the viewer's sensory and mental engagement produce shifts of consciousness. The somnambulistic movements and glassy stares of the actors intensify perceptual disorientation and blocks identification. With its long-held shots of clouds and swirling soft-focus mist as well as the unnerving quality of acting, the film induces a trance-like state that suspends the linear sense of time and opens up to duration.

Deleuze asserts that in cerebral and 'poetic' styles of postwar cinema, consensual time and space are modified, as customary perception of them becomes fluid. Non-linear time and spatial distortion can thus undermine conventional thought patterns. Here, I present *Heart of Glass* as a specific type of time-image, the crystal-image, which alters states of cinematic time. I want discover why Deleuze, whose references to *Heart of Glass* are tantalisingly brief, claims that it presents the 'greatest crystal-images in the history of cinema'.[54] To contextualise my discussion, I will outline Deleuze's concept of the crystal-image then move on to interweave Herzog's film aesthetics and Deleuze/Bergsonian temporal theories.

The Crystal-Image

Deleuze's crystal-image is rooted in Bergson's dual model of actual and virtual in *Matter and Memory* which maps concentric circuits of present and past.[55] Like a mirror reflection and its material stimulus, the present moment has two sides contemporaneously: its actual, physical extension and its virtual side that is already part of duration.[56] The process of remembering seeks to actualise the virtual via a recollection-image. In order to find this, memory searches through ever-wider circuits of duration made up of layers of the past by 'a thousand repetitions of our psychic life' that move ever further back from the ongoing present.[57]

When a recollection-image surfaces into consciousness, it retains two sides: actual and virtual. Like a mirror-image or a double, they coalesce.[58] For Deleuze, 'the real object is reflected in a mirror-image as in the virtual object which, from its side and simultaneously, envelops the real'.[59] Crystalline structures 'by nature double', such as mirrors, are 'consolidates' of actual and virtual'.[60] They are an objective correlative of what Deleuze calls the 'indiscernibility' of real and imaginary, present and past, actual and virtual.[61] Such indiscernibility is not an imaginary projection, but an inherent property of crystalline substances.

Deleuze uses Bergson's circuitry model to posit the operations of opsigns and sonsigns. He argues that such images, when cut off from their motor extension, form large circuits linking up to 'recollection-images, dream-images and world-images'.[62] The key, or, to use Herzog's own image as Deleuze does, the 'heart' of the opsign, is a point on the smallest internal circuit as its 'true genetic element', the crystal-image.[63] This is manifest when 'the actual optical image crystallises with *its own* virtual image' and the larger circuits of opsign compositions are, to continue the mirror figure, 'nothing other than slivers of crystal-images'.[64]

In the crystal-image, the actual and the virtual remain distinct. However small the circuit becomes, it retains discernible elements of each that 'undergo a process of continual exchange' of relative characteristics.[65] When the virtual is actualised, it 'becomes visible and limpid, as in the mirror or the solidity of finished crystal. But the actual image becomes virtual in its turn, referred elsewhere, invisible, opaque, shadowy, like a crystal barely dislodged from the earth'.[66] What Deleuze calls the 'crystalline circuit' involves three figures, 'the actual and the virtual (or the two mirrors face to face); the limpid and the opaque; the seed and the environment'.[67] Both Deleuze and Bergson use the irreducibility of actual and virtual as a philosophical tool to explore the indivisible continuum of time and our perception of it.

Cinematic expression operates a crystal circuitry in the time-image. The seed is the virtual image that causes an amorphous environment to crystallise, but when the seed is an actual image, that virtual environment requires the inherent structural potential to become crystalline. Deleuze's chief example of this is the shattered glass snowstorm from Orson Welles's *Citizen Kane* (1941). When the 'crystal' breaks, we have a special-effect close-up of gusts of snow that seem to come towards us, 'to impregnate the environment that we will discover', yet we do not know at this point whether the 'actual environment enjoys the corresponding virtuality'.[68] The next shot reveals Kane as a boy playing in real snow in the past world of childhood, a recollection-image that duration has opened up, perhaps as a consolation to the dying man. Deleuze also speculates whether the figure of the crystalline circuit helps us 'understand the splendour of the images in Herzog's *Heart of Glass*, and the film's double aspect', a question I return to later.[69]

Agitation of the Mind

Like Deleuze, Herzog asserts the power of cinema to offer a special and challenging mental experience. For the director, 'film is not analysis, it is the agitation of the mind'.[70] At this stage in our discussion, I will identify temporal techniques used in the opening sequence of *Heart of Glass* to alter the mental templates of spectators and engage us in the role of seer as brain and screen become one.

The film deploys trance-induction from outset by demanding intense concentration. The ground of the title sequence is a long-shot that could be a fixed still, apart from the almost imperceptible shifts of cattle feeding in a misty landscape. A static human figure sits with his back to the camera, blocking any view of his face and attendant identification. In the film, close-ups, which might have produced an unwanted effect of subjective empathy, are replaced by mid- or long-shots that refute this and distance us emotionally from the characters. This enables us to engage more directly in the meditative mode ourselves.

Yet the very concept of 'ourselves' is, of course, problematised in the time-image. Neither Deleuze nor Bergson works with a psychological model of subjectivity. According to Deleuze, for Bergson, 'the only sub-jectivity is time, non-chronological time grasped in its foundation, and it is we who are internal to time, not the other way round'.[71] For both philosophers, consciousness rather than personality *is* time. The temporal dynamics of art offer insight into the operations of the embodied mind as a 'centre of indetermination' amid the flow of time-images in perpetual motion.

When the man in the opening sequence finally turns to face the camera in medium shot, his gaze is unfocused. Hias, the herdsman (Josef Bierbichler), is a seer who looks off-frame or through images to contem-plate duration's elsewhere. Hias is a suitable medium for duration because of his own crystalline quality of transparency, later characterised by the deranged factory-owner Huttenbesitzer (Stefan Güttler) as a 'heart of glass'. Deleuze describes such characters trapped in the disjointed world of the time-image as 'pure seers [. . .] caught in certain pure optical and sound situations'.[72] They

> no longer exist except in the interval of the moment, and do not even have the con-solation of the sublime, which would connect them to matter or would gain control of the spirit for them. They are rather given over to something intolerable.[73]

Like Bergson and Deleuze, Hias gazes into the intolerable depths of 'time's abyss'.[74]

Time itself informs the contents of the herdsman's visions, and the director sets out to produce a similarly slow-motion experience of time on screen. Dramatic action is suspended and the engaged viewer is likewise compelled to adopt the seer's depersonalised gaze as images unroll in this entrancingly slow opening take that sets the pace for the rest of the film. Time is insistently present in each shot and the film forces us into con-sciousness of its unfolding.

Hias is no longer present even as a distanced intermediary in the ensuing shots. Rather, his vision is directly revealed to us in sublime images, accom-panied by the elevating strains of a Wagner-style horn melody. A panoramic sky, bordered only by the edges of the frame, and a low mist-swathed row of pines fail to contain the vastness of its grandeur. Fast-motion cinematography speeds up the swirling of the fog above the river. It makes it flow at the river's own pace as the gaseous element adopts aqueous characteristics. Time-lapse cinematography overtly displays the camera's ability to distort time. These shots make their own time by forcing the pace of nature into technological motion.

The film so far has been non-verbal, but at this point, Hias's voice-over begins his apocalyptic commentary to accompany images of avalanche and the lava-like bubbling of a sea of mud. His back remains turned to us to maintain the impersonal quality of prophesies that far exceed personal history. He pronounces that 'time will tumble and then the earth'. It is not only the avalanche and the earth itself that 'tumbles, falls, crumbles and collapses', but the rational, everyday consciousness of the hypnotised spectator.

In voice-over, Hias verbally describes his technique of self-hypnosis. He focuses on the centre of the cataract until 'a vertigo seizes upon' him and 'everything becomes light' as he flies upwards. Simultaneously, we share this experience as we also focus on the close-up image of falling water. A grainy lens filter blurs the water to offer us the reflection-image of elemental force rather than a reflective human face as our direct sharing of Hias's vision intensifies. Light further bleaches out the details of soft-focus grey and white images. A textured effect with a tactile quality is produced in a tactisign like fabric woven together on the loom of Time itself. The visionary world of cloud and mist closes in to sharper focus. A disorienting upward pan reveals a bridge across a ravine as beams of light cut through the shadow and bleach out details of the rocks below. When Hias again faces camera, his inner-directed gaze still looks out beyond the frame into duration's elusive elsewhere.

Crystal and Cloud

Hias predicts the end of a narrow world-vision that exceeds the locale of his village and its limited affairs, despite its temporary focus there. The narrative concerns a recently dead master glassmaker who has taken the secret formula for ruby glass, revealed by a mysterious traveller, with him to the grave. Without its industrial and creative *raison d'être*, the village falls under enchantment as though itself trapped within a crystal world. The crystalline nature of the diegesis is emphasised by sharp focus and the hyper-real brightness of its colours. This limpid, pristine quality is at the opposite pole to Hias's opaque visionary world of mist, yet it forms its complement. In the factory, aimless workers are 'sleepwalkers' who move in a dreamlike lethargy, eyes glazed and speech slurred. The only source of animation is the elemental force of their furnace fire with its scarlet flicker and roar.

Huttenbesitzer is a monomaniacal aesthete, obsessed by glass within glass, his collection shut away in a transparent case. The glass has malign magical force, power *in potentia*, like a seed crystal itself. The ruby of the goblets and carafes doubles in potency when filled with red wine, yet it craves a more intense red. Concealed in a darkened room, it only emits a soft red glow at first. When the young servant, Ludmilla, opens the cabinet to clean it and visualises 'a whole town made of glass', however, the light grows brighter, its vampiric force awakened in anticipation of her virgin's blood.

Having lost his protective talisman against time and change, the Factory Master is exposed to 'the evil of the universe'. In his baroque chapel, he prays not to God but to the spirit of glass. He treats his collection like a magical fetish, making passes over his goblets as he seeks to increase his own feeble energy. A close-up reveals a heart etched into the red glass of a goblet, linked to his own life-force and that of the village.

Deleuze applies Bergson's cone template to the film's contrasting worlds: the world of the crystal (the glass–obsessed village) and Hias's cloud world. Deleuze signals their interdependency, suggesting that 'the search for the alchemical heart and secret, for the red crystal, is inseparable from the search for cosmic limits'.[75] The end of the crystal world is necessary because 'crystalline perfection lets no outside subsist'.[76] Hias's apocalyptic vision also heralds the energy of a fresh beginning as 'like the submerged Atlantis, the earth rises out of the waters'.

At the end of the film, in an inexplicable spatial and temporal shift from the village to an isolated rocky island, a new world freed from the shattered crystal is imagined. A group of islanders, doubting the earth is flat, set sail to quest for a new land. Despite their 'pathetic and senseless' attempt, the energy of the crystal is now unbound as sea birds wheel across the vastness of the sky and the sea swell. Deleuze asserts that when the crystal-image breaks, 'a new Real will come out beyond the actual and the virtual'.[77] The end of the then-known order foreseen by Hias will produce a further new world in the actuality of history: the social and political upheaval of the industrial revolution and the future of Germany.

Herzog's intended experiment with hypnotic passes would have triggered interesting spectatorial responses, but his cinematic equivalent in *Heart of Glass* possesses an entrancing force of its own. Herzog's hypnotic cinematography uniquely expresses the opaque, virtual world and the limpid sharpness of actualisation as the distinct but contiguous processes of time and our human perception of it. In the final shot of the film, the seabirds blur into imperceptibility, flying faster than the film speed or the moving camera can follow. We also lose sight of the tiny boat, swallowed up by the ocean swell, as Herzog signals the limits of what film technology can capture. Like Deleuze, he insists that his intended 'agitation of the mind' should not be limited to the virtual world of the screen, but should be actualised in the spectator. Like *Heart of Glass*, *Stalker* offers an exemplary 'crystallised space' for Deleuze and we will resume our analysis of Tarkovsky's film, in some respects complementary to Herzog's own, very different work.[78]

Liquid Crystal: *Stalker*

liquid crystal which keeps its secret (Deleuze)[79]

Herzog's crystal is brittle glass and swirling mist, whereas Tarkovsky's world is liquid crystal. *Stalker* sets out to 'sculpture in time' by long, contemplative takes that induce metaphysical dimensions as the viewer directly experiences the slow passage of time. For 'time and its passing' to be powerfully revealed, the director intends it to be 'as if the whole film had been made in a single shot'.[80] To achieve this, plot details and 'external effects' are kept to a minimum and there is no time lapse between shots. Along with a strongly formulated central idea and clearly defined action at a local level, these techniques ensure that everything will 'reverberate in response to the dominant note: things, landscapes, actors' intonations'.[81] The 'dominant note' or 'diagrammatic component' of *Stalker* is the 'liquid crystal' time-image produced by the qualitative impact of light on water.

Like Deleuze, Tarkovsky contends that cinematography and editing act to induce a crucial temporal experience. What the viewer seeks in the cinema, Tarkovsky argues, is 'time lost or spent or not yet had. [S]He goes there for living experience'.[82] The technical capacities of cinema to modify our customary sense of time are uniquely placed to provide this because 'cinema, like no other art, widens, enhances and concentrates a person's experience'.[83] The temporal alterations in his films enhance the spectator's awareness of time's qualities and make time feel significantly longer.

Deleuze identifies the 'liquid' mode of perception in the earlier work of French directors Jean Renoir and Jean Vigo. Their images of water combine with fluid camera movements to produce the *reume* of liquid perception in a Bergsonian 'flowing-matter'.[84] Tarkovsky's method takes 'various time-pressures, which we could designate metaphorically as brook, spate, river, waterfall, ocean', and joins them together to engender as a 'newly formed entity' a special sense of time.[85] His cinema also uses water literally, as puddles, pools, lakes or cascades, to express temporal 'rhythmic design'.[86] Rather than the dramatic necessity of canals and the sea in Vigo's tale of life on a barge or Renoir's fast-flowing river where the lovers' boats sail, Tarkovsky's water is not a plot device, but nevertheless remains integral to his film's temporal qualities. His water both reflects and refracts light. The play of light and colour produces a variety of responses, ranging from tactile discomfort to meditative calm.

In the nostalgic sepia-tinted film stock that expresses durational overlay, Stalker takes time away from his companions for spiritual reflection. The disused factory well he prays at, polluted by oil that skins over its surface, produces a particular visual and temporal effect. The oil slows the water's natural motion down to make it unnaturally smooth and enhances its numinous impact. Like the sea of *Solaris* (1972), it pulsates and seems sentient, animated by a non-organic life-force. The circle of bright water in a dark well shaft, stirred by shimmering ripples and droplets in response to Stalker's supplication, has a lunar quality. Its properties of becoming are a physical correlative to his prayer that his companions become 'helpless like children', because 'hardness and strength are death's companions. Pliancy and weakness are expressions of the freshness of being, because what is hard will never win'. He hopes the others can share in his own state of fluid receptivity.

Tarkovsky's most significant use of water surrounds Stalker's vision or dream. In an unnerving spatio-temporal loop, Stalker and the Writer return to watery terrain they have just left, near a breach in the factory wall down which a torrent cascades. This place offered them temporary respite, but Stalker insists that it is time to move on, because 'things change here every minute'. When they leave, the embers of a fire by the water mysteriously ignite in an unnatural elemental mix. Alone on screen, it glows and fades with the gusts of wind that suggests the place and its objects are sentient presences responsive to change.

A tracking shot across the frame from the fire at the left reaches a pool of still, transparent water on the right, then travels back before entering the pool to reveal physical fragments of Stalker's personal memories, remnants of his previous trips to the Zone as well as more general human debris. The camera glides across these submerged objects that indicate times past: a rusted machine-gun, broken hypodermic needles and the torn pages of a calendar. Although clock time stops for people at the end of their personal time-line, the film powerfully implies that duration moves ever onward like a flowing current.

The travellers rest on mossy rocks that rise from the ubiquitous water. It saturates their clothes so that they 'become water' themselves. Stalker lies prone, partly immersed, embracing the Zone with abandon. In contrast, the bodies of the Writer and the Professor retain solid and uncompromising outlines. Significantly, they seek out the driest ground in this wet green space, just as they maintain attitudes of emotional aloofness and mental scepticism. The camera glides away from the ephemeral concerns of their argument (art versus science) to resume Stalker's vision of the 'flowing waters' of duration where machine guns, a bandage, the broken mechanism of a clock, a metal spring and a page from a calendar are material markers of mutability. Floor tiles from the factory and a single woollen glove are inexplicable remnants of attempts to destroy the Zone or to impose a human order upon it. Light flickers on ripples over mud and then an upward pan closes in on the sleeping Stalker's hand, dipped into the water. The vertically tracking camera comes full circle. In terms of Bergson's cone, it has explored one layer of past time and completed one cycle of memory.

The scene cuts back to the Writer and the Professor's temporary agreement: that music is a wordless art form with powerful emotional and spiritual affects. As they converse, the camera tracks up from rocks with their bright green moss to the grey flat expanse of the lake and beyond, to mist-shrouded, soft-focus trees. The featureless, watery space lends the abstract, metaphysical quality of music itself to their discourse and the act of recollecting the power of art brings brief respite to their suffering.

Near the end of the journey, aqueous effects again convey spiritual intensity and the limits of human mental capacity. After a physical struggle between the three men, the Professor, who secretly planned to blow up the Zone, discards the bomb in a pool on the factory floor. Each man is overwhelmed by intense despair at the failure of his personal hope. Yet, this draws them together physically by the water. A smooth tracking shot backs away from the signs of their grief and moves out into the silent, cavernous space of the chamber.

The camera, an embodiment of contemplative thought, is freed from the struggle of human emotions and shares its calm detachment with the viewer. Colour drains out of the world in the renewal of sepia tones that return to the virtual realm of duration and memory. Yet the tiles still glow with a soft golden light under the water. This dull gold spreads to the men and gilds them with its warmth, inducing a sense of comfort as their personal, ego-driven struggles are diminished in the larger process of time and change.

A curtain of rain falls, its redemptive and cleansing properties transforming the gold light quality to cool silver, as motion returns to the water's surface in glinting ripples. As the travellers gaze out across the pool, the rumble of distant thunder indicates the workings of a non-human order. The rain eases off, leaving a few silver sparkles of turbulence growing calm. Under water, fish swim curiously to the dark, bloodlike stain of oil that spreads from the discarded bomb. The submarine world, littered with human debris, expresses in miniature how the present moment's effluvia are absorbed into the layers of duration.

For Deleuze, water is the diagrammatic component of Tarkovsky's time-image *oeuvre*. The director's quest, in which 'the crystal turns in on itself, like a homing device', is stymied by an overwhelmingly opaque environment.[87] This quality of opacity is expressed through a totalising wetness in which 'the seed seems to be frozen in these sodden, washed and heavily translucent images, with their sometimes bluish, sometimes brown surfaces'.[88] Nature does not offer redemption in films like *Mirror* (1974), where 'the green environment seems, in the rain, to be unable to go beyond the condition of a liquid crystal which keeps its secret'.[89] Total saturation, produced by the rains 'that provide a rhythm for each film', repeats the question 'what burning bush, what fire, what soul, what sponge will staunch this earth?'[90] For Deleuze, the saturated environment that prevents Tarkovsky's crystal seed from clarification is the opacity of Russia itself.

To counter Deleuze's overwhelmingly pessimistic slant on Tarkovsky's crystalline properties, I offer the scenes above. In the Stalker's dream, water escapes opacity to become translucent in a potent cinematic expression of spiritual insight. Despite, or possibly because of its roots in human failure, it exhilarates us via the clarity of a vision at once sensory and metaphysical. Having considered the operations of the time-image in two 'classic' art house films already mentioned by Deleuze, I want to shift focus to a recent, more formally conventional film that drew wider critical acclaim than the cult following it initially targeted. Rather than focusing on the crystal-image, I will explore the temporally 'incompossible worlds' of an ostensibly movement-image film, *Donnie Darko* (Richard Kelly, 2001).

Donnie Darko: Incompossible Worlds

undecidable alternatives between circles of past, *inextricable differences* between peaks of present.[91] (Deleuze)

You have to have the vessel and the portal. And the vessel can be anything. (*Donnie Darko*)

At the end of *Donnie Darko*, time winds back to when the story began. This time round, Donnie (Jake Gyllenhall), angst-ridden high-school student as 'seer', rejects the time-line we have just assumed was the 'real' film narrative. In a free act, Donnie accepts his own death rather than being led to safety by Frank, his schizoid, demonic alter ego. As the film closes, Donnie chooses to stay in his bed in full consciousness of what is about to happen. When a jet explodes and the engine falls onto his room, crushing him, he dies with a smile on his face. I start at the end because in *Donnie Darko*, despite the sensory-motor links of its movement-image narration, the line between past, present and future becomes indiscernible.

I approach the temporal alterities of Kelly's film via Deleuze's 'incompossible worlds'. This is his cinematic adaptation of Leibnitz's philosophical solution to the contradictions of free will and predestination. Leibnitz, in his model of the crystal pyramid, posits a layered series of contingent futures within the 'simultaneity of all possible worlds'.[92] Deleuze deploys this concept to account for the anomalies of time and space in the New Cinema and the contradictions they raise by undermining notions of reality and truth. Rather than the one revealed truth of mainstream cinema, these more problematic films present a series of incompossible worlds.

In the work of Robbe-Grillet with Alain Resnais, such as *Last Year at Marienbad*, successively arranged presents are replaced by the 'simultaneity of a present of past, a present of present and a present of future, which make time frightening and inexplicable'.[93] These implicated, mixed presents are 'revived, contradicted, obliterated, substituted, re-created, fork and return'.[94] In this more 'genuine' use of the time-image, the narrativity of the movement-image is transformed because all successive action is abstracted from it. The narration comprises different presents for different characters. Although each is plausible in its own terms, they become incompossible when linked together so that 'the inexplicable is therefore maintained and created'.[95]

In Buñuel's late films, such as *The Discreet Charm of the Bourgeoisie* (1972) a further type of direct time-image is produced, featuring the simultaneous 'plurality' of worlds.[96] Here, the same events are not uniquely experienced in the present by different characters, as with Robbe-Grillet, but Buñuel gives us 'one and the same event in different objective worlds, all implicated in the event, inexplicable universe'.[97] Deleuze's discussion of the direct time-image in the work of Robbe-Grillet/Resnais and Buñuel sheds light on the split-off times of Kelly's very different film.

Deflecting Time's Arrow

Donnie Darko literalises temporal conundrums via the insights of modern physics, packaging complex issues in the accessible form of a predominantly sensory-motor movement-image movie. Like Bergson in his productive exchanges with Einstein, Deleuze draws on the paradigm of relativity to elucidate temporality. He uses Buñuel's cinema to exemplify a 'sidereal time, a system of relativity, where the characters would be not so much human as planetary, and the accents not so much subjective as astronomical' in the universe's multiple worlds.[98] In this 'pluralist cosmology', where coexistent worlds only *appear* to be one and the same, the same event is 'played out [. . .] in incompatible versions'.[99]

Donnie's physics teacher, Dr Monitoff (Noah Wyle), seeks to answer his troubled student's questions about time travel. Monitoff refers to Stephen Hawking's book *A Brief History of Time* (1988) and discusses the scientist's theory of wormholes, which could 'provide a short cut for jumping between two distant regions of space-time'.[100] One route for such a short cut would be an Einstein-Rosen Bridge, a theory produced by Einstein with Nathan Rosen in 1936. The tunnel or bridge is theoretically, as Monitoff puts it, a 'wormhole in space controlled by man'. It is imaged as a tunnel running through the intersected tips of two cones that represent a black hole and a white hole.[101]

In order to cross such a bridge between two distinct realities, a vessel is needed, and as Monitoff admits, this could be anything, including the mysterious plane that damaged Donnie's home earlier, the existence of which is denied by aeronautics officials. The second, diegetic source of the movie's temporal theme is an illustrated book, *The Philosophy of Time-Travel*, by a maverick 'mad scientist' Roberta Sparrow, which shapes Donnie's visions of time-lines.

While Donnie watches a Redskins match on TV, time's arrow is literally manifest, as the movement-image is flooded with 'a little time in its pure state'. The room is 'momentarily bathed in artificial white light, as if God had hit the slow-motion button during a flash of lightning'.[102] Out of his father's navel area, a thick spear of 'silvery plastic gel' iridescent with rainbow reflections extrudes.[103] Donnie likewise emits a time-spear, which curls over into a beckoning finger to lead him forward. The spear goes before him, tracing 'the exact geography of his movement through time [as it] It uses his centre of gravity as its axis point'.[104] Donnie has directly experienced his own and his family's individual time-lines that push into the future and lead them on along an already traced-out path. The bodily location of these lines at the navel links back intriguingly to Castaneda's image of the sorcerers' 'lines of flight' adapted by Deleuze and Guattari, which I mentioned in Chapter 2.

Donnie's vision of time-lines appears to offer evidence of predestination, for which he seeks validation from Monitoff. His teacher confirms the feasibility of time-lines, as 'each vessel travels along a vector-path through space-time . . . along its centre of gravity'. Yet Donnie posits that if God controls time, 'all time is pre-decided. Then every living thing travels along a set path'. Monitoff's relativism counters that if time-lines could be seen by us in advance of our actions, then the individual would have 'the choice to betray our chosen destinies', thus all pre-formed destiny would end.

Donnie replies, with a perspective that could be seen as either pious or passive, that such apparent free will might still remain under the divine aegis if we 'chose to stay within God's channel'. At this point in the discussion, Monitoff breaks off, fearing the loss of his job if he goes any further in this potentially blasphemous discourse. The film stresses the educational establishment's muzzling of speculative thought and stylistic innovation in both arts and sciences.

His parents absent, Donnie throws a party for his high-school buddies, who enjoy the traditional chaos of Halloween unaware that cataclysmic events are scheduled for that same night. Donnie and his girlfriend Gretchen cement their emotional rapport by making love for the first time. In keeping with the manic carnival atmosphere, the on-screen close-up image of Donnie is turned upside down and he envisions the time-lines of his party guests.

An 'abyssal tunnel of light' refracting rainbow colours approaches Donnie as his head is enveloped by Gretchen's time-line and he is sucked into her temporal vortex.[105] Drawn towards the glow at the centre, Donnie breaks through and, in a effect reminiscent of Scottie's descent into vertiginous insanity in Hitchcock's *Vertigo* (1958) his face is surrounded by light rays. In an earlier scene, Donnie had stabbed his sinister alter ego Frank in the eye when he appeared in the bathroom mirror, so here one of Donnie's eyes is deformed because of his schizoid identification with Frank. Donnie whizzes down a tunnel of bright clouds into an anomalous cobwebbed space.

After a fracas with the school bullies, Gretchen is run down by a car driven by 'Frank', who is shot by Donnie. With her corpse on the car seat next to him, Donnie drives home, his face pale and drawn by the sufferings demanded by his role as a seer compelled to gaze into 'time's abyss'. Black clouds in an inverted tunnel-formation like a twister hang above Donnie's house. In a blinding flash of lightning, he surveys the spectacle of a spiralling time-portal in the sky above the valley. At this point, Donnie wills time's arrow to fork back and adopt another path. The tunnel of cloud flows in rapid motion speeded up by time-lapse effects.

A jet engine breaks off from an exploding plane and falls through a hole in time. It 'approaches the hexagonal plate of light which accelerates downwards . . . forming a tunnel with walls made of swirling liquid marble'.[106] The engine falls on Donnie's room and crushes him. By refusing a future time in which his mother, sister and lover are killed, he decides to embrace his own death to save them rather than himself. Referring back to his discussion with Monitoff, it appears that Donnie has, perhaps, asserted his own free will in choosing 'God's channel'. The rejected alternative was the diabolical path that Frank offers in which Donnie triumphs over his enemies and 'gets the girl'. Frank's alternative world is also the attainment of conventional narrative closure. By being taken beyond its temporal cut-off point, the repellent ethical implications of the 'happy ending' in mainstream cinema are revealed.

The main body of events in the film occur in one layer or zone of time. When this forks, another distinct layer of unfolding time in another, incompossible world is accessed. In the new time-zone, Donnie's friends and enemies awake in a different time-line, suffering only the after-effects of a haunting nightmare. At the end of the film, Gretchen cycles by Donnie's house as his corpse is being carried out. Saddened at the death of this friend she will never know, she waves to Donnie's mother. The grieving woman returns the greeting with an unnerving expression of familiarity with this girl who is a stranger, as though she briefly glimpsed the other, incompossible world.

According to Deleuze, *Citizen Kane* is structured in coexisting sheets of present, alternate histories that arrive at the same point: Kane's death and the enigma of 'Rosebud'. *Donnie Darko*, on the other hand, presents Deleuze and Bergson's second type of temporal image, simultaneous 'peaks of present', in which 'two people know each other, but already know each other and do not yet know each other. Betrayal happens, it never happened, and yet has happened and will happen [. . .] all at the same time'.[107] In Buñuel's *Belle de jour* (1967), for instance, 'the husband's final paralysis does and does not take place (he suddenly gets up to talk about holidays with his wife)'.[108] Such films free the spectator from a position frequent in more formulaic modes, the submissive expectation of the inevitable clear-cut happy or tragic ending. By expressing the 'pure force of time', they problematise any fixed perspective on the real or on the objective notion of truth.[109]

The two time-lines in *Donnie Darko* and the hero's choice at the pivotal moment open up the paradox of 'contingent futures'. Leibnitz's incompossible worlds remain distinct, but for the second type of cinematic time-image, in which the incompossibles are part of the same world, Deleuze cites instead Jorge Luis Borges's short story 'The Garden of Forking Paths'.[110] The alternative time-lines of this tale describe 'the straight line as force of time, as labyrinth of time,' which is also 'the line which forks and keeps on forking, passing through *incompossible presents*, returning to *not-necessarily true pasts*'.[111]

Deleuze suggests that 'falsifying narration' goes one step further towards the 'indiscernibility of the real and the imaginary' than the crystalline description that forms one of its stylistic correspondents.[112] The narrative 'power of the false' problematises relations of present and past.[113] In Donnie's role of seer, and his dialogue with Frank on the other side of the schizoid mirror, Donnie adopts some of the properties of Deleuze's figure of the forger, who 'passes into the crystal' and thus makes the direct time image visible; he provokes undecidable alternatives and inexplicable differences between the true and the false, and thereby imposes a power of the false as adequate to time, in contrast to any form of the true which would control time.[114]

In applying Deleuze's power of the false to *Donnie Darko*, I am conscious that, in its movement-image generic components, the film lacks both the stylistic sophistication and the overtly philosophical complexity of my earlier examples of crystalline description. Nevertheless, my contention is that Deleuzian film theory, in its focus on the ontological properties of the medium, is applicable in some degree to *many* films, regardless of subject matter, style or genre. As well as this more general ontological applicability, I also want to extend the narrow range of art-house films chosen for analysis by Deleuze himself to include the rich suggestiveness of popular cinema with wider appeal to contemporary audiences.

For my second agenda here, *Donnie Darko*, despite its high-school movie plot and stylistic conventions of alterity, like time-lapse cinematography and CGI, is an outstanding recent example of a film that, like Resnais/Robbe-Grillet, maps out '*undecidable alternatives* between circles of past, *inextricable differences* between peaks of present'.[115] The time-image components thus, I would argue, gravitate against the extrinsic sensory-motor links of movement-images. My most detailed reading explores the temporal components of Stanley Kubrick's *2001: A Space Odyssey* (1968), with a brief side-step into its shorter experimental forerunner, Belson's film *Re-Entry* (1964). By their apparent location in 'outer space', I will argue that both films significantly alter intensive states of time.

2001: A Time Odyssey

A blank, dark screen and three long-held, sonorous notes open *2001: A Space Odyssey*. Seeing nothing but darkness, we may react with impatience for the film to 'start', or we may ourselves start speculating, projecting possible expectations into the gap. A further reaction might be simply to let the sonorous opening bars of Richard Strauss's tone-poem *Also Sprach Zarathustra* (1896) bombard the sensorium with the unfamiliarity of pure sonsigns without representational images.

The cinematic skewing of sensory-motor perceptions by darkness and pure sound here keys in the film's more self-consciously contemplative mode of expression. *2001* is renowned as an altered states film. Contemporary audiences compared its 'psychedelic wonders', particularly the star-gate sequence, to cinematic LSD.[116] Publicity posters likewise proclaimed it as 'The Ultimate Trip'. The trailer tempted punters by a 'dazzling array of visual happenings' and much of the film functions outside linguistic parameters. The conventions of dramatic interaction, linear plot and character psychology are withheld or kept to a minimum. Although the title promises a science-fiction voyage in space, its odyssey takes us instead on a trip through time.

In 1969, Annette Michelson celebrated *2001*'s 'disquieting' function.[117] She argued that the intensity of the film's physical presence and its perceptual disorientation demand complex affective adjustments. As well as offering new sensory perspectives, she noted the film's ability to stimulate metaphysical speculation. For Michelson, events happened 'somewhere between the screen and the spectator [. . .] an area defined and constantly traversed by our active restructuring and reconstitution' via Kubrick's 'outer' space and the body's 'inner' space.[118]

Although she still distinguished spectator and screen, Michelson seemed to anticipate a dynamic affective assemblage of inner body and outer screen. Her critique leans towards the bolder and more substantial premise to be developed in Deleuze's assertion that in Kubrick, brain and screen are one. Rather than continuing Michelson's focus on the spatially haptic disorientation of the body, I shift the film's displacements from space to time.[119]

In presenting us with what Deleuze calls the 'paradoxical characteristics of a non-chronological time', *2001* manifests 'the pre-existence of a past in general; the co-existence of all the sheets of past; and the existence of a most contracted degree'.[120] Kubrick expresses these temporal extremes via crystalline narration, in which vision is not 'a presupposition added to action, a preliminary which presents itself as a condition', but instead it 'occupies all the room and takes the place of action'.[121] Rather than the anomalies of movement being 'accidental or contingent' to the narrative, here they are central.[122]

Deleuze draws on the insights of physics to describe the crystalline spaces of the time-image as Riemannian or quantum. Riemann, who I cited regarding multiplicity, studied the theory of complex variables. He introduced topological methods into complex function theory via what are now known as Riemannian surfaces.[123] In a Riemannian space, the properties of location are path-dependent. Different paths to the same location will change its properties. Such locations are paradoxical and produce singularities of infinite density.

In Deleuze's cinematic application, Riemannian space is 'disconnected, purely optical, sound or even tactile' and the 'connecting of parts is not predetermined'.[124] In such 'empty and amorphous spaces', the landscape 'becomes hallucinatory in a setting which now retains only crystalline seeds and crystallisable materials'.[125] Although Riemannian time-images might appear spatialised, as 'direct presentations of time' they 'imply non-localisable relations'.[126] Their 'nonchronological' time produces movements 'necessarily "abnormal", essentially "false" '.[127]

The direct time-image appears in 'de-actualised peaks of present' and 'virtual sheets of past' produced by pure optical and sound situations.[128] The relation of forces in such cinematic material is not quantitative, but expresses pure quality. The two poles of the time-image, sheets of past and peaks of present, are evident in *2001*. Although I distinguish these, Deleuze cautions that a 'perpetual present' does not imply 'less time-image than an eternal past'.[129] I illustrate their qualities and interrelations via two contrasting sequences, starting with the first section of the film.

A Prehistory of Consciousness

After the blank darkness of the opening shot, bright light floods the screen to herald a portentous planetary alignment, the 'star-gate'. Although a first-time viewer is unaware of the anticipatory nature of this image, it keys in the film's eternal return of the same, and non-linear temporality. For Deleuze, Kubrick's temporal cross-cuttings move across the plane of an 'alien' cosmic time in 'undecidable alternatives between sheets of past' where apparent transformations are 'strictly probabilistic from the point of view of the coexistence of ages'.[130]

In a sense, the birth of the star-child at the film's end has already happened long before human evolution begins. The first image of earth's rocky desert landscape resembles a similar terrain on the 'alien' planet at the end of the star-gate corridor. Kubrick's temporal repetitions are informed by Nietzsche's concepts of the Overman (*Übermensch*) and the Eternal Return, and the choice of Richard Strauss's *Also Sprach Zarathustra* for the musical theme makes these associations overt.

One way in which Kubrick challenges customary spatio-temporal orientation is through his use of section titles. The first one, 'The Dawn of Man', implies objective documentation rather than dramatic engagement. The prehistoric setting compels a sense of time extended far from the classical unities of traditional narrative. Rather than reinforcing fictive verisimilitude, this world unfolds the power of the false in aesthetic spectacles that stimulate thought. Yet it does not seek to totally objectivise external spectacle as correlative to a subjective gaze. It operates directly in the BWO assembled with the spatio-temporal body of the film. Both mind/brain and on-screen image thus move together in unprecedented ways. Deleuze's reference to the films of Resnais is equally applicable to Kubrick's own 'brain as world', where the 'cartography is essentially mental, cerebral' and there is 'only one single character, Thought'.[131]

Deleuze suggests that in the time-image's anomalies of motion, 'movement can tend to zero, the character, or the shot itself, remain immobile'.[132] The prehistoric world at first makes little overt movement as a series of still, fixed shots. Despite their lack of extensive motion, though, the shots move with intensive temporal quality in the light vibrations of a bleached-out desert. Without dramatic sensory-motor action, our consciousness of the properties of time and its intensive motion is affectively engaged.

In *2001*, the viewer also moves haptically 'outward' from a fixed position, drawn into the wide-screen space that bends to enclose us within the edges of the frame. Via lenses with optical distortion and short focal length, straight lines become curved. The most extreme example of this is our direct sharing of the machinic point-of-view of HAL, the artificial intelligence computer, as the visual impressions of his glass 'eye' are replicated by the use of a fish-eye-lens. The effect is produced by the 'barrel' or Pinkerton distortion of a very wide-angle lens. The film's visual quality of a wide perspective is further intensified by the use of 70 mm film stock.

Overt movement begins not with an object passing across the frame but in the slow, smooth motion of the camera. It tilts upward to reveal the vast space of a barren plain stretching into a horizon with boundaries obscured by dazzling sunlight. Reinforcing the minimal movement, no clear 'plot-line' develops in the preparatory shots of animal bones, but the viewer is compelled to wait and watch a wide, chiefly empty, space. Searching the screen for non-existent clues of meaning, we relax into a more contemplative mode as the desertscape unfolds.

Deleuze identifies two key stylistic devices in the direct time image. Both 'cut-up and piecemeal montage' and the long sequence shot serve the same purpose: to cause a 'shock of forces', either within one image or between images.[133] The sequence shot is produced by long takes with deep or flat perspective depending on their temporal intention. Depth of field, however, creates a distinct type of time-image that evokes memory by 'virtual regions of the past, the aspects of each region', and corresponds more closely to Bergson's circuitry model.[134] Rather than dividing the film spatially by linear edits, the sequence-shot presents the simultaneous 'relation of forces in its variability, in its instability, its proliferation of centres and multiplication of vectors'.[135] Although horizons may be stressed in a sequence shot their affective impact is vertical (intensive) rather than horizontal (extensive).

The shadow silhouettes of proto-humans appear. The unnerving quality and anomalous appearance of these hominids is offset by the initially indirect style of presentation. Competing with other mammals for diminishing resources, they are prey to carnivorous predators while their own predatory potential lies dormant. The lengthy fade to black suggests that ages have passed during the gradual unfolding of evolutionary forces. The next scene of fierce competition between rival groups for a water hole has fast-forwarded into the future.

The bracketing of this scene within two fades indicates the further passing of ages. A few clouds subtly hint at impending change, delayed by the return to fixed landscape shots. At nightfall, the hominids huddle in fear of nocturnal predators and wait for dawn. In the slow progress of pre-historic time, the pre-human 'memory ages of the world' are recalled, without clear temporal markers apart from night and day.[136] The sense of prehistoric, 'timeless' time recalls André Bazin's location of Welles's *Macbeth* (1951) at the ' prehistory of consciousness at the birth of time and sin'.[137] By the stretching out of time in this sequence, Kubrick expresses the earliest forms of temporal perception before quantified time, based on the division of darkness and daylight.

The next long fade heralds total and unprecedented change with the inexplicable appearance of a black obelisk. Rather than assigning a fixed symbolic meaning to this mysterious object, Kubrick regarded it as a 'primal force' and an evolutionary catalyst.[138] At first it frightens and excites the hominids until its presence becomes familiar. A low-angle proto-human point of view of the obelisk with the sun rising over it pre-figures the star-gate sequence of the distant future. To the accompani-ment of the portentous theme tune, the obelisk enters into machinic connection with the boldest simian. Their physical and mental contact triggers the urge to kill that will ensure success in the Darwinian struggle for survival. It is unclear whether the extraterrestrial agent implants the lust for power in 'innocent' creatures or develops an already potential characteristic.

The hominid brandishes a thigh-bone as a weapon. The editing pace speeds up, with a jump-cut of him beating a herbivore to death. His motions express the thrill of increased force used for domination as well as food. Before sundown, his group eat meat. On the next day in terms of editing, but actually a much longer period, an internecine battle occurs between rivals. The group 'chosen' by the obelisk stand on their hind legs. They relish the brutal attack on a rival, who is struck down and repeatedly beaten. The predominant simian throws his bone high up into the air in triumph. These proto-humans have become greedily territorial, as a prelude to their descendants' urge to measure out space and time and colonise the universe.

The camera tracks after the flying bone then match–cuts to an orbiting spaceship in Kubrick's celebrated temporal cross–aeon ellipsis. This drastic fast–forward is an acceleration of previous ellipses in which the passing of days and nights stand in for centuries and fades into black for millennia. Further attributes of the time–image are expressed in the film's lengthy two–part finale.

Jupiter and Beyond the Infinite

Deleuze attributes the production of direct time–images to pure optical and sound situations in the crystalline system.[139] In the time–image, the anomalies of movement 'become the essential point instead of being accidental or contingent' and demand our total absorption.[140] *2001*'s star–gate sequence offers a crucial example of anomalous, intensive movement that outstrips perceptual capacities to process stimuli.

The pyrotechnics of the star–gate corridor travelled though by astronaut Dave Bowman (Keir Dullea) first impacts on us like a multiple montage of brief shots. On repeated viewing, though, it becomes evident that the corridor comprises long sequence shots of abstract kaleidoscopic effects. These are loaded with drastic in–shot movements of light and colour that dazzle the eyes and induce haptic disorientation, so they *feel* like rapid–fire editing in contrast to the film's generally contemplative pace of temporal elongation.

Reprieving the title shots, the moons of Jupiter align with an obelisk floating in space. The reflected lights of Bowman's control panel distort into the raw material of his impending trip into radical temporal and spatial alterity. For Deleuze, there are two states of time, 'time as perpetual crisis and, at a deeper level, time as primary matter, immense and terrifying, like universal becoming'.[141] Here, the sequence shot, which 'throws up a jumble of vanishing centres', belongs to the latter type.[142]

Kubrick makes disorienting shifts between horizontal and vertical compositions. An upward tilt reveals a vertically slit centre–frame from which parallel, horizontal lines radiate. The central line (which distinguishes the projections of the slit–scan machine's original images and their doubly virtual reflection) shifts to horizontal. Rich, saturated colours of purple, orange, red, blue and gold are initially grounded by black sky, then spread out to flood the screen. Vertical gold bars curve into parabolas. Central white light expands and explodes, to push the colours aside, leaving gold round the edges, like a sunburst or a combusting star with a shimmering corona.

During the corridor sequence, the viewer's awareness of the flat plane of the screen and its rectangular properties is wiped as we are engulfed by wide-screen compositions. The affective impact of the images combines outward-bending and inward-pulling. The distortions induced by diverging lines draw us forward and back along the sliding camera's track, alternately drawn deeper into the vortex 'within' the screen and enwrapped by the lines and colours coming out of it.

At the opposite pole to the fixed shot, movement in the time-image may also be exaggerated and incessant, becoming 'a world-movement, a Brownian movement, a trampling' to and fro in a multiplicity of movements and scales.[143] As noted earlier, Deleuze uses 'Brownian movement' to suggest random velocity and direction in which the volume of the space occupied increases over time. In this fractal-like cinematic world, 'force no longer has a centre precisely because it is inseparable from its relation to other forces' and, in the terms of Didier Goldschmidt cited by Deleuze, the forces 'constantly topple to right and left'.[144]

On entry into the star-gate corridor, the spacecraft shakes violently. The shuddering of Bowman's head exceeds the film speed to create blur and the illusion of his head physically expanding. The impact of brief intercuts of Bowman's shocked face is open to debate. For Scott Bukatman, it belongs to the film's rhetoric of the Romantic Sublime as seen in the German Romantic paintings of Caspar David Freidrich, where a depersonalised human figure contemplates the infinite and awe-inspiring landscape as our proxy.[145] The inserts of Bowman might also alienate us from total absorption and remind us of the supra-personal perspective engineered by the director.

The corridor ends as a circular composition of evenly balanced beams of light. A spiral of red/gold light spins outwards then a match-cut, extreme close-up of the astronaut's iris and pupil reflects blue and gold. The abstract flux of light and colour solidifies into the recognisable image of a supernova. At the same time, the frantic pace of sensational bombardment slows to a more stately rhythm. The corridor's confusion of perspective and direction is, however, extended as the camera appears to track towards the cluster of stars and at the same time to back away. It is difficult to gauge whether the supernova is exploding, imploding or both simultaneously. The circularity of this composition is replaced by the flat, horizontal image of a nebula.

The breadth of its diamond shape is smoothly scanned from left to right. Spheres form and burst until one develops a tail like a spermatazoon. Floating in space, the camera/brain glides through the central vortex in a loop of white vapour. Matter solidifies into cells bathed in a green glow. Inside an egg-like formation, a foetus-like shape floats in white haze. A solitary star shifts into a match-cut to Bowman's eye, rendered familiarly human by its blinking motion. When the slit-scan turns horizontal, five crystalline shapes appear: a literal embodiment of the crystal-image. Two more crystals enter, one from each side of the frame. As they spin, they flash rapidly transmuting patterns.

Insert: The Abstract Time-Image

An electronic roar assaults our ears as a dark horizontal bar appears in centre frame topped by shimmering, elongated crystals. These radiate outwards before moving into the central slit and vanishing. A blurred rainbow surrounds a planet-like sphere. Split by a horizontal white bar, the globe gleams like hammered copper. The colours shift from verdigris to gold, silver and turquoise then hot red on a purple ground. White clouds glide down a blue ground like a slow motion waterfall. Exploding spheres transmute from blue, turquoise and purple to white, red and gold. An eye-shaped disc blurs and floats down to be replaced by a fiery red one, which explodes to swallow up the screen, emanating grey smoke. A glowing planet is irised-in as it spins, to become a recognisable image of Earth haloed with light that fades to an afterglow.

My description here might easily have been an extension of *2001*. Yet I have paused Kubrick's movie to intercut a sequence from another, lesser-known film. This insert is of direct relevance to our consideration of time as a cinematic altered state. As I indicated earlier, experimental filmmakers in the 1960s were using cosmic images to induce a metaphysical experience via the expanded sensorium. Belson's interests combined the inner and outer space of Mahayana Buddhism and astrophysics. I want to acknowledge here how much the short film *Re-Entry* directly shaped the less complex and subtle effects of the more technologically advanced *2001*.[146] Kubrick, via special effects expert Douglas Trumbull, also adapted Whitney's slit-scan invention for the star-gate.

These short experimental animations seek to alter the viewer's sense of time as well as space. Mainstream film, particularly in its 'art house' varieties, tends to graft such pure optical and sound situations of the crystalline system with varying degrees of integration into the temporal expression of their own cinematic worlds.[147] With my brief acknowledgement of their radical contribution to altered states of space and time on film, our main feature will be resumed.

Time in a Room

After the desubjectified vision of the crystals, the astronaut's eye reappears, with a bright gold light reflected in its centre. Attention focuses on the upper frame as the camera tracks across a planet surface. The terrain both is and is not the Grand Canyon on Earth, its geographical features defamiliarised. Flickering time-lapse images speed up dawn and dusk as we glide across vistas of clashing colours in an intensive vibration of contrasts. Electronically mixed voices chanting long-held notes increase image potency by sonsigns.

The spectator's eye, collapsed with the image of the eye on screen, is hit by extremes of spectral colour before returning to the recognisably human shade of Bowman's grey eye, the lid and lashes clearly visible. It blinks in a more familiar movement after being fixed wide-open. The vortex of the corridor has been replaced by the solidity of the space-pod, but Bowman sees anything but a reassuring locale. He looks out though a convex porthole at the totally unexpected image of a white room.

The room first appears framed within the frame by the oval window of the space-pod, surrounded by the lights of the control panel that register 'no function'. In sharp contrast to the visual chaos of the star-gate, this room is too regular and calm in its neoclassical balance. The flux of boundless space is replaced by stasis, containment and sensory deprivation. Nothing moves here but the intensive vibrations of white light. There are two statues in niches and likewise twin neoclassical paintings facing each other from opposite walls. Both the floor and the ceiling are included in the shot, inducing claustrophobia. The translucent floor tiles, lit from below, bathe the space in ubiquitous brightness without shadow. Later shots position Bowman against this ground of light, which recalls a computer-screen grid and reduces the room's presence to virtual abstraction.

A fixed shot of the space-pod reveals it as actually located inside the room. Rather than producing visual disjunction, the pod's pristine whiteness and uncluttered shape make it strangely at home. An image of the pod through a convex lens further harmonises it with its setting via a commonly distorted image. Furthermore, the pod and the room are spatially bent together by the receding parallel lines of the floor tiles. The traumatised Bowman, as he shudders and shakes inside the pod, is the only diegetic element in motion. Yet the bare minimalism of the room offers plenty of scope for intensive, speculative thought.

A temporal jump-cut pushes Bowman out into the room, a vividly prominent shape in his red spacesuit. Although the camera's point of view is located in the darkness of the control console, there is no other visible watcher. This perspective produces a schizoid split. Bowman is no longer recognisable as his former 'self' but his identity is fragmented. This subjective dissolution suits the objective nature of his role as a vehicle for the monolith's intent. In a sense, he has been anaesthetised for an operation to produce total transformation.

Although he is discussing Welles's *The Lady from Shanghai* (1947), Deleuze's description of 'mad' characters is strikingly applicable to Bowman's temporal state and mental condition here. In Welles's film, sheets of past are no longer evoked by means of recollection-images. Instead, it is as though 'the past surfaces in itself', in the disturbing form of

> personalities which are independent, alienated, off-balance, in some sense embry-
> onic, strangely active fossils, radioactive, inexplicable in the present where they
> surface [as the film presents] not recollections, but hallucinations.[148]

Like Welles's sinister noir characters, Bowman's mental derangement opens him up to 'pure' time. In such characters, according to Deleuze, 'madness, the split personality, now shows the past'.[149]

In distinction to Welles's characters, however, Bowman's derangement is not inherent, but induced by his traumatic experience. The radical contrast of the star-gate's primal chaos has exploded the rigid disciplinary structures of his training as an astronaut. In the room, Bowman is now literally both 'embryonic' and a 'strangely active' fossil as the aliens' laboratory animal used to gestate the star-child. Rather than showing marks of the past in distinction from the present and the future, Bowman figures the continuity of duration.

Deleuze distinguishes 'pure recollection' from the recollection-image derived from it, but nevertheless, it remains as ' "magnetiser" behind the hallucinations which it prompts'.[150] Bowman has experienced the polarities of time. After encountering 'not recollections, but hallucinations' in the corridor, Bowman's personal memory bank seems to have been wiped. In its place is a generic memory of Western human civilisation expressed in the room's neoclassical abstraction. He has special access to a pure, virtual time not available to the usual processes of recollection. There is nothing in the room to disturb Bowman's state of calm except traces of his former self and the remnants of a human time-frame.

Moving into close-up of Bowman's anxious face in his visor, the camera registers his white hair and wrinkled skin. The temporal ellipsis of passage through the star-gate has aged him drastically. His expression of disbelief on recognising his own reflection as a suddenly older man marked by finite, human time suggests that despite his trauma, he retains some degree of subjective identity. Through the doorway, a black-clad man with his back to the camera is seated at a table, turning to reveal himself as an even older version of Bowman. Rather than being a doppelgänger of the present Bowman, he exists on a different temporal plane, where his 'past' self briefly intrudes and disturbs his 'future' self. In this overlaid site of past and future, the temporal ellipsis of editing is sharply foregrounded as distinct layers of duration are given simultaneously.

The elderly Bowman is a tiny figure dwarfed by the room, but his solid black robe marks a degree of singularity. His expression still flickers with curiosity when he is disturbed by the intrusive virtual presence of his own former 'self'. Bowman's physical motion is slowed down. He is compelled to shuffle slowly across the floor: first by his weighted space-boots and second by his rapid ageing. In the slowing down enforced by the ageing process, our actual physical speed decreases, but our virtual experience of time speeds up as we spend more of our time in recollection. The operations of memory and an intensive experience of pure duration take over from extensive spatial motion.

At the table, with its perfectly arranged serving dishes, Bowman disturbs the room's unnatural balance by shattering a wine glass. This sudden, violent movement is a harbinger of his impending death as a human. He looks helplessly at the shards and beyond them to his own supine figure on his deathbed. Both the living and dying Bowman appear in the same frame as the back of the standing man overlooks the shrivelled corpse-like figure. Past, present and future overlap in a version of time far removed from human norms. To an alien consciousness, these time periods, which we experience as highly compressed and overlaid, occur together.

The dying Bowman reaches out towards the flat black monolith materialised again at the centre of the room. His gesture recalls that of his proto-human ancestor touching the first monolith. In place of the aged man, a glowing ball of white light lies on the bed. In this globe of light that replaces a human womb, Bowman is reborn as the star-child, an embryonic over-man who heralds a new cycle of human evolution. The newborn child has delicate skin and large eyes that resemble his own. The camera moves in to the monolith and engulfs the screen in total darkness. The next shot of a white planetary sphere locates the event simultaneously both inside and outside the room. A track down to planet Earth shows the star-child suspended in a globe equal in size to Terra that slowly turns to confront us with the final shot of the film, the star-child's wide blue gaze.

Bergson identified 'durations which are inferior and superior to man'.[151] Like human temporal divisions, the Cartesian split of interior brain and exterior world is not valid for an alien intelligence. Neither does it hold for Kubrick's own film-philosophy and his cinema of the time-image. The distortions of temporality in *2001* are experienced directly by the spectator's embodied mind in a fusion of screen and brain. As with the other films in this chapter, we have seen how the viewer's own perceptions of time are distorted and extended both during and after the screening. Time is permanently changed for us. In their experiments with the time-image via cinematography and editing, these films succeed in 'inventing these paradoxical hypnotic and hallucinatory sheets whose property is to be at once a past and always to come'.[152] To conclude the book with new beginnings, I would like to suggest some future possibilities for Deleuzian film theory and practice.

Notes

1. Smith, 'introduction', p. xviii.
2. Deleuze, *Cinema 1*, p. 67.
3. Ibid.
4. Ibid.
5. Tarkovsky, *Sculpting in Time*.
6. Deleuze, *Cinema 2*, p. xi.
7. Bogue, *Deleuze on Cinema*, p. 19.
8. Ibid.
9. Deleuze, *The Logic of Sense*, p. 164.
10. Ibid., p. 165.
11. Deleuze, 'The Brain is the Screen', p. 371.
12. Rodowick, *Gilles Deleuze's Time Machine*, p. 79.
13. Deleuze, *Cinema 2*, p. xi.
14. Bergson, *Time and Free Will*, p. 30.
15. Bergson, *Matter and Memory*, p. 98.
16. Ibid., p. 107.
17. Ibid., p. 101.
18. Ibid., p. 128.
19. Ibid.
20. Ibid.
21. Ibid., p. 112.
22. Ibid.
23. Deleuze, *Cinema 2*, p. 79.
24. Ibid., p. xii.
25. Ibid.
26. Bergson, *Matter and Memory*, p. 114.
27. Ibid., pp. 138–9.
28. Bogue, *Deleuze on Cinema*, p. 14.
29. Bergson, *Matter and Memory*, p. 100.
30. Ibid., p. 134.
31. Ibid., p. 104.
32. Ibid., p. 100.
33. Ibid., p. 171.

34. Ibid., p. 133.
35. Ibid., p. 134.
36. Ibid., p. 135.
37. Lacan, *Écrits: A Selection*, p. 319.
38. Deleuze, *Cinema 1*, p. 23.
39. Ibid., pp. 23–4.
40. Ibid., p. 32.
41. Ibid.
42. Ibid.
43. Ibid.
44. Ibid., p. 106.
45. Ibid., p. 23.
46. Monaco, *How to Read a Film*.
47. Deleuze, *Cinema 2*, p. 24.
48. Rodowick, *Gilles Deleuze's Time Machine*, p. 89.
49. Deleuze, *Cinema 2*, p. 23.
50. Rodowick, *Gilles Deleuze's Time Machine*, p. 84.
51. Werner Herzog, in Cronin, *Herzog on Herzog*, p. 139.
52. Deleuze, *Cinema 2*, p. 74.
53. Ibid., p. 125.
54. Ibid., p. 75.
55. Bergson, *Matter and Memory*, p. 152.
56. Ibid., p. 79.
57. Ibid., p. 162.
58. Ibid., p. 68.
59. Ibid.
60. Ibid., p. 69.
61. Ibid.
62. Ibid.
63. Ibid.
64. Ibid., p. 69.
65. Ibid., p. 70.
66. Ibid.
67. Ibid., p. 71.
68. Deleuze, *Cinema 2*, p. 34.
69. Ibid., p. 74.
70. Ibid., 139.
71. Ibid., p. 82.
72. Ibid., p. 41.
73. Ibid.
74. Ibid., p. 78.
75. Ibid., p. 74.
76. Ibid., p. 83.
77. Ibid., p. 86.

78. Ibid., p. 129.
79. Ibid., p. 75.
80. Tarkovsky, *Sculpting in Time*, p. 193.
81. Ibid., p. 194.
82. Ibid., p. 63.
83. Ibid.
84. Deleuze, *Cinema 1*, p. 80.
85. Ibid.
86. Ibid., p. 121.
87. Deleuze, *Cinema 2*, p. 75.
88. Ibid.
89. Ibid.
90. Ibid.
91. Ibid., p. 105.
92. Rodowick, *Gilles Deleuze's Time Machine*, p. 98.
93. Deleuze, *Cinema 2*, p. 101.
94. Ibid.
95. Ibid.
96. Ibid.
97. Ibid.
98. Ibid.
99. Ibid., p. 102.
100. Hawking, *A Brief History of Time*.
101. For a definition of an Einstein-Rosen Bridge, see: http://www.krioma.net/articles/Bridge%20Theory/Einstein%20Rosen%20Bridge.htm (accessed 9 February 2006).
102. Richard Kelly, *Donnie Darko* screenplay, at: http://www.script-o-rama.com/movie_scripts/d/donniedarko.pdf, p. 46 (accessed 30 December 2006).
103. Ibid.
104. Ibid.
105. Ibid.
106. Ibid., p. 74.
107. Deleuze, *Cinema 2*, p. 101.
108. Ibid., p. 102.
109. Ibid., p. 130.
110. Borges, 'The Garden of Forking Paths'.
111. Deleuze, *Cinema 2*, p. 131.
112. Ibid.
113. Ibid.
114. Ibid., p. 132.
115. Ibid., p. 105.
116. McKee, 'Out of the Silent Planet', p. 205.
117. Michelson, 'Bodies in Space', p. 56.
118. Ibid., p. 59.

119. Ibid., p. 57.
120. Deleuze, *Cinema 2*, p. 99.
121. Ibid., p. 128.
122. Ibid.
123. http://www-groups.dcs.st-and.ac.uk/~history/Mathematicians/Riemann.html (accessed 06 February 2006).
124. Deleuze, *Cinema 2*, p. 129.
125. Ibid.
126. Ibid.
127. Ibid.
128. Ibid., p. 130.
129. Ibid., p. 123.
130. Ibid., p. 120.
131. Ibid., p. 122.
132. Ibid., p. 128.
133. Ibid., p. 139.
134. Ibid., p. 109.
135. Ibid., p. 139.
136. Ibid., p. 19.
137. Ibid., p. 116.
138. Lobrutto, *Stanley Kubrick*, p. 284.
139. Deleuze, *Cinema 2*, p. 130.
140. Deleuze, *Cinema 1*, p. 128.
141. Deleuze, *Cinema 2*, p. 115.
142. Ibid., p. 142.
143. Deleuze, *Cinema 1*, p. 128.
144. Deleuze, *Cinema 2*, p. 142.
145. Bukatman, 'The Artificial Infinite', p. 260.
146. Gene Youngblood was first to acknowledge Kubrick's debt to Belson in *Expanded Cinema*, p. 156.
147. Belson's work with 'outer space' began with the Vortex series of concerts at the Morrison Planetarium, San Francisco (1957–60). His early 'light shows' accompanied music by John Cage, Karlheinz Stockhausen and Toshiro Mayusumi. Synaesthetic sound and vision were induced by star and aurora borealis machines.
148. Deleuze, *Cinema 2*, p. 113.
149. Ibid.
150. Ibid., p. 123.
151. Ibid., p. 118.
152. Ibid., p. 123.

Conclusion: Becoming-Fractal

the plane is the formless, unlimited absolute, neither surface, nor volume, but always fractal.[1] (Deleuze and Guattari)

an unidentifiable surface becomes the matrix out of which brief, specific images appear.[2] (P. Adams Sitney)

chaos has three daughters, depending on the plane that cuts through it: these are the *Chaoids* – art, science and philosophy – as forms of thought or creation.[3] (Deleuze and Guattari)

'Title 18': rainbow-coloured clouds form starfish spirals that pulse outwards and spread endlessly. Between the wavering 'arms' of the main spiral, innumerable self-same patterns shimmer in anticipation of the zoom that will enter their own shifting formations and on into relative infinity. 'Title 22', a classic Mandelbrot fractal, is monochrome with filigree edges of shimmering silver. 'Title 10', a circular formation in fiery red and gold, flows out of a black hole at its centre to fill the screen, its jagged points spreading into abstract patterns.[4]

These clips from basic fractal video 'films' (and my basic descriptions of their complex detail) typify millions in current circulation on the Internet. Automated fractal art of the zoom or flyover animation type has proliferated and its sheer volume is overwhelming. It is difficult to single out examples from a plethora ranging from adventurous to formulaic. It is relatively easy to play with existing fractals and to make our own with computer software. Though scientific application is also widespread, the philosophical and cultural significance of digital imaging technologies is harder to map.

In this speculative conclusion to my study of altered states and film, I want to suggest some future directions for digital technologies of the moving image and how they might be thought. My introductory focus on fractals here is twofold. I consider the potential of 'film' fractals to engineer shifts in consciousness and I connect them with Deleuze and Guattari's philosophical project.

Fractals result from the application of a diverse family of equations. On one level they diagram concepts in chaos and complexity theories. They can be used to model physical systems ranging from the weather to the structure of plants. As well as these scientific applications, the aesthetics of fractals circulate more widely. Today, their 'deterministic chaos' is familiar as dance club projections, where their rhythms are self-synchronised with the music.[5] They are also common on computer screens as screensavers used to 'space-out' from goal-driven work.

On the more experimental side of fractal 'films', video feedback loops produce self-similar fractals generated not by mathematical algorithms but by pointing a digital video camera at its own output. Modelling forms that recall 'biological morphogenesis' and neuronal networks, they express a machinic kind of molecularity inherent in the medium.[6] Their reaction-diffusion processes also resemble the 'hallucinogenic dynamics'[7] of the visual cortex identified, for example, in Oliver Sacks's work on the 'self-organising displays' of the migraine aura.[8]

So how can fractal films engineer altered states and ways of thinking them? Fractals change self-similar forms from frame to frame and a sense of fluid movement is created by the sequential display of frames. Recent consciousness studies experiments with fractal video report that the brain of an engaged subject 'attending to the high event rate' of the moving image enters hyper-arousal.[9] This distinctly hypnoid state of receptivity produces certain responses encountered earlier in my study, including stimulation, focusing and 'spontaneous accessing of emotions and memories'.[10]

So how can fractals be used to express Deleuzian concepts more specifically and thus elucidate them? Unsurprisingly, the use of the term by Deleuze and Guattari is late given the period over which they worked. Although fractals were 'discovered' by Mandelbrot in 1975, they only entered wide public circulation with the spread of computer literacy by the late 1980s. Yet in *What Is Philosophy?* (1992) Deleuze and Guattari rapidly adopt the fractal by aligning it to the plane of immanence in a series of figures beginning with the body: skeleton (concepts) and breath (plane), which are used to distinguish the plane from the concepts arising from it.

If concepts are 'absolute surfaces or volumes, formless and fragmentary', Deleuze and Guattari argue, then the plane itself is the 'unlimited absolute' and 'always fractal'.[11] One use of Lacan's diagrams of the Borromean knot was to distinguish the symbolic, the imaginary and the real with their Möbius strip-like torsions ever turning on each other yet not touching. Instead of this more static kind of model which moves yet retains an overall fixed form, they choose to apply the deterministic chaos of the fractal, its emergent properties continuously open to the elsewhere.

Deleuze and Guattari borrowed another scientific figure to distinguish the plane of immanence from concepts: the event horizon around a black hole.[12] If 'concepts are events, but the plane is the horizon of events, the reservoir or reserve of purely conceptual events' then the event as concept is 'independent of a visible state of affairs in which it is brought about'.[13] An event horizon is the boundary round a black hole at which escape velocity exceeds the speed of light.[14] Physically, everything in the event horizon collapses to a singularity. Deleuze's use of singularity to mean the specificity of a particular component or assemblage, its distinctive quality as well as its infinite potential, has, I would argue, fractal properties.

Conventionally, member points of the Mandelbrot set are coloured black. Like contours on a map, the colours trace the distance of the points away from the set. In one sense, the event horizon corresponds to the boundary of the Mandelbrot set, whose member points collapse to zero. At the event horizon, there is an infinite time-dilation effect and the 'endless' outpouring of self-similar, yet completely new, patterns in fractal film has durational qualities.[15]

So how might this fractal model be applied in Deleuzian film-philosophy? David Neo uses fractals to figure the operations of memory as transcendental time-image in *Mother and Son* (Aleksandr Sokurov, 1997).[16] He asserts that the memory-images of the film, like 'magnified "mini Mandelbrots"', interact with our psyche, 'forming and evolving our perception with variations' to produce a new stage in the process of singularity. Neo refers to the similarity of actual experience and its virtual memory in Bergson's account, via which 'memory grafts distinctions upon resemblances that are spontaneously abstracted'.[17] According to Neo, this also describes how fractal geometry works, via 'the self-similarity of fractals constantly creating and reconstructing'.[18]

Neo goes on to argue that the film's photograph, sound and language images arise from ' "similarity" (of pure recollection) or "self-similarity" (of fractals) of the collective unconscious – they become archetype-images of Memory which in turn helps shape our being and identity'.[19] In a sweeping move, Neo elides Bergson, Deleuze, Jung and fractals. His interpretation of the film's intensive states thus develops the director's own avowed Jungian inclinations and the philosophical rigours of the time-image are swallowed up in the archetypal collective unconscious.[20]

Despite its more facile commercial forms, the fractal retains further potential as a tool for DeleuzeGuattarian speculation. Yet, fractals are just a small segment of the much broader emergence of digital aesthetics. Digitalisation, whether mainstream CGI or more experimental work, is impacting directly on traditional cinematic images and demanding new modes of theorisation in ways that are only just beginning to emerge.

Virtual States/Actual Implications

today we live in the imaginary world of the screen, of the interface and the reduplication of contiguity and networks.[21] (Jean Baudrillard)

the life or afterlife of cinema depends on its internal struggle with informatics.[22] (Deleuze and Guattari)

I start this section on digital futures by citing a deeply pessimistic critique of contemporary trends. For Jean Baudrillard, nostalgic for the comparatively human-sized 'home' of Lacanian psychoanalysis, we lived formerly in 'the imaginary world of the mirror, of the divided self and of the stage, of otherness and alienation'.[23] Since the informatics revolution, he contends, not only have machines become screens, but humans have too, so that 'the interactivity of men has become the interactivity of screens'.[24] Baudrillard's world of hyperreality is run by simulacra and the masses are swallowed up in the black hole of informatics where the only ecstasy is that of communication.[25]

Baudrillard's pessimism raises substantial questions. How might cinema reflect such simulacral ecstasy and would technological shifts in the medium be an entirely repressive series of developments as he asserts? How far does digitalisation stymie 'live' performance and audience interaction? If informatics formations are indeed 'erasing the history of film that is grounded in the concept of "recording reality"' are they still film?[26] How do they impact on traditional forms of cinema and what might be their potential to induce altered states of consciousness in their users?

In Chapter 3, I foregrounded the complex and subtle abstractions of artisanal and analogue computer films in the 1960s. On one level, new technologies are extending these experiments in 'expanded cinemas' celebrated by Youngblood in his eponymous book of 1970. Animation arts have gained enormous momentum from digitalisation, with far-reaching implications. On the positive side, they have replaced small countercultural audiences of cinetheques and clubs with interactive DIY methods available to the computer-using public. Individual accessibility is unparalleled in the late capitalist West.

Of course, Hollywood had been quick to incorporate new digital imaging from the introduction of morphing in the early 1990s showcased in such films as *Terminator 2* (James Cameron, 1991) to today's heavy use of CGI in fantasy material to enhance special effects and create virtual worlds. A case might be made for the 'democratic' interchange of popular cultural acceptance and bottom-up as well as top-down interactivity. Movie-based tie-in computer games modify the mainstream narrative templates that have already incorporated them by the game's 'assembling and reconfiguring' elements from compiled image sequences.[27]

Interactive software, such as macromedia and flash, enable the easier creation of 'movies' by combining video, animation and multimedia elements.[28] Public spaces as well as galleries host interactive projections using narrative or non-narrative film footage in ways different to those it was originally designed for.[29] Haptic 'force feedback games', that translate phenomena in virtual world to physical sensations for the gamer, are also being developed.[30]

Digital art theorist Christiane Paul argues that when hyperlinked textual narrative incorporates elements of montage or jump-cuts, the 'visual translation of a scene remains an entirely mental event that will be informed by the interpretation and meaning the reader supplies'.[31] Fired by the creative and outlet potential of digitalisation for artists and filmmakers, she does not question the nature or political implications of the 'mental event'. Rejecting Baudrillardian pessimism, she describes these developments in glowing quasi-Deleuzian terms as 'nomadic networks' with their multi-user environments and avatars.

I began to explore the implications of the new digital media from a Deleuzian viewpoint in my reading of *Strange Days*. Here, I want to consider the ambivalence of Deleuze both solo and with Guattari towards what was, when they wrote, a relatively new development. In his survey of the time-image, Deleuze scrutinises the issues raised by the new media in full awareness of their potential to deal a death blow to the traditional forms of cinema so rich in philosophical and political possibilities.

Deleuze conducts his scrutiny of digital media though a series of speculations. Identifying the 'new computer and cybernetic' automata of motion, composition and thought with their controls and feedback, he asks whether there might be a 'new regime of images like that of automatism?'[32] Digitalisation certainly accompanied a change in the political landscape that appeared to 'invert' older power structures with charismatic leaders and political figureheads. Deleuze's account of the new configurations of power produced by the 'information superhighway' seems to anticipate William Gibson-esque hackers and cyberpunks who need to know the very codes they want to crack and may be working the system for their own purposes.

The oppositional computing of Neo (Keanu Reeves), the hacker hero, and his digital guerrilla team of *The Matrix* (Wachowski Brothers, 1999) might, it could be argued, be implicitly informed by some of Deleuze's insights as well as the more explicit nod to Baudrillard via the (hollowed out) copy of *Simulation and Simulacra* in his apartment. For Deleuze, traditional hierarchies of power have become 'diluted' in a network of information that incorporates opponents as well as willing operatives, where ' "decision-makers" managed control, processing and stock across intersections of insomniacs and seers'.[33]

So how does digitalisation impact on the existing grammar of moving images in cine film? As Deleuze indicates, electronic-type effects were already being anticipated by more adventurous cinematography prior to widespread digitalisation. The art-film examples he cites include Bresson, Ozu, Resnais and Godard. Electronic film lacks the focal depth of the camera lens. Yet earlier 'high modernist' works like those of Brakhage and some abstract animators deliberately chose to flatten depth of field for specific purposes.

Deleuze indicates another significant change in the dynamics of framing. He argues that electronic images do not have an 'outside (out-of-field) any more than they are internalised in a whole: rather, they have a right side and a reverse, reversible and non-superimposable, like a power to turn back on themselves'.[34] This property impacts considerably on the films' spatial and temporal dimensions as they do not seem to offer an opening on to elsewhere. Again using terms reminiscent of fractal dynamics, Deleuze notes that the new images are 'objects of a perpetual reorganisation, in which a new image can arise at any point whatever of the preceding image'.[35] Their moving plane of immanence thus has a chaotic quality of unpredictability.

The spatial composition of the screen is another area affected by electronic media. Although he is not referring to overblown CGI, Deleuze notes the spatial gigantism of 'huge *mises en scènes*' that could be applied to them.[36] Rather than the vertical human-centred screen of Renaissance perspective, the new screen 'constitutes a table of information, an opaque surface on which are inscribed "data", information replacing nature'.[37] Of course, the society of the spectacle is also the society of increased electronic surveillance. What Deleuze calls the city's 'third eye, replacing the eyes of nature', is depicted literally in the super-computer in *The Matrix* and its simulacral city impregnated with 'subjectivised' computer surveillance programmes like Agent Smith.[38]

As well as other electronic effects that have still 'undetermined relations' with traditional cinematic images, a further area singled out by Deleuze is digitally enhanced audio.[39] He indicates that as sound is achieving 'autonomy which increasingly lends it the status of an image, the two images, sound and visual, enter into complex relations with neither subordination nor commensurability and reach a common limit'.[40] So the earlier subordination of sound to image is undermined via Dolby stereo and other electronic enhancement as heard, for example, in the hallucinatory sound quality of the horror film *From Hell* (Hughes Brothers, 2004) with its preternaturally enhanced heartbeat thuds, gloopy liquid spurts and nerve-grating scratches. Having highlighted its transformative impact on traditional cinema images, Deleuze contends that 'new spiritual automatism in turn refers to new psychological automata'.[41]

But how far can electronic images attain the 'autonomous anticipatory functions' of the time-image? Deleuze insists that they need to be driven by 'another will to art, or on as yet unknown aspects of the time-image'.[42] His speculations on the future of digitalised cinema close on a somewhat Baudrillardian note of caution. He warns against over-hasty intoxication with the dizzying possibilities of the new images, reminding us of the politics of control and that 'the life or afterlife of cinema depends on its internal struggle with informatics. It is necessary to set up against the latter the question which goes beyond it, that of its source and that of its addressee'.[43] The impact of digitalisation on thought also demands further inquiry.

Forms of Thought or Creation

As we have seen, altered states cinema induces virtual derangement via affective distortions of cinematography and *mise-en-scène*. Yet the brain's functions are only partly dependent on the sensory array of percepts and affects. Some forms of cinema, such as silent and black-and-white films, appear to reduce the range of stimuli by their lack of colour and sound. It could be argued, though, that these connect the on-screen image and the realm of pure ideas in a closer-knit assemblage of brain and screen than the techno-sensory overload of digitally enhanced film. For Deleuze, the question remains whether the 'flatter' electronic image, with its negative connotations of postmodernist superficiality, still deploys a conceptual scope as wide as traditional cinema.

Nevertheless, *What Is Philosophy?*, Deleuze and Guattari's last joint work and written at the juncture of a shift 'from gnosiology (in modern art) to ontology (in postmodern art)',[44] sounds a more optimistic note of cross fertilisation between the exploratory planes of art, philosophy and science as 'forms of thought or creation'.[45] Each plane, in its own way wants to 'tear open the firmament and plunge into chaos', from which they bring back a 'chaosmos', a 'composed chaos neither foreseen or preconceived' specific to their field.[46]

For the philosopher, this takes the shape of 'variations', for the scientist 'variables' and for the artist 'varieties'.[47] The three, irreducible planes thus comprise:

> plane of immanence of philosophy, plane of composition of art, plane of reference or coordination of science; form of concept, source of sensation, function of knowledge; concepts and conceptual personae, sensations and aesthetic figures, figures and partial observers.[48]

Art transforms 'chaotic variability into *chaoid* variety' and composes chaos into sensation images.[49] Science is attracted to the chaos that necessarily delimits it.[50] For Deleuze and Guattari, 'if equilibrium attractors (fixed points, limit cycles, cores) express science's struggle with chaos, strange attractors reveal its profound attraction to chaos' as well as constituting the 'chaosmos internal to modern science'.[51] A strange attractor is fractal by definition. If a system with a limit-cycle attractor is moved to one with a strange attractor, the original limit cycle unfolds or explodes. The strange attractor opens up an infinite family of self-similar cycles. Here the fractal is intensive rather than extensive. It is not self-similar in terms of scale but is infinitely thick.

In Deleuze and Guattari's three-plane model, the brain, as a centre of indetermination in the durational flux of forces, acts as a vital junction-box of circuitry exchange. It operates as '*the junction* – not the unity' of the chaoid planes.[52] In order to counter recognition's 'derisory model' of reality that seeks to police the creative forces of desire, the three planes can fruitfully cross-fertilise in the brain to produce new thought.[53] Thus the 'vital ideas' offered by each chaoid operate durationally 'in the deepest of its synaptic fissures, in the hiatuses, intervals and meantimes of a nonobjectifiable brain'.[54]

Despite the irreducibility of planes, Deleuze and Guattari welcome, and themselves consistently practise, productive 'interference'. Three types of interference between disciplines fuel conceptual progress. In the first 'extrinsic' kind, the interfering discipline keeps its own methods intact.[55] 'Mixed plane' interference involves more subtle and mutual 'sliding' between them.[56] 'Becoming indiscernible', the most extreme interference, is shared by functions (science), sensations (art) and concepts (philosophy).[57]

This type of interference is determined by the negative. As well as the broader challenge of chaos, each plane must confront the distinctive challenges of other disciplines, hence philosophy needs '*a nonphilosophy that comprehends it, it needs a nonphilosophical comprehension just as art needs nonart and science needs nonscience*'.[58] In its triple-headed plunge into chaos, the creative brain will discover 'the shadow of the "people to come"'.[59] If, as Deleuze contends, the twentieth-century creative brain has been the cine screen, the brain screen of the future will be digital.

Yet, despite enriching cross-fertilisations of science, philosophy and art, the political agendas of the latest technology are not, of course, inherently progressive. Ronald Bogue argues the 'essential mutability' of the digital image,[60] referencing Edmond Couchot's amorphous 'immedia' of 'transformable emissions' without origin or destination.[61] The main use of television for Bogue has been for 'social control rather than artistic invention'.[62] As Rodowick rather more polemically reminds us, the philosophy of audiovisual and information might espouse 'communication, consensus and universal values', but these are likewise the values of global capitalism and liberal democracies.[63] The duty of 'the simulacral arts and a philosophy of resistance' combines interpretation and evaluation in order to 'invent alternative ways of thinking and modes of existence immanent in, yet alternative to' capitalist hegemony.[64]

Deleuze and Guattari express their own concepts via a blend of poetic delirium and conceptual rigour itself productive of alterity. For them, art's aim is not simply to stimulate a *frisson* and the altered states of the cinematic encounter are not just recreational. The agenda of schizoanalysis is driven by a politically anarchic desire that opposes repressive power structures by thought, image and deed. Deleuze approves Welles's cinematic dictum to make 'each shot a blow, a counter-blow, a blow received, a blow struck'.[65] In some ways Deleuze and Guattari endorse traditional avant-garde agendas to radicalise consciousness in order to effect progressive change.

Yet some forms of contemporary art/film practice are bringing into being new digital creative initiatives specifically Deleuzian in inspiration.[66] Italian video artist Mattia Casalegno, for example, finds inspiration in ' "painting the forces", the visual languages as an aim to extend the field of visible', and seeks to express 'the rhizome, the levels of immanence, the body without organs and abstract machines'.[67] He addresses the painting of sounds and the hearing of images via 'affections in their pure state', in an 'unbodily universe' with 'undiscursive blocs of emotion, deterritorialised bodies'.[68]

Casalegno's film *X-scape* accompanies live electronic music performance. The screen develops an aspect ratio of 2 : 3. On the right, the image's rhythm is jagged staccato and on the left flows more smoothly, like an unfolding map or graph. The two uneven images spread, slide and change, invading the other's territory and swapping sides. The perceiver's eyes are presented with two distinct rhythms to assimilate at the same time. Predominantly black and white with an intermittent blue tint, Casalegno's film reveals an intensively moving plane minimalist in symbolic content but dense in affective force.

American Victor Liu's work with the delter program reworks the grammar of the digital matrix to create Deleuzian becomings.[69] Within the video stream is encoded data, designed to be 'read' only by the machine. Delter renders the movement of 'informatical percepts' encoded into film images to 'approximate a zero-order level of perception, a machinic vision' and to reveal their movement patterns as perceived by the camera eye.[70]

Drawing on Deleuze's concept of the camera eye as non-subjective consciousness, Liu asserts its increased applicability in the digital age. By 'visualising only the inter-frame motion vectors [we obtain] a glimpse of the movement of (a-subjective, machinic) thought' that reveals 'the percepts of the machine, the units of transaction by which images act and react according to their own rules' via the interplay of images.[71]

Liu's bouncing ping-pong ball sequence has a liquid, melting effect and subtle colour tones. It enables awareness of movement as a force that extends much further than the ball's pale trajectory. The clip of the shower sequence from *Psycho* would make an ideal tool for teaching the quality of molecular movement to newcomers. The affective force of Norman's knife-thrusts are foregrounded. The sequence conveys the fluctuating movement of Hitchcock's camera-eye to reveal a surprisingly liquid mode of perception.

The deltered clips range from more abstract trajectories of motion to familiar movie scenes. All are interactive, via zoom, colour range and motion speed. The zoom toggle takes effect gradually to slide us further into the fractal-like world. Each part of the screen simultaneously engages the eye rather than being ruled by perspective. Nets of pixels form a molecular mesh as the image shifts in automated self-modification. Its infinitely layered density appears as a fluctuating plane of immanence.

My model in this book has not been a flat plane but a multidimensional manifold. If the plane of immanence is fractal in nature like Deleuze and Guattari suggest, or is even *a* fractal, concepts form like whirlpools made by waves stirred by turbulence. The fractals of the Mandelbrot set are actually self-different not self-similar. We are not sucked down into tunnels at the centre of fractals but, rather, new formations rise up to be discovered, each with their own qualitative singularity. To shift figures, the intrusive virus disturbs genetic balance to cause mutation. Or, perhaps, the viral contagion of the art encounter works as a strange attractor to draw thought processes along unpredictable paths in a kind of fractal logic.[72]

I suggest that film techniques used to express altered states of consciousness are, by means of a singular cluster of floating affects and percepts, one method of producing such turbulence in the plane of immanence. By gathering and channelling the turbulence that passes through them, new forms of thought arise. The virtual force of concepts can energise the BWO, impelling extensive motion to actualise change. The encounter with moving images can alter perception, melting the frameworks of everyday being into more intensive states of becoming.

Yet, however much we might study and discuss their texts, Deleuze and Guattari cannot do all the work for us. If we allow their concepts to harden into schema and merely teach them to others as such, we limit the possibilities they offer to our work in the field. We are not the same viewer before, during or after the cinematic event. The movement of film images continues to reverberate as memory transforms them into a force of virtual potential for actual change. Above all, I have asserted the encounter with film as altered state. Yet this state is far from being static or limited to its medium. Fuelled by the lucid optimism of Deleuze and Guattari, it is up to us to alter it further by setting new kinds of meta-cinematic images in motion.

Notes

1. Deleuze and Guattari, *What Is Philosophy?*, p. 36.
2. Sitney, *Visionary Film*, p. 179.
3. Deleuze and Guattari, *What Is Philosophy?*, p. 208.
4. There are millions of fractal videos available on the Internet. The very basic examples here are from *Fractal Worlds – A Visual and Musical Journey into the Strangely Beautiful World of Chaos*, DVD Cymru Wales Ltd, 2002.
5. Mandelbrot, 'A Geometry Able to Include Mountains and Clouds', p. 50.
6. http://www.transphormetic.com/Talysis01.htm (accessed 31 May 2006).
7. Ibid.
8. Sacks, *Migraine*.
9. Humphreys and Eagan-Deprez, 'Fostering Mind–Body Synchronization and Trance Using Fractal video', p. 101.
10. Ibid., p. 96.
11. Deleuze and Guattari, *What Is Philosophy?*, p. 36
12. Hawking, 'Black Hole Explosions?'.
13. Deleuze and Guattari, *What Is Philosophy?*, p. 36.
14. Sciama, 'Time "Paradoxes" in Relativity', p. 16.
15. Ibid.
16. Neo, 'Fractal Images of Memory in *Mother and Son*'.
17. Bergson, cited without reference in ibid., pp. 208–9.
18. Ibid., p. 4.
19. Ibid.

20. Ibid., p. 2.
21. Baudrillard, *Xerox and Infinity*, p. 9.
22. Deleuze and Guattari, *What Is Philosophy?*, p. 270.
23. Baudrillard, *Xerox and Infinity*, p. 9.
24. Ibid.
25. Baudrillard 'The Ecstasy of Communication', pp. 126–34.
26. Paul, *Digital Art*.
27. Ibid., p. 97.
28. Ibid., p. 108.
29. Ibid., p. 105.
30. Ibid., p. 125.
31. Ibid.
32. Deleuze, *Cinema 2*, p. 264.
33. Ibid., p. 264.
34. Ibid., p. 265.
35. Ibid.
36. Ibid.
37. Ibid.
38. Ibid.
39. Ibid.
40. Ibid., pp. 265–66.
41. Ibid., p. 266.
42. Ibid.
43. Ibid., p. 270.
44. Severin, 'From Comparative Cultural Studies to Post-literary Study'.
45. Deleuze and Guattari, *What Is Philosophy?*, p. 208.
46. Ibid., p. 204.
47. Ibid., p. 202.
48. Ibid., p. 216.
49. Ibid., p. 204.
50. Ibid., p. 205.
51. Ibid., p. 26.
52. Ibid., p. 209.
53. Ibid.
54. Ibid.
55. Ibid., p. 217.
56. Ibid.
57. Ibid., p. 218.
58. Ibid.
59. Ibid.
60. Bogue, *Deleuze on Cinema*, p. 195.
61. Ibid.
62. Ibid.
63. Rodowick, *Gilles Deleuze's Time Machine*, p. 205.

64. Ibid.
65. Interview with Orson Welles in *Cahiers du Cinema*, cited in Deleuze, *Cinema 2*, n. 17, p. 304.
66. In this section on new Deleuzian-inflected work, I want to acknowledge the helpful pointers of Alan Hook, the artistic director of *A/V* webjournal.
67. Personal communication with the author, 31 May 2006.
68. Programme notes from Mutek Festival, Montreal – project by martux_m.
69. Delter uses a modified MPEG-1 codec. Liu doctored a sample MPEG-1 decoder implementation in Java >> written by Dr-Ing. Jörg Anders at the Technische Universität Chemnitz. Codes released under the GNU General Public Licence.
70. Victor Liu's delter work was premiered as part of the Info@blah; artists respond to information overload exhibition at the Mills Gallery Boston Centre for the Arts April–June 2003. It also features on the Web biennial 2003, in http://www.neural.it/nnews/delter.htm (accessed 31 May 2006).
71. http://www.n-gon.com/delter/istanbul.html#remarks (accessed 16 April 2006).
72. http://www.whatrain.com/fractallogic/page2.html (accessed 15 July 2006).

Bibliography

Works Cited

Anger, Kenneth, in Jack Hunter (ed.), *Moonchild: The Films of Kenneth Anger*. London and San Francisco: Creation Press, 2002.

Aranda, Francisco (1976) *Luis Buñuel: A Critical Biography*. New York: Da Capo Press.

Artaud, Antonin [1927] (1972) 'Introduction to The Seashell and the Clergyman', rep. in *Collected Works*, Vol. 3. London: Calder & Boyars.

Artaud, Antonin [1971] (1976) *Les Tarahumaras*, trans. Helen Weaver, *The Peyote Dance*. New York: Farrar, Strauss & Giroux.

Baudrillard, Jean (1983) 'The Ecstasy of Communication', in Hal Foster (ed.), *Postmodern Culture*. London: Pluto Press, pp. 126–34.

Baudrillard, Jean [1987] (1988) *Xerox and Infinity*. London: Touchepas/Agitac.

Bergson, Henri [1910] (1971) *Time and Free Will: An Essay on the Immediate Data of Consciousness*, trans. F. L. Pogson. London: George Allen & Unwin.

Bergson, Henri [1911] (1983) *Creative Evolution*, trans. Arthur Mitchell. Lanham, MD: University Press of America.

Bergson, Henri [1908] (1991) *Matter and Memory*, trans. Nancy Margaret Paul and W. Scott Palmer. New York: Zone Books.

Bergson, Henri [1923] (1999) *Duration and Simultaneity*, ed. Robin Durie. Manchester: Clinamen Press.

Bogue, Ronald (2003) *Deleuze on Cinema*. London and New York: Routledge.

Bordwell, David (1989) *Making Meaning: Inference and Rhetoric in the Interpretation of Cinema*. London and Cambridge, MA: Harvard University Press.

Bordwell, David and Noel Carroll (1996) *Post-Theory: Reconstructing Film Studies*. Madison, WI: University of Wisconsin Press.

Bordwell, David and Kristin Thompson (eds) [1999] (2004) *Film Art: An Introduction*. New York: McGraw-Hill Education.

Borges, Jorge Luis (1970) 'The Garden of Forking Paths', in *Labyrinths*, trans. Donald A. Yates. Harmondsworth: Penguin.

Boundas, Constantin V. and Dorothea Olkowski (eds) (1994) *Gilles Deleuze and the Theatre of Philosophy*. London and New York: Routledge.

Bourdieu, Pierre (1984) *Distinction: A Social Critique of the Judgement of Taste*, trans. Richard Nice. Cambridge, MA: Harvard University Press.

Brakhage, Stan (1963) 'Metaphors on Vision', *Film Culture*, Fall.

Brakhage, Stan (1967) 'The Camera-Eye: My Eye' (from 'Metaphors on Vision', *Film Culture*, Fall, 1963) reprinted in Geoffrey Battcock (ed.) *The New American Cinema: A Critical Anthology*. New York: Dutton.

Brakhage, Stan (1982) *Brakhage Scrapbook: Collected Writings 1964–1980*. New York: Documentexte.

Breton, André [1924] (1969) 'Manifesto of Surrealism', in Richard Seaver and Helen B. Lane (eds), *Manifestos of Surrealism*. Ann Arbor, MI: University of Michigan Press, pp. 49–110.

Buchanan, Ian (2000) *Deleuzism: A Metacommentary*. Edinburgh: Edinburgh University Press.

Buchanan, Ian and Claire Colebrook (2000) (eds) *Deleuze and Feminist Theory*. Edinburgh: Edinburgh University Press.

Buchanan, Ian and John Marks (eds) (2000) *Deleuze and Literature*. Edinburgh: Edinburgh University Press.

Buchanan, Ian and Marcel Swiboda (eds) (2004) *Deleuze and Music*. Edinburgh: Edinburgh University Press.

Bukatman, Scott (1999) 'The Artificial Infinite: On Special Effects and the Sublime', in Annette Kuhn (ed.), *Alien Zone II: The Spaces of Science Fiction Cinema*. London and New York: Verso.

Bürger, Peter (1984) *Theory of the Avant-garde*. Minneapolis, MN: University of Minnesota Press.

Burroughs, William [1953] (1984) *Junky*. Harmondsworth: Penguin.

Cameron, James (1995) *Strange Days* (original text). London: Penguin.

Carroll, Noel (1990) *The Philosophy of Horror or Paradoxes of the Heart*. London: Routledge.

Carroll, Noel (1998) *Interpreting the Moving Image*. London: Routledge.

Carroll, Noel (1999) *A Philosophy of Mass Art*. London: Routledge.

Castaneda, Carlos (1973) *A Separate Reality*. Harmondsworth: Penguin.

Castaneda, Carlos (1973) *The Teachings of Don Juan: A Yaqui Way of Knowledge*. Harmondsworth: Penguin.

Castaneda, Carlos (1976) *Tales of Power*. Harmondsworth: Penguin.

Chayefsky, Paddy (1980) *Altered States*. London: Corgi.

Chayefsky, Paddy (1995) *Altered States* screenplay, in *The Collected Works: Screenplays Vol. II*. New York and London: Applause Books, pp. 233–331.

Chion, Michel (1995) *David Lynch*, trans. Robert Julian. London: BFI.

Clarke, Arthur C. et al. (2004) *The Colours of Infinity*. London: Clear Press.

Colebrook, Claire (2000) 'Inhuman Irony: The Event of the Postmodern', in Ian Buchanan and John Marks (eds), *Deleuze and Literature*. Edinburgh: Edinburgh University Press, pp. 100–34.

Colebrook, Claire (2000) 'Introduction', in Ian Buchanan and John Marks (eds), *Deleuze and Literature*. Edinburgh: Edinburgh University Press, pp. 1–17.

Colebrook, Claire (2002) *Gilles Deleuze*. London and New York: Routledge.

Conley, Verena Andermatt (2000) 'Becoming-Woman Now', in Ian Buchanan and John Marks (eds), *Deleuze and Literature*. Edinburgh: Edinburgh University Press, pp. 18–38.

Crowley, Aleister [1904] (rep. undated) *The Book of the Law*. New York: Magickal Childe Publishing.

Curtis, David (1971) *Experimental Cinema: A Fifty Year Evolution*. New York: Delta.

Deleuze, Gilles (1983) *Nietzsche and Philosophy*, trans. Hugh Tomlinson. London: Athlone Press.

Deleuze, Gilles (1986) *Cinema 1: The Movement-Image*, trans. Hugh Tomlinson and Barbara Habberjam. Minneapolis, MN: University of Minnesota Press.

Deleuze, Gilles (1988) *Spinoza: Practical Philosophy*, trans. Robert Hurley. San Francisco: City Lights Bookshop.

Deleuze, Gilles (1989) *Cinema 2: The Time-Image*, trans. H. Tomlinson and R. Galeta. London: Athlone Press.

Deleuze, Gilles (1990) *Negotiations*, trans. Martin Joughin. New York: Columbia University Press.

Deleuze, Gilles (1990) 'Porcelain and Volcano', in *The Logic of Sense*, trans. Mark Lester and Charles Stivale. New York: Columbia University Press.

Deleuze, Gilles (1990) *The Logic of Sense*, trans. Mark Lester. London: Athlone Press.

Deleuze, Gilles (1991) *Bergsonism*, trans. Hugh Tomlinson and Barbara Habberjam. New York: Zone Books.

Deleuze, Gilles (1991) 'Coldness and Cruelty', in Gilles Deleuze and Leopold von Sacher-Masoch, *Masochism*. New York: Zone Books, pp. 9–142.

Deleuze, Gilles (1994) *Difference and Repetition*, trans. Paul Patton. New York: Columbia University Press.

Deleuze, Gilles (1997) 'Bartleby; Or, the Formula', in *Essays Critical and Clinical*, trans. Daniel W. Smith and Michael A. Greco. London and New York: Verso, pp. 68–91.

Deleuze, Gilles (1997) 'Literature and Life', in *Essays Critical and Clinical*, trans. Daniel W. Smith and Michael A. Greco. London and New York: Verso, pp. 1–7.

Deleuze, Gilles [1991] (1997) 'Re-presentation of Masoch', in *Essays Critical and Clinical*, trans. Daniel W. Smith and Michael A. Greco. London and New York: Verso.

Deleuze, Gilles (1997) 'Real and Imaginary: What Children Say', in *Essays Critical and Clinical*, trans. Daniel W. Smith and Michael A. Greco. London and New York: Verso, pp. 61–7.

Deleuze, Gilles (1997) 'The Exhausted', in *Essays Critical and Clinical*, trans. Daniel W. Smith and Michael A. Greco. London and New York: Verso, pp. 152–75.

Deleuze, Gilles (1997) 'To Have Done with Judgement', in *Essays Critical and Clinical*, trans. Daniel W. Smith and Michael A. Greco. London and New York: Verso, pp. 126–36.

Deleuze, Gilles (2000) 'The Brain Is the Screen', in Gregory A. Flaxman (ed.), *The Brain is the Screen: Deleuze and the Philosophy of Cinema*. Minnesota, MN and London: University of Minnesota Press.

Deleuze, Gilles (2002) 'Dead Psychoanalysis: Analyse', in Gilles Deleuze and Claire Parnet, *Dialogues II*, trans. H. Tomlinson and B. Habberjam. London: Athlone Press.

Deleuze, Gilles (2003) *Francis Bacon: The Logic of Sensation*, trans. Daniel W. Smith. London and New York: Continuum.

Deleuze, Gilles (2004) *Desert Islands and other Texts 1953–1974*, ed. David Lapoujade, trans. Michael Taormina. Los Angeles and New York: Semiotexte.

Deleuze, Gilles and Félix Guattari (1984) *Anti-Oedipus: Capitalism and Schizophrenia*, trans. Robert Hurley, Mark Seem and Helen R. Lane. London: Athlone Press.

Deleuze, Gilles and Félix Guattari (1988) *A Thousand Plateaus: Capitalism and Schizophrenia*, trans. Brian Massumi. London: Athlone Press.

Deleuze, Gilles and Félix Guattari (1991) *What is Philosophy?*, trans. G. Burchill and H. Tomlinson. London: Verso.

Deleuze, Gilles and Claire Parnet (1987) *Dialogues*, trans. H. Tomlinson and Barbara Habberjam. London: Athlone Press.

Deren, Maya (1946) *An Anagram of Ideas on Art Form and Film*. New York: Alicat Bookshop Press.

Deren, Maya (1960) 'Cinema as an Art Form', in Lewis Jacobs (ed.), *The Art of the Movies*. New York: Noonday Press.

Deren, Maya (1960) 'Cinematography: The Creative Use of Reality', *Daedalus*, Winter, pp. 150–67.

Deren, Maya (1965) 'Maya Deren: Notes, Essays and Letters', in *Film Culture*, No. 39, Winter.

Deren, Maya [1953] (1970) *Divine Horsemen: The Voodoo Gods of Haiti*. New York: Dell Publishing.

Fitzgerald, F. Scott [1936] (1945) *The Crack-Up*. New York: New Directions.

Flaxman, Gregory (2000) *The Brain Is the Screen: Deleuze and the Philosophy of Cinema*. Minneapolis, MN and London: University of Minnesota Press.

Fleiger, Jerry Ann (2000) 'Becoming-Woman: Deleuze, Schreber and Molecular Identification', in Ian Buchanan and Claire Colebrook (eds), *Deleuze and Feminist Theory*. Edinburgh: Edinburgh University Press.

Fremantle, Francesca and Chogyam Trungpa (trans.) (1987) *Bardo Thodol/The Tibetan Book of the Dead*. Boston and London: Shambala.

Freud, Sigmund [1922] (1940) 'Medusa's Head', in *The Standard Edition of the Complete Psychological Works of Sigmund Freud Vol. 18*, trans. James Strachey. London: Hogarth Press and the Institute of Psychoanalysis, pp. 273–4.

Freud, Sigmund [1919] (1955) 'The Uncanny', *The Standard Edition of the Complete Psychological Works of Sigmund Freud Vol. 17*, trans. James Strachey. London: Hogarth Press and the Institute of Psychoanalysis, pp. 218–56.

Freud, Sigmund [1913] (1986) *Totem and Taboo*, Penguin Freud Library Vol. 13. Harmondsworth: Penguin.

Freud, Sigmund [1905] (1987) 'Three Essays in the Theory of Sexuality', *On Sexuality*, Pelican Freud Library Vol. 7. Harmondsworth: Penguin, pp. 33–169.

Freud Sigmund [1918] (1990) 'From the History of an Infantile Neurosis ("The Wolf Man")', *Case Histories II*, Penguin Freud Library Vol. 9. London: Penguin, pp. 227–366.

Freud Sigmund [1900] (1991) *The Interpretation of Dreams*, Penguin Freud Library Vol. 4. Harmondsworth: Penguin.

Freud, Sigmund [1915] (1991) 'The Special Characteristics of the System *Ucs*', *On Metapsychology*, Penguin Freud Library Vol. 11. Harmondsworth: Penguin, pp. 167–222.

Freud, Sigmund [1920] (1991) 'Beyond the Pleasure Principle' in *On Metapsychology*, Penguin Freud Library Vol. 11. Harmondsworth: Penguin, pp. 269–339.

Freud, Sigmund [1924] (1991) 'The Economic Problem of Masochism', in *On Metapsychology*, Penguin Freud Library Vol. 11. Harmondsworth: Penguin, pp. 409–26.

Goddard, Michael (2006) 'The Surface, the Fold and the Subversion of Form: Towards a Deleuzian Aesthetic of Sobriety', *Pli: The Warwick Journal of Philosophy, Diagrams of Sensation: Deleuze and Aesthetics*, Vol. 16, pp. 1–27.

Goethe, Johann Wolfgang von [1840] (2002) *Theory of Colours*, trans. Charles Lock Eastlake. Cambridge, MA and London: MIT Press.

Golding, Robin (1982) Sleeve notes to Leo Janacek, *Glagolitic Mass*, conducted by Simon Rattle, EMI digital CD.

Griggers, Camilla (1997) *Becoming-Woman*, Theory Out of Bounds series, Vol. 1. Minneapolis, MN: University of Minnesota Press.

Grosz, Elizabeth (1994) 'A Thousand Tiny Sexes: Feminism and Rhizomatics', in Constantin B. Boundas and Dorothea Olkowski (eds), *Gilles Deleuze and the Theatre of Philosophy*. London and New York: Routledge, pp. 187–213.

Guattari, Félix (1984) *Molecular Revolution: Psychiatry and Politics*, trans. Rosemary Sheed. Harmondsworth: Penguin.

Guattari, Félix (1995) *Chaosmosis: An Ethico Aesthetic Paradigm*, trans. P. Bains and J. Pefanis. Sydney: Power Publications.

Guattari, Félix (2000) *The Three Ecologies*, trans. Ian Pindar and Paul Sutton. London and New Brunswick, NJ: Athlone Press.

Harding, James (1980) *Jacques Offenbach: A Biography*. London: John Calder.

Hawking, Stephen (1974) 'Black Hole Explosions?', Letter, 1 March, *Nature*, No. 248, pp. 30–1.

Hawking, Stephen (1988) *A Brief History of Time*. New York: Bantam.

Herzog, Werner (2002), in Paul Cronin (ed.), *Herzog on Herzog*. London: Faber & Faber.

Humphreys, Reginald B. and Kathleen B. Eagan-Deprez (2005) 'Fostering mind-body synchronisation and trance using fractal video', *Technoetic Arts: A Journal of Speculative Research*, Vol. 3, No. 2, pp. 93–104.

Hunter, Jack (ed.) (2002) *Moonchild: The Films of Kenneth Anger*. London and San Francisco: Creation Press.

Huxley, Aldous [1954] (1994) *The Doors of Perception, Heaven and Hell*. London: Flamingo.

Iser, Wolfgang (1978) *The Act of Reading: a Theory of Aesthetic Response*. London and New York: Routledge.

James, David E. (1989) *Allegories of Cinema: American Film in the Sixties*. Princeton, NJ: Princeton University Press.

Jancovich, Mark, Lucy Faire and Sarah Stubbings (2003) *The Place of the Audience: Cultural Geographies of Film Consumption*. London: BFI.

Jancovich, Mark, Joanne Hollows and Peter Hutchings (2000) *The Film Studies Reader*. London: Arnold.

Kaleta, Kenneth C. (1993) *David Lynch*. New York: Twayne.

Kennedy, Barbara M. (2000) *Deleuze and Cinema: The Aesthetics of Sensation*. Edinburgh: Edinburgh University Press.

Kerrigan, Justin (2000) *Human Traffic*. London: FilmFour.

Klein, Melanie (1988) *Envy and Gratitude and Other Works 1946–1963*. London: Virago.

Klüver, Heinrich (1966) *Mescal and the Mechanisms of Hallucinations*. Chicago: University of Chicago Press.

Lacan, Jacques (1977) *Écrits: A Selection*, trans. Alan Sheridan. New York and London: W. W. Norton.

Lacan, Jacques [1972–3] (1982) '*Encore: Le Seminaire XX*', trans. Jacqueline Rose, in Juliet Mitchell and Jacqueline Rose (eds), *Feminine Sexuality: Jacques Lacan and the École Freudienne*. Basingstoke: Macmillan.

Leary, Timothy [1965] (1971) *The Politics of Ecstasy*. London: Paladin.

Lilly, John C. (1973) *The Centre of the Cyclone*. St Albans, Herts: Paladin.

Lobrutto, Vincent (1997) *Stanley Kubrick: A Biography*. London and New York: Penguin.

Lynch, David (1997), in Chris Rodley, *Lynch on Lynch*. London: Faber & Faber.

McCabe, Colin (1998) *Performance*. London: BFI.

McKee, Mel (1969) 'Out of the Silent Planet: Review of 2007', *Sight and Sound*, Vol. 30, No. 4, pp. 204–7.

Mandelbrot, Benoît (2004) 'A Geometry Able to Include Mountains and Clouds', in Clarke et al., *The Colours of Infinity*. London: Clear Press, pp. 46–53.

Martin-Jones, David (2006) *Deleuze, Cinema and National Identity: Narrative Time in National Contexts*. Edinburgh: Edinburgh University Press.

Masson, Jeffrey (1985) *The Assault on Truth: Freud's Suppression of the Seduction Theory*. Harmondsworth: Penguin.

Michelson, Annette (1969) 'Bodies in Space: Film as "Carnal Knowledge"', *Artforum*, Vol. 7, No. 6, pp. 54–63.

Mitchell, Juliet and Jacqueline Rose (eds) (1982) *Feminine Sexuality: Jacques Lacan and the École Freudienne*. Basingstoke: Macmillan.

Metz, Christian (1982) *The Imaginary Signifier: Psychoanalysis and the Cinema*. Bloomington, IN: Indiana University Press.

Modleski, Tania (1988) *The Women Who Knew Too Much: Hitchcock and Feminist Theory*. New York: Methuen.

Monaco, James (1981) *How to Read a Film*. Oxford and New York: Oxford University Press.

Mulvey, Laura (1975) 'Visual Pleasure and Narrative Cinema', *Screen*, Vol. 6, No. 6, pp. 6–18.

Neville, Richard (1995) *Hippie Hippie Shake*. London: Bloomsbury.

Nietzsche, Friedrich [1883–92] (1969) *Thus Spoke Zarathustra*, trans. R. J. Hollingdale. Harmondsworth: Penguin.

O'Sullivan, Simon (2005) *Art Encounters Deleuze and Guattari: Thought Beyond Representation*. London: Palgrave Macmillan.

The Oxford English Dictionary (1989) Second Edition, Vols I, II, XVI. Oxford: Clarendon Press.

Paul, Christiane (2003) *DigtalArt*. London and New York: Thames & Hudson.

Penrose, Roger (1986) 'Big Bangs, Black Holes and "Times Arrow" ', in Raymond Flood and Michael Lockwood (eds), *The Nature of Time*. Oxford and New York: Blackwell, pp. 36–62.

Peterson, James (1994) *Dreams of Chaos, Visions of Order: Understanding the American Avant-garde Cinema*. Detroit, MI: Wayne State University Press.

Pisters, Patricia (2003) *The Matrix of Visual Culture: Working with Deleuze in Film Theory*. Stanford, CA: Stanford University Press.

Plant, Sadie (1999) *Writing on Drugs*. London: Faber.

Powell, Anna (2005) *Deleuze and Horror Film*. Edinburgh: Edinburgh University Press.

Rabinowitz, Lauren (1991) *Women, Power, Politics in the New York Avant-Garde Cinema 1943–1971*. Urbana and Chicago: University of Illinois Press.

Rinpoche, Trungpa (1987) Commentary to *Bardo Thodol/ The Tibetan Book of the Dead*, trans. Francesca Fremantle and Chogyam Trungpa. Boston and London: Shambala.

Rodley, Chris (1997) *Lynch on Lynch*. London: Faber & Faber.

Rodley, Chris (2005) *Lynch on Lynch*, revised edn. London: Faber & Faber.

Rodowick, David N. (1997) *Gilles Deleuze's Time Machine*. Durham, NC and London: Duke University Press.

Russett, Robert (1976) 'Contemporary Imagists', in Robert Russett and Cecile Starr (eds), *Experimental Animation: An Illustrated Anthology*. New York: Van Nostrand Reinholt, pp. 150–3.

Russett, Robert and Cecile Starr (eds) (1976) *Experimental Animation: An Illustrated Anthology*. New York: Van Nostrand Reinholt.

Sacks, Oliver (1993) *Migraine*. London: Picador.

Savage, John (1993) 'Snapshots of the 60s', *Sight and Sound*, Vol. 3, No. 5, pp. 14–19.

Sciama, Dennis (1986) 'Time "Paradoxes" in Relativity', in Raymond Flood and Michael Lockwood (eds), *The Nature of Time*. Oxford and New York: Blackwell.

Selby, Hubert [1978] (2004) *Requiem for a Dream*. London: Marion Boyars.

Severin, Constantin (2003) 'From Comparative Cultural Studies to Post-literary Study: Gilles Deleuze and Central-European Thought', *Internet-Zeitschrift für Kulturwissenschaften*, No. 14, February. Translation available at: http://www.inst.at/trans/14Nr/inhalt14.htm (accessed 30 December 2006).

Shaviro, Steven (1993) *The Cinematic Body*. Minneapolis, MN and London: University of Minnesota Press.

Shulgin, Alexander (1995) *PIHKAL*. Berkeley, CA: Transform Press.

Silverman, Kaja (1988) *Acoustic Mirror: The Female Voice in Psychoanalysis and Cinema*. Bloomington, IN: Indiana University Press.

Sitney, P. Adams (1979) *Visionary Film: The American Avant-Garde 1943–1978*. London: Oxford University Press.

Smith, Daniel W. (1997) 'Deleuze's Theory of Sensation: Overcoming the Kantian Duality', in Paul Patton (ed.), *Deleuze: A Critical Reader*. Oxford: Blackwell, pp. 29–56.

Smith, Daniel W. (1998) 'Introduction', in Gilles Deleuze, *Essays Critical and Clinical*, trans. Daniel W. Smith and Michael A. Greco. London and New York: Verso, pp. xi–lv.

Stacey, Jackie (1993) *Stargazing*. London: Taylor & Francis.

Tarkovsky, Andrey (1987) *Sculpting in Time*, trans. Kitty Hunter-Blair. Austin, TX: University of Texas Press.

Thoburn, Nicholas (2003) *Deleuze, Marx and Politics*. London: Routledge.

Truffaut, François (1983) *Hitchcock by Truffaut: The Definitive Story*. London: Paladin.

Vogel, Amos (1974) *Film as Subversive Art*. New York: Random House.

Weiss, Allen S. (1992) 'Pressures of the Sun: Manifesto Against the Electric Drug', *Continuum: The Australian Journal of Media and Culture*, Vol. 6, No. 1: 'Radio Sound'; rep. and ed. Toby Miller – see under electronic resources.

White, Allon (1982) 'Pigs and Pierrots: The Politics of Transgression in Modern Fiction', *Raritan*, Vol. 2, Part 2, pp. 51–70.

Whitney, James and John Whitney (1947) 'Audio-Visual Music', in P. Adams Sitney (ed.), *Art in Cinema*. San Francisco: San Francisco Museum of Modern Art.

Williams, Linda Ruth (1993) *Sex in the Head: D. H. Lawrence and Femininity*. Hemel Hempstead: Harvester Wheatsheaf.

Youngblood, Gene (1970) *Expanded Cinema*. London: Studio Vista.

Zimmer, Heinrich (1946) *Myths and Symbols in Indian Art and Civilization*. New York: Harper & Row.

Žižek, Slavoj (ed.) (1992) *Everything You Always Wanted to Know About Lacan . . . But Were Afraid to Ask Hitchcock*. London: Verso.

Electronic resources

Aronofsky, Darren Interview, 'Before Tackling Batman, Darren Aronovsky Has a Dream', conducted by Michael Marano, Scifi.Com, 23 September 2001; rep. at: http://aronovsky.tripod.com/interviews.html (accessed 28 February 2006).

Bradshaw, Peter, 'Living in Oblivion: Darren Aronofsky's *Requiem for a Dream*', in *The Guardian*, 19 January 2001, at: http://film.guardian.co.uk/News_Story/Critic_Review/Guardian_Film_of_the_week/0,4267,424064,00.html (accessed 2 February 2006).

Casalegno, Mattia, *X-Scape*, at: http://www.kinotek.org/bootstrap.html (accessed 9 September 2006).

Liu, Victor, at: http://www.neural.it/nnews/delter.html (accessed 31 May 2006).

Neo, David, 'Fractal Images of Memory in *Mother and Son*', in *Offscreen* web-journal, 30 November 2001, at: http://www.horschamp.qc.ca/new_offscreen/fractal_images.html (accessed 14 May 2006).

Severin, Constantin, 'From Comparative Cultural Studies to Post-literary Study: Gilles Deleuze and Central-European Thought', *Internet-Zeitschrift für Kulturwissenschaften*, No. 11, February 2003, at: http://www.inst.at/trans/14Nr/severin14.htm (accessed 10 October 2005).

Weiss, Allen S., 'Pressures of the Sun: Manifesto Against the Electric Drug', *Continuum: The Australian Journal of Media and Culture*, Vol. 6, No. 1: Radio-Sound (1992); rep. and ed. Toby Miller in: http://wwwmcc.murdoch.edu.aU/ReadingRoom/6.1/Weiss.html (accessed 19 September 2005).

http://www.bbc.co.uk/dna/h2g2/A6083633 (accessed 14 May 2006).

http://www.chocolate.org/index.html (accessed 10 June 2006).

http://www.english.uiuc.edu/maps/poets/m_r/olson/life.html (accessed 2 May 2005).

http://www.eri.mmu.ac.uk/deleuze/ (accessed 12 November 2006).

http://www.horschamp.qc.ca/new_offscreen/fractal_images.html (accessed 20 June 2006).

http://www.ica.org.uk

http://www.inst.at/trans/14Nr/severin14.htm

http://www.krioma.net/articles/Bridge%20Theory/Einstein%20Rosen%20Bridge.htm (accessed 9 February 2006).

http://www.lux.org.uk

http://www.release.org.uk/html/~drug_menu/ecstasy.php (accessed 6 January 2006).

http://www.script-o-rama.com/movie_scripts/d/donniedarko.pdf, p. 46 (accessed 30 December 2006).

http://www.whatrain.com/fractallogic/page2.htm (accessed 11 November 2005).

http://www-groups.dcs.st-and.ac.uk/~history/Mathematicians/Riemann.html (accessed 6 February 2006).

Filmography

2001: A Space Odyssey (1968) Stanley Kubrick.
L'âge d'or (1930) Luis Buñuel.
All About Eve (1950) Joseph Mankiewitz.
Altered States (1981) Ken Russell.
Apocalypse Now (1979) Francis Ford Coppola.
At Land (1945) Maya Deren.
Austin Powers: International Man of Mystery (1997) Jay Roach.
Belle de jour (1967) Luis Buñuel.
Black Moon (1975) Louis Malle.
Brigadoon (1954) Vincente Minnelli.
The Cabinet of Dr Caligari (1926) Robert Wiene.
Cat's Cradle (1959) Stan Brakhage.
Un Chien andalou (1928) Luis Buñuel and Salvador Dali.
Citizen Kane (1941) Orson Welles.
Cleopatra (1963) Joseph Mankiewitz.
Le coquille et le clergyman (1928) Germaine Dulac.
Dante's Inferno (1935) Harry Lachmann.
The Discreet Charm of the Bourgeoisie (1972) Luis Buñuel.
Dog Star Man (1961–1964) Stan Brakhage.
Donnie Darko (2001) Richard Kelly.
Easy Rider (1968) Dennis Hopper.
Entr'acte (1924) René Clair.
The Fall of the House of Usher (1928) Jean Epstein.
Fire Walk with Me (1992) David Lynch.
The Flicker (1965) Tony Conrad.
Fractal Worlds – A Visual and Musical Journey into the Strangely Beautiful World of Chaos (2002) DVD Cymru Wales.
From Hell (2004) The Hughes Brothers.
Fuses (1967) Carolee Schneemann.
Heart of Glass (1977) Werner Herzog.
Hiroshima, Mon Amour (1959) Alain Resnais.
Human Traffic (1999) Justin Kerrigan.
Inauguration of the Pleasure Dome (1954) Kenneth Anger.
Jacob's Ladder (1993) Adrian Lyne.
The Lady from Shanghai (1947) Orson Welles.
Lapis (1966) James Whitney.
Last Year at Marienbad (1960) Alain Resnais.
Loving (1957) Stan Brakhage.
Macbeth (1951) Orson Welles.

The Man with the Golden Arm (1955) Otto Preminger.
The Matrix (1999) The Wachowski Brothers.
Meshes of the Afternoon (1943) Maya Deren.
Mirror (1974) Andrei Tarkovsky.
Mother and Son (1997) Aleksandr Sokurov.
Mulholland Drive (2001) David Lynch.
Night of the Hunter (1955) Charles Laughton.
Nosferatu (1922) F. W. Murnau.
Pandora's Box (1926) G. W. Pabst.
The Passion of Joan of Arc (1927) Carl Theodor Dreyer.
Performance (1970) Donald Cammell and Nicolas Roeg.
Piece Mandala: End War (1966) Paul Sharits.
Psycho (1960) Alfred Hitchcock.
Puce Moment (1949) Kenneth Anger.
Ray Gun Virus (1966) Paul Sharits.
Re-Entry (1964) Jordan Belson.
Reflections on Black (1955) Stan Brakhage.
Requiem for a Dream (2001) Darren Aronofsky.
Ritual in Transfigured Time (1945–6) Maya Deren.
Le sang d'un poète (1929) Jean Cocteau.
Sherlock Junior (1924) Buster Keaton.
Singing in the Rain (1952) Stanley Donen.
Solaris (1972) Andrei Tarkovsky.
Spellbound (1945) Alfred Hitchcock.
Stalker (1979) Andrei Tarkovsky.
Strange Days (1995) Kathyrn Bigelow.
The Tales of Hoffmann (1951) Michael Powell and Emeric Pressburger.
Terminator 2 (1991) James Cameron.
Trainspotting (1996) Danny Boyle.
The Trip (1968) Roger Corman.
Vertigo (1958) Alfred Hitchcock.
Yantra (1955) James Whitney.
X-scape (2006) Mattia Casalegno.

Index